The Big Balloon

(A Love Story)

RICK BERLIN

Table of Contents

Prologue

"Small is large to me."
— **Suzanne Vega**

There is no linear structure to this book. No over-arching narrative. Each entry is self-contained. One piece can relate to another, but it isn't necessary to make that connection. The reader can pick it up, crack it open anywhere, read a section and put it down. The 'chapters' are just the rooms in my house.

It could be said that I chose this odd-ball format for bathroom reading. For those with short attention spans. On the other hand, much as I love the twists and turns of a full blown story, the Haiku simplicity of disparate entries exposes Berlin as if opening the paper window flaps of a Twelve Days Of Christmas holiday card in no particular order.

The Big Balloon is super personal. Most art, at least the art I love best, is personal. From another's truth one extrapolates one's own echo, wisdom, embarrassment and laughter. That's what I'd hope for you, dear reader. That you'd laugh or at least find something self-relevant in these independent passages of my peculiar life.

A brief encounter can sometimes be the most efficient dart to the heart.

Why The Title, *The Big Balloon (A Love Story)*?[1]

Not sure when this happened or who said it, but it goes like this:

"Rick, I've seen three of your apartments. The rooms always look like you blew up a big balloon and your stuff wound up on the walls and floors like Bang! Drag this mess around."

He's right. In honor of his comment, I took photos of the inanimate in my house and wrote about each one. In so doing I fell down unexpected rabbit holes of memory, unlocking doors long shut. Portraits, observations and déjà vu recall, as humorous and amorous as they are disturbing. I pray that *Balloon* is not the Berlin edition of Capote's *Answered Prayers*, the book that, once published, lost him all his friends. He betrayed them, exposed their secrets and burned every bridge. I also hope it doesn't bore the shit out of you. Some are close to frivolous, but I think they offer relief from the headier, deeper cut pieces.

And this – a love metaphor:

"The balloon. It's something you hold on to, but can also let go. But at least when you let go, it rises."'
– Margie Nicoll

---

1   See 'Double Dedication'

KAMA KAZI & THE ADDED FAT

KAMA KAZI is mis-spelled. It should be *KAMIKAZE*, but I opted for the split.

I've stolen words from the past, written in my long lost Dear Diary, typed onto construction paper and folded into parts of The Balloon. I kept the day-to-day archived in my silver room on Ridgemont Street[2]. I didn't want *Balloon* to be a puff piece for The Ladies Homosexual Journal. Diving back into *KAZI* I was assaulted by details long forgotten, submerged or hidden out of fear of brutal self-sabotage. Nevertheless, they belong here. A subterranean, even painful return to those early years when I was trying to figure out who the fuck I was as an artist, a lover, an identity.

I thought I'd lost it, *KK*. I'd given a copy to Oedipus. He gave it back and I left it with Chet Cahill for safe keeping. Billie Best shuttled it home to me after Chet died. Re-reading it took me back to those first days when Orchestra Luna I and then II were formed. The writing isn't bad. I made edits, but not many. I was in my late twenties when I tapped away on a hospital blue Smith Corona portable – snap, snap, SNAP! I miss the clickity clack, as everything I write these days is on a Mac.

KK, which I had printed and bound at Copy Cop years ago, was falling apart. I transcribed it. In so doing I realized that that period of my life, the people I loved and the work I was attempting startled me. That long ago Self seems so unlike the dude I imagine myself to be today. It's way more gay than I remembered. I guess back in the 70's I didn't give a shit about how I'd be perceived. I still don't, but (maybe) I'm less gay, gay, gay in my old age.

Why the title, *KK*? When I was in Grenada[3], West Indies, shooting a never to be completed, edited or released film for an Amherst grad and drug

---

2   See 'Ridgemont Street'

3   See 'Busted In Grenada' ('The Paragraphs')

dealer, Frank Height, he said, from behind his reflector sunglasses and in his slow, Jack Nicholson drawl:

"You know what you are, Rick? You know how you lead your life?"

"How's that?" I asked.

"You live it like a Kamikaze pilot."

Not sure if this was a compliment, but I gotta say, I'm in favor.

> *"The person who loves you has picked you out of the great mass of uncreated clay which is humanity to make something out of, and the poor lumpish clay which is you wants to find out what it has been made into. But at the same time, you, in the act of loving somebody, become real, cease to be a part of the continuum of the uncreated clay and get the breath of life in you and rise up. So you create yourself by creating another person, who, however, has also created you, picked up the you-chunk of clay out of the mass. So there are two you's, the one you yourself create by loving and the one the beloved creates by loving you. The further those two you's are apart the more the world grinds and grudges on its axis. But if you loved and were loved perfectly then there wouldn't be any difference between the two you's or any distance between them. They would coincide perfectly, there would be a focus, as when a stereoscope gets the twin images on the card into perfect alignment."* – All The King's Men[4]
>
> **– Robert Penn Warren**

> *"Love is just friction and ego."*
>
> **– Michael Stipe**

---

4   (from in my scrapbook)

The Big Balloon (A Love Story) Double Dedication:

1. MICHAEL DIRTBIKE

(A Sensitive Boy)

"There are somethings you don't even know you know until you're asked. But it's so seldom you find anyone who'll ask the right questions. Most people aren't that much interested...."
— Christopher Isherwood

It's fair to say, at this late winter in my life, that I met someone. A notice-r. Someone who, visiting my house, sees what's here. Asks about it. Pointed questions. Questions that, being asked, move me to answer fully. To be interrogated, even about something as offbeat as a heating pad for a cat or as memorable as reading out loud the liner notes on the cd of my first band ever, Orchestra Luna, is a savage gift, an awakening about parts of my life I'd lost interest in re-examining, forgot, or was weary of the autobiographical tape loop. To produce long buried details and anecdotes required an unusual heat lamp, an in-your-face, genuinely interested detective, someone who I could open up to from the heart and for real.

Had he not been like this – intelligent, empathetic, inquisitive, hilarious, gentle and beautiful – these bits and pieces (I had sworn off a second book after 'The Paragraphs' was published) would have never been typed up.

So, Michael, thank you. Thank you for Everything.

Love,

A 74, now 75 year old tree.

Michael Dirtbike:

"It's unfinished but whatthefuck:

74 isn't old if you're a tree

Spanish moss hangs atop his Iowa christened crown.

Cold noreastern wind propagates his sound.

No gale's strong enough to uproot him from our jungle,

His roots run deep, his soul is underground.

Sonic saplings, tapsters, and albino squirrels attract him.

The sentinel of JP supports a unique ecosystem.

In his shadow we sit after a long fought day,

With a yeunger, a miller, singing the 'ol Behan hymn."

2. FRIENDS & FAMILY PAST, PRESENT, FUTURE

This project has unearthed friends (along with their object references) I've lost touch with or who've left this world entirely. A lucky man am I to have known so many that I love and who give a shit. Let me never forget. Please forgive me, those I've left out or those not bubbled up from the litter in my house. It's just that I've kept my 'balloon'[5] MO intact.

---

5   See 'Why Am I Calling This The Big Balloon (A Love Story)?

The Love Map. Guess you can't have a map like that until you've driven cross-country miles along the Love Highway, but I can see those lines, the lines of love, etched in my face. Love has been given to me, time and time again. Beautifully, in crazed heat, in darkness, in truth, in falsehood. Who I am are those who have opened their hearts to me, and I them. Nothing else much matters.

NOTE: In some cases I've used pseudonyms to protect the innocent as well as myself from incrimination.

Foyer

Lock That Box

This 10-nippled beauty I picked up at True Value. It saved our ass. Robby had lost his keys. Robby never loses anything. The fistful that he needs for work and home probably plopped into a snow bank on his way to Bella Luna where he runs the kitchen. With an employee turnover revolving door, he often has to work extra hours. Sometimes seven days a week. The band adjusts set times at shows to his schedule. He needs the work. He needs the money. We need Manochio.

He never planned on being a chef, or keeping a job in The Industry. He's an ace musician and an ace guitarist. When he was a teenager he won First Prize at a jazz recital in Montreal. These days he's a Jersey rocker who can play sensitively when required or burn a hellfire solo like Hendrix – I'm not kidding.

He always brings an original, on the money, out-of-the-blue guitar part to my songs, piloting the music down an unpredictable runway. His solos sing. He's assembled an airplane cockpit of recording gear that he works on whenever he has the time. Much of *Great Big House* was recorded on his console. All that equipment makes it possible to practice with headphones and not disturb the neighbors. It also allows us to record rehearsals so that what the band comes up with can be recalled.

For me, having art/music made in the house, inspires. It helps hearing work done in the background. Makes me just another worker bee and not a pompous queen.

Robby's a poet when drunk (which he no longer is). A visual artist (I've seen the dorm wall paintings from his time at Berklee). A natural athlete. Golf, football, baseball. He and his best friend, Ricky McLean, hit the links at Franklin Park every morning from spring through fall. Up at dawn playing 18, sometimes 36 holes. Listening to the roar of lions from the zoo.

"Whack and walk," he calls it.

An unassuming foot soldier who keeps to himself and stays clear of romantic discord (one hard felt broken heart too many). He carries the dark stoically. He wears a cheerful face and makes subtle Obi Wan suggestions.

"Move along and practice with a metronome."

He lets Carlotta sleep and drool at the foot of his bed. He always shows up, a super reliable on time pro. I trust him completely – with my songs, with my car (which he calls the *"GG"* as in Gay Green), with his sense of himself. He's getting restless, especially with the shutdown. We might lose him which would be an immeasurable vacancy.

When he lost his keys, including the mailbox key, we were fucked. The landlord never gave us a spare. We could be locked out, an emergency nightmare. Hence, the lock box. Robby set it up with a cool code. We're always able to open the door with the key dead in that miniature grey coffin. It's not an easy reach for me coming home from the Brendan Behan after four Miller Lites and a gummy, but I fumble with numb fingers and open the door.

We've since gotten new keys, but kept one in the nipple box – our gatekeeper.

Hallway

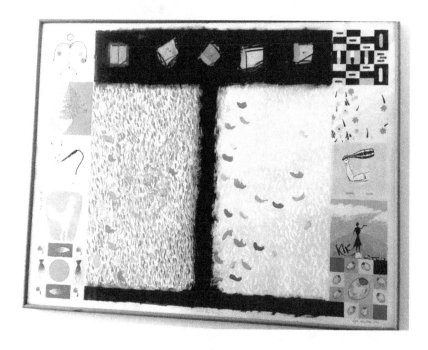

Kick Step Ducky

Wes Kalloch, 1993. I can't picture his face; too long ago. Pretty sure he was a part-time regular at Jacques during my ten year installment. He showed up one night with the painting, framed, and handed it over with a big smile. The title and the work, a puzzle unsolved. A portrait of me or a map of Wes's psyche? It has a disquieting quiet about it. An implication of undeciphered codes and images. My eyes land on the rooster, then the bombs, then olives, a candlepin weapon, a fir tree, an I-beam. It has a message in a frame which tells me something different every time I look at it. An A-plus in art.

I have been kicked by this duck and glad of it. Fuck a duck.

Pony Express

with no saddle sores. Hey, I'm the key kid. The roommate with mailbox access. Always have been. At 370B I had the one and only. I dropped off mail at each roommate's door. Same here at OVT[6], even though we each have a key, or did before Robby lost his.[7] But like he says, I'm *"regimented"*. My day is scheduled like a Adderall Marine. First this task, then that until the day is done and each item on the list is checked off. I start the same way every day, bustling about the apartment with tiny step, on purpose Chinese bound feet, daily ducks in a row, breadcrumbed clue reminders in soldierly rows.

When Clinton was asked the day he was elected President, what his first priority in office would be, he answered:

"After civil rights, delayed gratification. Americans want everything right away. Change takes time."

An interesting comment considering the cigar. My chorus of ablutions represent delay. Delay of breakfast. Delay of coffee. Delay of art-for-the-day. Delay of phone calls to sisters. Delay of secretarial out-boxing. Delay 'til midnight to hit the Behan and booze up.

Robby's right. I am a choreographed regiment waving a rainbow flag at half time on a college football field, same marching orders day in and day out. Marathon Mommy at the tiller on repeat. The Kentucky Derby giddyup deliverer of bills and birthday cards.

---

6   Our new street

7   See 'Lock That Box'

Put Your Glasses On

Berlin and give it a second look. Nick Kent is an art changeling. His work shifts gears every few months or even weeks. Abstract for the most part and of varying size and component parts, but ever evolving. This one, given to me, felt at first as if I was going to be bowled over by a tornado. If I put on my specs, however, I realize that those yellows might be Wordsworth daffodils fluttering in a grassy field. (Nick would stroke his chin at my analysis.)

Met him at the Behan. Caulk it up one more time to Brendan, The Mad Poet bringing disparate souls into one small, dark corner bar. A talking bar. A haven for the honest. No home for the phony. All others welcome.

Nick looks a lot like W. H. Auden, the amphetamine poet who's words have always carried weight with me. A shock of red hair up off the forehead like a flame. Tall and slender, a runner's build. He ran long distance at Northeastern with a team of friends he keeps up with to this day. One's in the CIA. Another's a cop. Another a one-of-a-kind character.

His day gig: graphic artist. Nick designed all but one of The Nickel & Dime Band's cd's and did the heavy lifting on *The Paragraphs* even though the publishers knocked the stuffing out of him with endless edits. He was my initial go-to when the idea of a book first surfaced. He mocked it up, got it Amazon rough printed and as a result I was able to turn it over to Kate and Katie for review. It became their first published book – Cutlass Press. This never would have happened without Nick's early effort and belief in my writing.

He used to live nearby, on Forbes St, a third floor walk-up with several empty rooms. He lived alone. Work, paint, run. He was busy with the broads back then. Crazy women who, after a break up, would camp out on his door step tearfully hoping for reprieve. Then his Dad died. They were deeply close. Hit him hard. A long grief. He left the hood and moved back to Marblehead. Got his own place. Hung out with his high energy Mom, but kept to himself. Not a loner, more that he's self-possessed. The calm silence of a solo universe.

He owns a boat. He tries to coax me and Margie[8] up for a sail at sea. We never seem to get it together. Someday, one day. He sets up museum trips for the three of us, caging out which artist is showing at which gallery. It's always worth the trip. Taking it all in as he 5th gears references for his constant output.

I'm lucky he can do what he does for me, although, like Chet said:

"You don't hear from Berlin unless he needs something from you."

---

8   See 'The House That Margie Built'

Stolen

Dad landed on the Vineyard with Lisa's high school friend, Priscilla Bohlen. How he found me (swimming naked on an acid trip in a pond that even I could hardly locate after living there for months) I'll never know. He was toting vodka and ice in a Styrofoam cooler and hitch-hiking all over the island looking for god knows what. Me, I guess. Strange, as I'd never told him I was there.

He was always, as he put it, half in the bag. The courage of the Dutch inspiring insane behavior. He'd revert to his seventeen year old teen Dick[9], which, I have to say, much as he was heavy to be around, I was proud of. Nothing held back, insult or praise. My friends loved hanging with him, middle-fingering the pretentious. He should never have been a 1950's money-man cocktail cliché. An author? He did have a knack for words. He took wild stabs at life once free of his miserable Estate Planning job at the Girard Trust & Corn Exchange Bank and he felt unleashed after the divorce. Truthfully, he was on borrowed time, the booze eating up his liver and far along on his chosen path: death by drink. He and Priscilla were bunked up at some fancy-assed hotel in Edgartown. He coveted the hallway frame. It housed a tepid scene-at-sea, but the frame itself was exquisite. So he stole it, laughing about the get-away-with-it as he ran down the hall.

My friend, Gabe, painted this self-portrait while he attended art school in Portland. He gave up art after landing in JP and became an ace chef. Maybe someday he'll return to art. Set up an easel on a beach and paint whatever comes into his head. He could. He should. He won't.

---

9   See 'Me, Dick & A Cactus'

I like the fictitious Chinese stamp in the lower right identifying as signature. I could be wrong, but I think he hated the thing and gave it to me just to get rid of it. The shaded eyes, missing left forearm and naked smeary torso, none of which actually look like him, still say something about his take on himself. Dad, had he seen it in the ripped off frame, would have dug it.

Dad – frame. Gabe – art. A Siamese union of ne'er-do-wells.

About this dude.

Not good at specifics. I fabricate and then believe the fabrication. I don't think it matters much in the truth department only because the essential person is likely made up anyhow. I do that. Don't we all a bit? Invent the new friend as one invents one's self in their context? An old harangue of mine doubtless repeated whenever I become close to some brand new character. Interaction is the mother of invention.

What I do remember is that I ran into him on the sidewalk outside and around the bend from Machine, the gay bar of choice where I'd wind up after work and where I stood on the sidelines, like a dope, hoping for conversation when anonymous sex was the only sport in town. Gabe was hanging with his friend Eliot, high on whatever. Underage. No bar would have them. We drove back to Doyle's (closed, but open for me), filled a gallon jug with hard cider and returned to the park. We drank it empty, lying in the grass.

Never verbose, he spoke with his eyes. Sad. Ironic. Mischievous. Early eye-bags. We met up here and there. Spent time at the Factory. Snorted heroin, though the high never took, thank god. Just a weak, short-lived nausea. We might have had a moment that night, a vague muscle memory. He's a looker, in a disgruntled Bukowski sort of way. You don't want to fuck with him if he's in a mood.

It was Gabe who, one night at the end of the Behan bar told me the story of Michiko (the name I gave her), his Japanese roommate whom he'd never seen eat. Anything. It became a song. I ripped him off word for word.

The Family Skirt

My Great, Great Grandfather, a Porteous, supposedly looks like I did as a boy. He kinda does.[10] I might have had fun myself in that breezy, no-underwear kilt. The print is a pale copy of the original. Like Great, Great, Grandpa Porteous, it will fade to white as the years go by. As will I.

I never quite get it, how unearthed history can flatter, corrupt or distort the present. Would the anemic aspects of my character improve/ whitewash with an upbeat bio from a yesterday relative? Will I architect a famous building or die of an overdose? Will I be more handsome or look away hideous? Make a pile of money or go broke following an impossible dream? Add brogue to my speech or attempt a phony impersonation in a bar? Play the bagpipes as easily as falling out of bed? All and none of the above.

G. G. Gramps went on to create Porteous, Mitchell & Braun[11], the biggest department store in Portland. My Mom shopped there until it shuttered. She got a stipend from her share in the company which put Dad's teeth on edge given there were two bread winners in the family. We'd stop in when we summered at Prouts Neck. T-Shirts, bathing suits, dresses. We felt as out of place in there as we did at the bank where Dad played hooky, drank his lunch and openly despised. We might have been happier kids playing Spit on the porch during a summer rain instead of family shopping in downtown Portland and feeling singled out.

I do puff up a bit thinking about the Scot heritage thing. Gramps's

---

10   See 'Pastel Rick'
11   See 'Once She Was Blonde'

shiny buttons. His chubby hands which might have gingerly lifted the plaid skirt and promised a naughty curtsy. I would have watched from a closet keyhole and worried about myself.

A 70'S SIDEWALK SKIRT OF A DIFFERENT CLOTH

It was Peter's idea: The Combat Zone. Cruise the porn, all three of us – Peter Barrett[12], Charlie Isenberg and myself. Three fairies on a Friday night quest.

The Kenmore bus stank of puke and exhaust. We sat in the back, in separate seats, staring out dirty windows. A Beckett-faced old fart struggled onto the bus. He wore a tent-shaped light grey raincoat fastened by three big buttons. He was muttering to himself, bobbing up and down on dirty unlaced sneakers. Peter was squealing with delight. His hands were fluttering at his sides like moths, hooked on the odd behaviors of old men and old ladies.

We got off in Chinatown and wandered from one dirty store to another. Once in the door – a bee line trio to the fag section. Up and down the aisles. A new line on the racks: Continental Gay. Young Swedes, the kind of kids a priest might appreciate in church and offer a hot meal. We flipped through the rags free of their plastic prophylactic wrappings, mortified by ferocious fist-fucking, dog-fucking and the boring, eyes-wide endless fellatio. Out the door and onto the next. Sarcastic commentary, sidewalk asides.

At The Scene it's all movies. We squeezed into a smelly stall and shoved a quarter in the slot. You have to keep feeding quarters if you want to watch the full flick. It looked inane, the fucking. It ended with one dude jerking off onto the other's please-don't-please-do face. Hot wax on the chin. I was disinterested. Maybe another night.

Out on the street, Pete and Charlie are way out front with me tailing behind like a dour Geisha. In the mist appeared an Empire State Build-

---

12   See 'Peter Barrett & Moosup, The Musical'

ing of a black transvestite in a bright orange fright wig and a hot pink leatherette mini-skirt. Charlie and Peter were doubled-over laughing, covering their mouths with cupped hands.

"What are you laughing about?"

"Did you hear what she said?*"*

"No."

"It was incredible."

"What was it?"

In unison:

"Haaaayeee. Ya out for a bloooow?"

An endlessly repeated refrain. Wear that skirt, baby, and don't walk away. I will follow.

Back Porch

Adirondack In Jamaica Plain

It's beginning to look like driftwood – bleached and slightly contorted. A gift from my Mom when I was living at the Piano Factory. Spanking new then; blonde wood, hard but comfy. It wound up in our kitchen at 370B[13] and would creak and shift under your ass, threatening collapse, a lonely Adirondack without a wrap-around porch and a view of Lake Michigan, or sinking its heels into wet sand at Jungle Beach, stark naked and scanning for action.

There are multi-colored plastic versions. They don't come close. This one's a classic. I bought tie-on flowery cushions from Home Depot. They collected cat hair and got greasy with use. I threw them out when we moved. I put the chair outside on our rotting back porch. The arms are good to balance a can of beer, a plant or a coffee cup. I could step outside in my pajamas and Daddy bathrobe and read the Globe out there in the summer, but I don't. It's become one more object d'art, as idle on the weathered gallery as Lisa Osborn's ceramic bust[14]. Looking closely, I see that the floorboards of the porch mirror the grain. Hopefully it's just fine out there. Hopefully they've become friends, porch and chair. Maybe it likes not being interrupted by a cat or person larding themselves onto a spindly frame.

The crud on each arm is disturbing. How did it get like that? Who's elbows were that disgusting? Did skunks spar, one per arm and spray the flat wood? They started out pristine, but have become a pair of encrusted afterthoughts. Glad Mom isn't around to notice. There's a *lot* I'm glad she's not around to notice.

---

13   On Centre St, JP, where I loved for 15 years.

14   See 'Statuesque'

Old Girl Ain't What She Used To Be

Poor dear has been relegated to the back porch and out of the kitchen where she used to promised Snow White a bite of the apple. Where she cast off evil cooking spirits and dangerous visitations, human or otherwise, in silent decree.

The ever creative, ever resourceful Barry Keating made this puppet. You could reach up under her skirt, wiggle a forefinger into the hole of her neck and have her talk in witchy slang. Her face, glue-gunned, so closely resembles Queen Grimhilde I expect her to make me a handsome prince, but she never does.

The butterfly wings I added have slipped. They no longer lift her into a diamond sky, or flutter her safely to the porch below. She's stuck up there, a coat hanger hooked in her neck. She's been rained and snowed on. If she weeps, I won't hear it. I pretend that she likes it out there. She can rest on her hook and hang out with the Adirondack chair, the plants and the terracotta statue.

I can't throw her out. I'm afraid of bad juju and no way would I toss a present from Barry. So there she resides in gradual decay. Her robe will fray and disintegrate. The nylon stocking wings will drop off. Her scarf will rot. Her head and face, last to die, will roll across the porch like an eight ball.

Statuesque

I met Lisa Osborn at Doyle's. She was married at the time, with two kids. Lived up the street. Since divorced and on her own. Lisa has, like all great ones, an idiosyncratic take on life, love, herself, art and the world. She works in ceramic, sculpting larger than life statues in extended Giacometti poses. They seem to be a part of some noble obsolete family. Or akin to those long buried and since unearthed 3rd Century Chinese terracotta armies; hundreds of soldiers in full battle armor lined up in military rows. Lisa's workshop is likewise filled with heads, torsos and tall clay beings, some as high as nine feet. It overwhelms. They seem to silently intone, to have profound thoughts, melancholy longings as wounded, insufficiently healed, souls.

"I sometimes think that they're my only friends," she laughs.

She'll conjure the image of her brother or her former husband, an oblique everyman reference, but more often it is her own face that she chooses. Not as self-portrait, but as a universal testimonial, a multidimensional voice.

At one point, when I was designing and booking Marlene Loses It At The Lizard, Lisa planted six of her statues in the club. Solemn personae bearing witness to the night's shenanigans. Afterwards, she gave me one. It came in three sections. Feet/knees, waist, torso/head. I stood him proudly in my loft at the Piano Factory. The pale grey, ghostly creature scared the shit out of whomever was a first time visitor. One night an infuriated drunk punched it in the face and ran out of the building. It shattered into a thousand dusty fragments. When I told Lisa what happened, she shrugged it off, said she'd give me another. That tiny waisted, contemplative girl/boy now presides on our back porch.

It had once been tall, but during the move, the two bottom sections cracked and broke. At half mast, she seems at peace, rain, snow or shine. The red is brilliant and bloody like hot mama fingernail claws.

Lisa taught at Mass Art and Harvard. She was helpful and encouraging to countless fledgling artists. The Mayor of Boston Art. She left town. Moved to her home state of Louisiana and lives on an island just off the coast of New Orleans.[15] May she survive all hurricanes and continue to marshal her own massive terracotta army.

I once asked her to make a water fountain statue of a dude, crouched backwards with his ass in the air, shower douching. She passed.

---

15   "I am not the only person living on the island, although it often feels that way, which is nice for an introvert. It is a salt dome in the Louisiana coast. It belongs to my larger—several gens back and forward—fam. It is pretty wonderful. I am "Staying Home" with 2 OTTB mares, a fully operating studio, and my kids, Herbert and Charlotte (remember them?), both graduating seniors—College and High school respectively— who have been here since March school closings. It has been kind of glorious with all of this sub-tropical outdoors (boats in the marsh, endless wildlife and astonishing bugs)." – Lisa Osborn

Basement

Electrocution Solution

New house, new basement, first time washer and dryer and a place to park the things we didn't want upstairs, but couldn't throw out. We considered setting the band up down there for rehearsal, but it's dirty, dusty and dank and who knows who'd want to yell at us about the volume or take a peek at gear they could sell on Ebay.

The basement has that smell, the one that assaults you first thing on your way into the below decks dark *("eau de mildiou"* – Peter Barrett); a musty, dirty things done dirt cheap aroma of blindfolded kink sex. Or of a pit hiding a terrified *Silence Of The Lambs* captive oozing savagery and tears.

I've always been a bit afraid in these dungeons. In Wayne, when my parents were at a party and I was watching a Laurel and Hardy flick in a wood paneled basement rec room, I heard a soft click. I looked behind me in a sweaty panic and saw that the door to the deeper darkness was being pushed open. It stopped moving and hurried footsteps receded. I did not make it up. The bulkhead was open. Whomever I imagined had been down there, had been. Who knows what the intruder had in mind for Little Ricky. I doubt he wanted to sketch my portrait.[16]

All these memory waves curl around my legs when I descend the backstairs with a bag of laundry. At the top, the light switch. Small time fear warns me to flick it on. Without light, the bogeyman will hide behind the hot water heater, jump out and stab me in the neck before I can stuff my dirty laundry into the washing machine maw.

---

16   See 'Pastel Ricky'

An over the shoulder swinging bag of filthy clothes cracked the brown plastic switch plate on my way downstairs and exposed the wiring, inviting a killer zap! Been there before. Chet, at an OL rehearsal at the Allston house, was fuse-connected from his bass to a wall plug. He hovered horizontally above the rug, teeth clenched, eyes screaming at us to fucking do something, to save his ass. We kicked the amplifier cord out of the socket and he hit the floor safe and sound, his curly head of hair a bit more 'fro'.

As a moderate spending improver of house and home, I picked out the shiny chrome. It didn't screw in all the way. The plate wobbles when I hit the double switch, but it is oh so pretty and helps me believe that the downstairs gremlin has fled the scene and uninterrupted happy laundry washing awaits.

Laundromat In The Basement

The last time there was an inhouse washing machine and dryer was when I was a kid. Since then, no apartment has had the amenity. Not that I hated leaving the house. Sitting in the window and reading while the at attention soldierly line up of machinery whirled and washed was a pleasure. Sometimes I'd throw the stuff in and to-and-fro from house to 'mat and multitask. It got me out of the house on a sunny day.

I love the quarter machine that swallows rumpled bills and spits out metal money, heavy in the pocket and zinged into the slot. But honestly, having that gear here, at home, down into the bowels of the basement is awesome. Multitasking a mere climb upstairs instead of a two block trot. No awkward encounters with a bag lady hoping for a handout from tightwad Berlin. No fight to grab the last dryer available. No tiny detergent box to bite open with my teeth and spit soap flakes on the floor. All that is taken care of right here. Hump the Santa bag into the gloom and load 'er up.

I feel like a rich person, like we have a maid. Looking online at ads for apartments the tag line *"washer and dryer included"* was astonishing to read. I didn't care if it was offered or not. It had been so long since that was an option. But now I'm hooked. Or spoiled.

I *am* a maid.

Pantry

A Tisket, A Tasket

Karla DeVito (now DeVito-Benson) gave me this cheerful chub when she left the Luna house in Newton Highlands to join the Meatloaf tour as The Girl. Steinman, Meat and his manager saw OL2 play Alice Tully Hall, our last gasp grasp for attention before we fell apart. I saw Meat play The Paradise just as they were climbing the charts. Karla, fabulous in a day-glo white onesie, was French kissing the be-Jesus out of Loaf and chewing up the torrid lifestyle of a world tour.

What a voice – widescreen, powerful, dramatic, flexible, searing hot. She brought us Billie Best, who managed band incarnations of mine for years. She and Billie, forever friends, have both been supportive of the Berlin dustbin catalogue. Karla did us a solid when she got Steve Popovitch (Meatloaf's exec for Cleveland International and the guy who dumped Orchestra Luna from the Epic roster) to see a third incarnation, no girls, no choreography, just plain Luna. Pop loved us, wanted to sign the band, got Ian Hunter and Mick Ronson (whom we met in a hotel room after Ian opened for The Kinks at the Garden) on board as producers. An almost but not quite signing. Had it worked out it would have been our best shot ever.

"I'm going to send you to Europe, Rick. Every artist deserves to walk the streets of Paris."
– Steve Popovitch,

forever endearing himself to me. If only...

But Pop had to let us go after a protracted battle with a local, coke addled son-of-a-bitch, to whom we'd signed over our recording rights.

We were industry babes-in-the-woods and it took us five beleaguered years to extricate. A rock n roll memoir cliché if ever there was one.

Back to the basket.

"If I hear the word basket one more time, I'm gonna throw up."
— Tex, a fifty something peroxide waitress at Machine.
I wrote a song about her for a Karla solo. She nailed it.

I love the green and yellow weave, the happy hat on top, a bellyful of needles, thread, scissors and buttons. During the hippie years, hitch-hiking Kinscherf kept his overalls in repair. Patching holes with bright colors, utilizing a special hook-n-ladder stitch for durability, Wheatena or ramen boiling over in a pot on a crash pad stove. Of late, like my Mom, I'm a thrower-outer. Out go ripped shorts, dead T's, worn out socks. Obsolescent County, USA. No time to curl up under a reading lamp and sew listening to Woodstock outtakes. But here it stayed, Karla's sewing basket on a pantry shelf, pretty as a pinafore.

And another thing: If Karla was pissed, she'd middle finger:

"Blow me!"

Number 1. I don't think girls get blowjobs, right? They give, get munched, but can't be blown. Wrong gear.

Number 2 (pet peeve). One doesn't 'blow', one sucks. Wouldn't it hurt if you actually blew?

Karla, weigh in.

THE CONTRACT

Charlie Isenberg, our roommate at the Ridgemont OL house, was always in our landlord's face, keeping our rent reasonable, repairs kept up. We thought he was super effective and so, once we started Orchestra Luna 2, Steven, Peter and I thought he'd be a terrific manager. He met

Jane Friedman during a trip to the city and duplicated her contract with Patti Smith and had us sign. It was thirty pages deep. I think it claimed we'd owe him everything in sight if we decided to get out of it down the road. No one else in the band went for it. We signed as three, the three queer amigos in solidarity, as long as Charlie promised to tear it up if we got into deep water.

He and I, took the OL record to New York and leaned on every and any A&R exec who would give us a meeting. We'd sit there and be asked:

"What is it you want?"

"We want a record contract," Charlie'd say, straight up, smelling his fingers.

The finger smell was a particularly grating habit. I'd glower at him, hoping he wouldn't do it, but he did. He always did. It was the nicotine on his fingers that he'd sniff as a way to remind him to smoke or quit. We got nowhere. OL was old news. Nobody gave a shit. Charlie did befriend Hilly Kristal at CBGB's and we were booked in there a lot and attracted a modicum of interest. But Charlie's days as our manager were numbered.

Billie arrived, full of smarts and instantly trusted by the rest of the band. We had to ask Charlie to tear it up. Tear up that encyclopedic contract. He came over to Danny Fields's loft where Steven and I were staying and did it. Literally tore it up. He is the only one, in a long list of dishonorable separations, the *only* person who settled a business matter as a human being first and as a businessman second. He could have tied us up for years. It was one of the saddest experiences of my life. I will always appreciate and respect him for doing it, but it became the trigger of an extended downward spiral for my friend. He felt defeated and betrayed. He never fully recovered.

After he left Danny's, Billie showed up. We explained what had happened and entered new territory. Billie never asked us to sign anything.

Hers was a handshake agreement. She hoisted the sails as we hit the turbulent wave that is the music industry.

Billie left, Danny came home.

"I smell cunt," he said. I'll never forget it. Our ears blushed. I think I told Billie. If anyone could take it, she could.

Bad Boy Boots

When the snow is piled high, when my parking spot is a precious, fought for commodity and my car needs to stay where it lays, I walk to work. To Doyle's. I love the trip. House windows glow like Jack-O-Lanterns, fuzzy warm and greeting card cute. Even better when it's still snowing. Those big fat flakes float like petals, melting on your nose.

Thing is, I never had a decent, no-snow-down-the-pantleg pair of boots. My sneakers soaked up the slosh and left watermarks all over the floors at work. Even with snowfall an increasingly rare phenomenon around Boston, I had to spring for the real deal. Boots that would keep my feet dry and that would last winter after winter.

At Eastern Mountain Sports I found this pair of beauties lined up and lonely against a wall in a fitting room, the only pair of it's kind. No one seemed to want them. They were gargantuan, elephant boots, too big for me, but my feet, my Triple E flippers, slid into them like old friends, thwump! No huffing and puffing. No lower back strain to pull them on. Because nobody wanted them, because they were the only pair of its kind, they were reduced to a paltry $35 bucks. I wore them home.

With my sneakers in my back pack, bad boy boots on foot, I clump through the snow drifts or on the street avoiding plows and cars with a giddy smile. The snow falls softly, almost totally silent. I think I can hear the flakes ping as they hit the ground, but I know that's silly. What I do hear is the scuffling of my badass boots. They squeak against new snow, feet toasty warm inside like boobs in a cashmere sweater. Once at work I'm a laughing stock.

"What are those?! Where did you get them?!"

Stand out ludicrous, my calling card. I'll give you one and you can call me up when you're in the mood for a moment of absurd embarrassment. If I could charge for it, I'd be a rich man.

Dance With Me, Baby

The go-to wig for a Three Stooges comedy. God knows what vile germs infest the grey spaghetti. I haven't used it at the new place, but once every two months I slopped the 370B sty all proud of myself.

Much as I enjoy my impersonation of a sing-along Gilbert and Sullivan cabin boy swabbing the deck, mopping kills my lower back. The lift of the heavy pail, the bending over, the push and pull takes a toll. The floors *look* shiny and clean, but the mop itself is so encrusted with backwash it can't possibly do a decent job. The step-and-squeeze-out is cool. I enjoy the one-legged choreography, the hot dribble into the bubbly pail and the darkened mop hair drained of dirt. I feel like a charwoman hipster or a near destitute mother working a shit job so her kid can go to college.

After the work is done, the longhair dank and wet, I thrust its neck out the window to hang until it dry, stiff and frozen in place, Iron Lady coiffed until the next time. I'll hang on to it. I like seeing it in the pantry as if I might actually use it, that day when I revive the swill and stroke the floors. Then again, employ a handsome intern?

Dance that decadent dance, Berlin, one more time.

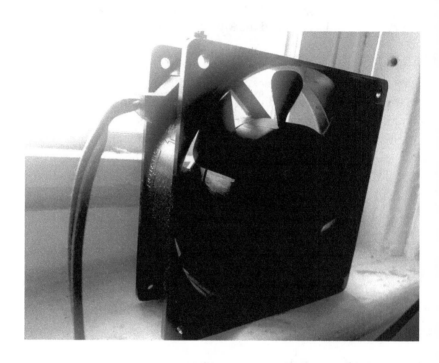

Darth Fan

I wanted a tiny fan in the pantry during the summer to suck litter box vapors out the wee window. Bought one online, plugged it in and it hummed along sounding like the bumble bee buzz of a tattoo needle. Putrid cat fumes were teased out the window into the back yard.

I wanted to see if it had varying speeds. It was fan-spinning away as I reached in to grab it, to see how it might be controlled and it chopped up my fingers. A little person Light Sabre. Tarantino blood spattered all over the walls, pantry floor and kitchen table. I washed it off and band-aided my never-should-have-happened wounds. Rope a dope.

After the fiasco, Robby pulled the plug, lifted it gingerly off the sill and straightened me out.

"This not a window fan. It's for a computer. An old school computer. It's supposed to be installed inside. It has no protective covering. It will cut you up."

Wrong fan. Wrong location. Weaponized. A shiny black Vader.

"Rick. I am your father."

Hide The Bottle

It's plastic. It can't break which is a good thing, because when Robby or Alex is in the bathroom and I can't hold it a second longer, I piss in it. I hide in the pantry and fill her up hoping against hope the no one will see. I hold tight for fear that a loose fingered drop will splishy splash yellow all over the floor, into litter boxes and onto trash cans. Cleaning lady Berlin will have to squat on hands and knees, sop it up and cope with the stench of his own piss. So yes, iron grip.

Afterwards, in a frenzy, I

1. Pour the yellow down the drain with precise, surgical aim.
2. Tap pretty orange dish soap into the container and fill her up with boiling hot water.
3. Stick it, foamed to the brim, onto the hidey hole shelf, relieved and naughty ashamed.

A long time ago, knowing that my roommate, Travis, liked Wild Turkey, I persuaded John Casey at the Behan to give me the wee pitcher with the Turkey logo so I could give it to Trav as a present. In an emergency I used it for a nefarious purpose. I did burn it clean and waited months to confess, but when I did, Trav refused to go anywhere near it.

An ongoing, secretive, puissant performance. Some things you can't help.

Hydrating The Plants

It used to be that one said:

"I'm drinking water."

Now you say:

"I'm hydrating."

How much do I hate that? Stands the hairs up on the back of my neck as defiantly as hearing people use *"like"* in front of every fucking word. Or worse: *"That's what she said"*. I swear off the colloquial habit even as, fraud that I am, I speak it. When I do it's like slapping myself in the face. When did it start, this hydrating shit? Now we're fucking stuck with it.

Maybe my three plants will like, *like* being hydrated. Maybe they'll think they're getting more than just a Monday watering. Maybe I'll spoon in some steroidal root and leaf stimulus. What*ever*. (There I go again.)

Moving right along.

Part 1.

I water once a week, every Monday so that I regularize and won't forget. With the addition of The Fig Tree (babysitting for Mike), I add a Thursday hy-fucking-dration as The Fig is more thirsty than his adopted brother and sister plants. Somehow all three remain vital and survive my historically inadequate attention. Like I said, plants die around me, but these? They persist. I should give them each a pink hat and a #metoo button.

Part 2.

The squirt bottle. A pleasing hair salon mist imitating a drizzly day. Their little leafy chests swell up with appreciation.

"Mmm, MMM. Thank you, Ricky! Thank you for the misty moisty. Feels like a l'l bit o' Heaven."

They recommend that you talk to your plants. Instead, they talk to me.

Push Pin Diamonds

are a girl's best friend. One of those rare times when, instead of throwing shit out, I save. At the old place I used them constantly. For a photo, a note, a piece of string, a stuffed mouse. Christmas decorations ate 'em for breakfast. The tin emptied as the pins pushed up colored lights in the hallway, fake pine needle loops looping in wedding cake U's, a green star in the bathroom, a plastic silver ball drooping like a chime above a fake tea candle.

They hurt my fingers twisting them into hard plaster. I'd take breaks from the rush to decorate. Pulled out and put away they look terrific altogether in the box, sparkling in the pantry, unaware of their beauty.

The most beautiful are always unaware of their beauty. On the other hand there's something magnetic about a narcissist. You want to knock them off their pedestal. You're pretty sure they don't think they're as handsome as they hope to be and are secretly grateful to be found out, to not have to live up to the man in the mirror. These glittering plastic jewels have no vanity. Like flowers, they are what they are, no admiration required.

Carlotta, however, is an admirer. She will balance on her haunches and pull at a pin holding up a postcard. Gnaw and yank 'til it falls free, the card lost under my bed, the pin bounced god knows where. If I catch her in the act, I can stop her, but I need to shuffle the furniture around so she can't repeat the kitty crime. What if she punctured her little black chop-ettes with a push pin? How would she like that?

Red Dude In The Forest

Got him when I lived at the Piano Factory. Can't recall the artist. It wasn't expensive and I really liked the rock hard naked ass, hair-do flip and fat moon so I bought it, a rare art purchase. I hung him upside down for a while, voodoo style. Upright he's more friendly, although I'd for sure hide behind the evergreens if I ran into him. I don't think he wants to be bothered. There's a lot on his Devil's plate. I'm glad he's red. Keeps his naked booty warm out there in the cold forest. I'd want to be red too, commie red. Better red than dead.

I'd bet he can run super-fast. A hottie who can score the girl or the boy of his choosing, but won't love you tomorrow. Places to go, people to seduce. A fiery force for badass good. A Pan. A practical joker. An imp. He prefers the no frame, just a canvas rectangle push-pinned into a wall.

I hide him in the pantry. Too many eyes could send him packing. Being in the shade, however, I see him every day when I rake out the litter box and feed the cats. He watches over their visits to the toilet with hand-over-mouth glee. He is, however, evacuation free.

A COMMITTED DANCER

In Stockbridge, shooting yet another unfinished movie with Colter (cameraman for the incomplete 'Sad-Eyed Lady' in Grenada)[17] I met an Italian actress/dancer who decided to 'become' a tree. She stayed in the woods overnight, hugging a single oak. I have no idea if she transformed, if her skin turned to bark or moss, but I admire the dedication. I wouldn't have lasted more than five minutes. I wouldn't

---

17   See 'Busted In Grenada' ('The Paragraphs')

have thought up the idea, unless high on peyote and wanting to show off to some hoped-for Person Of Interest.

The Ritual

"Repetitio est mater studiorum"[18]

I first heard this from my Latin teacher in high school. It's true, but I hate it. I don't like to practice my songs. I like to write 'em and move on. I don't like to do anything more than once. Nevertheless, I find comfort in repetition, in ritual.

My cats live by ritual even as they are unpredictable beasties. They know that somewhere between 10:30 and noon they'll get breakfast. Between 11:30 and midnight, dinner. Same half can of wet, tablespoon of dry. They don't begin to act up or cry out to be fed until those hours. I think they like it, the for sure regularity. They live by it. Ah, domestication; a two way street. I control their lives, they control mine.

Brings me to the ritual of the litter box. Before breakfast (mine or theirs) I rake out yesterday's Tootsie Rolls and piss clumps. Stinky hard candy. I want them to have a clean toilet. More importantly, I don't want them looking for new territory to do their business. The results are plopped into the trash can above. For one week. Then hot bagged and side-walked.

The duct tape? Cat piss is pernicious. We know that. A toxic stench that curls nostril hairs, makes for squinty eyes and held breath. My guys results, I have to say, don't smell that bad. My bias. I don't think my farts stink either. (Grain of salt on that one.)

At the same time, urine is a powerful eroding chemical. I've read that

---

18   Repetition is the mother of students.

the latches on hog pens need to be replaced once a year. Pig gas corrodes and rusts the latches. They fall quietly into the mud. Same with kitty piss. The handle on their litter trash can lifted off one morning. It came apart in my hands. Two holes were left through which the fumes crept. Duct tape plugged 'em up. Problem solved. Roommates happy.

There are many simple repetitions in my routines. Keeps me sane. Maybe, when I was younger, I had room for the less regimented. Championed pushing myself off a cliff. Curve balls against routine. But at seventy-five, racing towards the golden goal posts, I'm partial to ritual.

MY FAVORITE
Mike walks me home from the Behan. Or I walk him home. He started it. I was taken aback. This has never happened. One here, one there, but never on so regular a basis. His idea. I tear up thinking about it. I'm a romantic sap, but it means the world.

"I'm walking you home," he said that first night.

And again. And again. A leitmotif, a simple, gracious, romantic, gentlemanly gesture. Says more than any collection of words about how we are with each other.

Kitchen

Blue

is my favorite Joni Mitchell album. *"I could drink a case of you and still be on my feet"* – a killer line anywhere, anytime. It is also my favorite sponge. I plop six of 'em into the grocery cart admiring their tight, bite-through-'em cellophane packs. I replace with a fresh one after I've used the latest in the once-a-month litter box soak-and-clean. You don't want cat fungus on bowls, forks, spoons, knives, plates and glasses. I do double dip, however. I use the blue for the morning scrub of the cat bowls. I used to be more circumspect, one for cats, one for dishes. Then I loosened up. One sponge for all, but not for litter boxes. If low on spares, I spread usage across the kitchen DMZ and into the bathroom.

The braided dish came from my landlady. It was for cheese spreads which I'll never eat or buy. I was going to give it the heave, and then, forefinger to forehead, I thought:

"Perfect for the blue sponge."

Of course it's not a real sponge. It was given birth in a factory, not in the ocean. A crisp Sponge Bob rectangle, a handsome Gainsborough Blue Boy in the morning sun. Rough side – my side of choice. Sandpaper food scabs off any surface. The soft side best used as a wiper upper or on a vulnerable Teflon complexion.

I find it far afield. Wasabi sniffs leftover bacon bits and cradles it to the kitchen floor like a bird-in-mouth. Will the dish soap make him sick? I doubt it. He has an iron stomach, just like his Daddy.

Joni, if you're listening, I have a sponge you could skate away on. I'd send it to you in Vancouver, but you'd never open the package. Nam-

ing a sponge after your phenomenal record would have you throwing a beer across a crowded room.

A Forever Cat

After I put my dear Sofi down (one of the saddest days of my life) sobbing with her alone as she expired, watching her quietly fade into oblivion, Robby and I went to Angell Memorial and picked out Wasabi and Carlotta, brother and sister, two tiny kittens staring up at us and sharing the same cramped cage. These two were brand new, the first kitties I didn't get used.

While TJ (Wenzl) lived with us, he showed up one night carrying a ceramic, found object cat he rescued from a sidewalk. It was heavy as a cinder block. He was honoring Sof with this life-sized replica. A cement girl who is thirsty, but can never drink. Hungry, but can never eat. Starved for affection, but can't feel a pat. She licks a frozen paw like Nefertiti mummied in an Egyptian kitty sarcophagus.

Back then he was a lush, running sound at The Midway, constantly high and handsy (affectionate late night hallway hugs you had to peel off with considerate care). He has a stutter, cute to us, annoying to him. He's an ace engineer/producer, Bitch Kitty Studios, his kingdom and refuge. He used to save his ex-wife's dresses, hung like Miss Havisham memories in his closet from one apartment to the next. I think he got rid them after I kept bringing it up. I wrote a god awful, prog rock song about it: *TJ's Dresses*. Nowadays he's got a terrific girlfriend and a kid on the way. He's an ecstatic son of a bitch, off the sauce. He had a brutal battle with the butts, scary mean when trying to quit, yelling and screaming, throwing and breaking shit, but he won that fight and is one happy fella.

When we first met he was assembling and running his first recording studio with his longtime pal, Tanner. They called it The Temple. It floated on the top floor of a building on Centre St. above City Feed & Supply. They were pouring a ton of someone else's money into the joint. As checkout boys at the Whole Foods store near Berklee School of Music they met this dude who asked what their dream gig might be – an obvious hit on, right? But the money was real and the Temple came together; a lotta pot and a lotta *"fuck me hard"* action in those rooms. Nickel & Dime recorded their first song ever in there – *Pull Up To The Bumper Baby*, inspiring a long standing relationship and friendship with Herr Wenzl. The Temple encouraged an unstable identity: rock n roll, house parties, hip hop, fundraisers. TJ slept on the floor, food wrappers littered the rooms, noise complaints proliferated. Whatever. It didn't hurt to have another decent, well-heeled studio in the hood.

Because he and Tanner are short, 5'2" tops, we called them Hobbits behind their backs (they knew). I suggested they change the name of the studio to The Shire. They did not. Things went south and The Temple lost its luster. They'd been recording local rap groups pro bono. Dudes would get pissed off and start call-the-cops fights. Teej got his face smashed in in front of the console, one of several times he'd been jumped or accosted. I think he was picked on because of his size, but he does have a wicked short, Napoleon complex fuse.

The lad has evolved into a grown-up without losing what's best about him: hard work, a full-on professional ethic, a curiosity about new audio techniques and gear and a deep loyalty to his friends. Even after he moved out of 370B, he'd sign up for our annual trip to Allendale Farms with me, Robby and Alex to buy our Christmas tree. We take a selfie, big, sleepy shit-eating grins.

One incident I'll never get over. I got up to pee, old man's dilemma. Through the door that connected our bedrooms, I heard sounds, sex sounds, over-the-top moaning and groaning. I thought:

"Hmm. Good for you, Teej. You go girlfriend."

I tip-toed into the kitchen not wanting to disturb, where he sat, lo and behold, smoking a bowl in the sun room. What the fuck?! His iPad, nonchalantly alive on a pillow, was bedroom broadcasting aggressive porn. Hard thrusting, no holds barred fuck films.

"Ah, TJ, I, ah, heard sounds? Coming from your room?"

He looked at me. I looked back.

Shrug.

We burst out laughing.

A Watched Pot

It could be shinier. It gets crusty, no fun mirror reflections. SOS does the trick though I worry the bubbly foam will slosh into the spout, poison my coffee and make my stomach bleed.

The extent of my cooking chops:

"You only boil water."
— **Charlie Isenberg**

It's true. I'm the James Beard of boiled water.

With the stay-at-home, I spend more time at the stove. I don't suck as badly as I expected. I defensive maneuver chopping garlic, making sandwiches, prepping a frying pan as Wasabi tries to horn in, tail whipping like a rogue windshield wiper, any dropped spot on the floor a kitty gourmet. (He should write a coffee table cookbook for cats.) The cutting board wobbles on the stove as I chop. Vegetables and sausage perch on top of the fridge before W can figure it out and snatch and steal. I wash as I prep and cook, a poorly executed all-at-once.

I covet the spanking new kettles I see in kitchen supply windows. Fanciful, Art Deco shapes glistening like polished silver wanting to sing and dance just like Disney's *Beauty And The Beast*. But I am faithful to mine. Cheerful, chubby and partially reflective. I don't pop the whistle. It's way loud. My inner Swiss clock tells me when to get back in there, brew a fat pint of Bustelo and fruit up the cereal bowl.

Confession.

More than once I've left the burner on and run out of the house unaware. Water boiled down to nothing and scorched the bottom of the kettle red hot and blackened, a near fire starter. Time to strap on your brain, Berlin, or teach Wasabi how to shut off the stove.

Are Two Better Than One?

They're both presents. The big guy, Todd Drogy. The little squirt, Pamela Ruby Russell. I honor them both. I would sit under a Bodhi tree with either as enlightenment hop-scotched skeptically in my direction.

I always say that one of something is better than two. If I make a sandwich, peanut butter and avocado and it's wonderful and then I make another because the first one was so fabulous, it always disappoints. It never tastes as good. I scarf it down in a rush, upset with myself for not trusting my maxim. I was addicted to the chocolate cake they used to sell at Doyle's. A scoop of vanilla on the side and I'd gulp it down like a dog with his head in the garbage. I'd wait five minutes and sure enough, I'd be back at the fridge shoveling out another. Seconds are the devil.

In the case of the Two Buddhas, I think not. My rule does not apply. They preside separately. My spiritual health is not compromised by shared icons. They pray, intone, each to his own mantra without sacred interruption. I do think, however, that you can't follow two gurus. I don't think Jesus, Muhammad and the *Buddha* would drink tea on a mountain top, yuck it up and fist bump guru war stories. They'd argue paths and complicate the other's route to wisdom. So it's up to us. We need to choose, it's trial and error. We need to go where the heart beckons. All we have to do is listen, pay attention and let go of the steering wheel.

I doubt that it matters which choir sings the Ultimate Truth. That's inside us, patiently waiting to be revealed.[19] I don't think it even has a name or a denomination. I do think it's essential that we keep a watchful

---

19   See 'The Guru Is You'

eye for that which cracks open the Big Book, the one with mainframe clues and answers. Each of us has our personal tome in his or her soul library, the Library of Consciousness. Someday we will find it, lift it off the shelf, dust off the cover, open it up and read. If not today, then tomorrow, standing in the university of the universal beside our dearest friends.

It could be argued that my spiritual mumbo jumbo is decorative. The peace which surpass-eth a simple hunk of plaster on a shelf, a con. Its gaze an inherent calm, but empty without the discipline of practice. Meditation. Silence. I'm both a practitioner and a new age phony. My monk's robe is made of chintz and besotted with disclaimers.

Ariel

Ariel[20] is the sprite in the watery portrait, peering through leaves, a camouflaged mane of black and white green. Ink-penned by my ginger-haired friend, Chris Nash, a rare homo pal, a MassArt student, more tattoos than open skin and possibly a dungeon aficionado.

He told me, after he moved from East Coast to Left:

"It's weird here. It's like it's a full moon every night. Complete strangers say hi, plan a meet up for a drink or coffee and never show. They live so in the present they forget anything promised in the past and flake."

We hung out a bit. Always a good time, but the spark never caught fire. Ariel kept an eye out for magic elsewhere. Maybe that's what my friend was saying.

"If not us, another."

Magic is real, like Fate.

"Fate brought us together, Rick. Brought me to the Behan that night and I somehow stayed late enough to meet you at your predictable midnight hour."
– MD

Fate, magic or just because. There are few rational explanations for these encounters. As if a silver bell is struck by an initiate in a cave on

---

20   Ariel's name means Lion of God. – Wikipedia

top of a mountain in Nepal, the reverberation awakening a dormant heart and love comes to town.

Might be Ariel who dings that bell. It just might be.

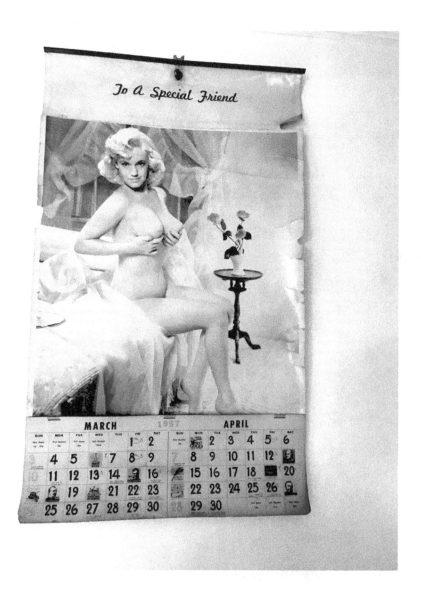

Because She's Special

A gift from Chet. Pinup fabulous. Those knockers are perfect, 1957 Hollywood chic. Yours for the feeling up. Her bed, a wonder world of pleasure. Fake flowers, odorless and soon to be kicked over in a seizure of passion.

As a teenager I discovered the Marylyn Monroe Playboy in my Dad's bureau drawer. Didn't do a thing for me, but her boobs were the exact same as the Special Friend who must have taken her cue from the Blonde Bombshell. Peroxide and voluptuous well before the overly muscled workout babes. Left toe on point. Right, poking around for pink mules. She looks cold, the mock-up bedroom, unheated. Bet she has goosebumps. What would her voice sound like? Nasal, squeaky? Marylyn breathy? Bacall low, dark and gravely? What would she say?

"C'mon over here soldier boy and give us a smooch."

She's adorable. Maybe someone's Mom, saving up for a dishwasher now that her husband flew the coop. Maybe she has a girlfriend on the side. Maybe she thinks you might have studio connections and can get her a screen test. For the horny teenager, the elderly shut in, the unfaithful husband, Special Friend is, no doubt, *Very* Special.

A DIFFERENT GIRL, DIFFERENTLY SPECIAL

We met Belle during the Luna Band era. She showed up at a gig in a floor-length, red sequined dress, a black sash pulled tight at the waist, a rhinestone brooch the size of a fried egg that clamped sash to hip. Stilettos (I think she slept in them) flared up at the ankles like B-movie boots, blood red with a floss thin, useless strap over the instep. She never shut up, gesturing the whole time as if manipulated by an invisible marionette string. She's tiny. Her dance moves petite and undeveloped. Her hoped-for poise and grace communicate a melancholy, wistful girl, as if to falsely indicate, as she called it, *"balletetic"* training, first in London and then Paree. We never believed her, but pretended to. Why break a heart already broken? She invited us to see her dance in a strip club north of Boston on Rt 1.

We watched her lift one leg, a high wobbly extension followed by a nose-to-floor dip, a twirl, a pout, a bend over. Hardly anyone was there. God knows what she had to do to get hired. She overworked a strobe light and dry ice fog. They hid her flaws. She's a stripper because she hurt her foot in an *"accident"*, or because she felt lost when she came back from Europe, hoping to join the corps de ballet of an American company, but was sidelined by drugs. That's when the wandering took over. That's when she was anybody's Special Friend. She needs to have her phone numbers changed or disconnected every week to keep the wolves at bay.

A few days ago, Patrick, who deals coke and manages another local band, took her into a back room and *"wanted sex"*. He forced her to whisk off her flimsy second hand blouse. She obliged. Belle, like Ado Annie, c'ain't say no.

She lost weight after a breakdown at the Pussy Cat Lounge. She'd hitched up from the south shore in the pouring rain, soaked to the gills, her heavy costumes in a sack over her shoulder. She caught the flu, lost thirty-five pounds, shrank to an unhealthy seventy-five and was fired from The Cat. She shrieked and screamed and threw things.

"Nobody treats me like a human being!"

She did not want to push drinks on rumpled, two-bit businessmen at the Lounge. She continued to dance under the flickering Rt 1 strobe for a year until she got the heave. Now she's on welfare and out of the circuit. In and out of the hospital. She looked lovely tonight, however. Full lips, tiny upturned Michael Jackson nose, immaculate barely

visible make-up and her trademark Fleetwood Mac shag, evenly tint-
ed with bottle-blondes-have-more-fun. She spoke in soft, modulated
phrase bubbles explaining that she was serious and professional about
her work. Her wispy dream about becoming a singer in a country and
western band seemed a stretch. She insisted that she's a *"good girl"* and
not what one might think. Fiction piled upon fiction.

She suggested that she and I *"take tea"* at some dump on Newbury
Street, or bring a picnic to a foreign film. She reminds me of Giulietta
Masina (*La Strada*), because she's nobody's girl. At the same time she's
not herself. Not all the way there. Loveless. I have a feeling that, if
asked, she'd be happy to pose as someone's special girl.

THE CLOSEST I GOT TO MAKING OUT
WITH A VERY SPECIAL GIRL

Me and Karen Isaacson went to a reunion party for high school friends
after being away freshman year. I'm home from Yale. I didn't know
who or what I was, except that it was impossible to re-introduce my
personality in the old way. The jokes and memories didn't apply. The
loud music, loud talk, knuckled up beer cans felt fake. To indulge
myself felt like an on parade performance of my former, EA senior
class president self. Since I couldn't cut it, I overdid it. Drank a few in
the car on the way there, beer bottle nestled between my legs, forefinger on the steering wheel, top down on the white VW Bug. I drove
fast on the narrow curving suburban roads, the spoiled brat careening
through the Main Line. A Yale show-off sticker on the rear bumper.

Thank god Karen was there. We were, as usual, laughing and mis-
behaving. We remembered how we crawled around on hands and
knees at a party last summer. She goosed the girls and I felt up the
boys. We'd report back and recount their histrionic reactions. So much
filthy fun. She had her forever mod haircut. High hairline at the nape
of her neck, long quotation mark 'side burns' and her omnipresent
death pink lipstick. She talked slow and lazy, with a southern Tallulah
affect, a hint of irony and sex.

We took a walk. Everything was rain wet. Past the rosebushes was a rabbit hutch on stilts. We talked baby-talk at the rabbit, slurry messages to flattened ears. Then we began to make out. My hands and arms up under her skirt, collapsing on the grass next to the rabbits. Moonlight softened the edges of her face. Kiss and rub. God it felt bizarre, although easier for being drunk. She let me do it and seemed to like it and for fuck's sake I was supposed to do *some*thing, so I did. No stiffy of course. We laughed off the self-consciousness of it. I tried a move, fingers on tip-toe, up from below, past the garter fortress and tight underwear, inside the edge of her panties to locate the real deal, soft hairs parting against the tips of my fingers and oh my god, for the first time in my life, I'm in! I kept wanting to feel something, but it was really unpleasant and dishonest. We stopped. I don't know how we knew when to stop, but we did. Maybe she reached for me and was disappointed. Maybe she didn't like it any more than I did. Snap the bra back together. Tidy up. Karen was the only girl I ever touched like that.

Seven years later, out of the blue, I got a midnight call, long distance.

"*Rickeee?...Hiiieee...Do you know who this is?*"

"*I don't.*"

"*It's me, Karen.*"

"*Oh my god?! Karen?!*"

"*Look. I'm in New York and I wanted to talk to you. I called your Mother and she gave me your number. Anyhow...I heard that you were gaaaay. Is that true?*"

"*Yup. That's what I am.*"

"*Well pay no mind, my dear...so...am...I.*"

Long slo-mo laugh.

*"Just don't spread it around. I don't want those bitches back on the Main
Line to find out. God, Ricky, I think it's just the biggest fake-out on all those
climbing Philadelphia snobs. I mean they were all after you down there.
Thinking you were going to be a big success and so on. They wanted their
daughters to marry you and you turned out to be a fruit. I love it."*

"Jesus."

*"Well, maybe we'll see each other soon. I love New York, I'm very happy
here. You should be here too. I'll never leave. I'll never go anywhere."*

I heard later that she died of a heroin overdose. I worry about my
effect on people.

Being A Sports Fan

is combat in my apartment. When all revved up about the Sox, Pats, Celts, Bruins (I'm a fair weather cunt in hockey-land) I forget that fans in other towns are as hard core as we are in Boston. Hurt with loss, euphoric in victory. Also, duh, sports is a bonding for dudes who can get safely worked up without embarrassing themselves with homo hugs and hi-5's. Loathing the Yankees or our fav jock stars who trade out is hot lather and overturned cars, but a safe-ish landing for violent impulses.

I wouldn't have gotten into sports were it not for the flat screens at Doyle's. Not the over-sized fatties in an actual sports bar, but substantial enough to not ignore. Nervous about where a game might be headed, I duck into the kitchen and wait for the bar crowd to cheer or groan. Then I hurry out and watch the replay, too much a coward to see in real time.

Once hooked, like watching a soap, I'm addicted. I ask stupid questions about the rules. About a ref call. About a player. Jill Petruzziello (server/bartender) has quick smart answers and doesn't make me feel like a wind tunneled, bouffant 50's housewife. I vied for her to be a sideline commentator/interviewer on NESN. She's terrific looking, but without those ridiculous egg beater hair jobs and knows her shit. Hard fact info clearly articulated, she'd be girl next door perfect. She'll never apply and thinks I'm nuts to want this for her. Maybe the most knowledgeable are more effective out of the spotlight. Girls are as avid fans at the guys and maybe even better informed.

In our apartment we're split. two Sox fans and one *"all rise"* Yankee. Alex is by far the most sports educated. He scooped up the bobble doll of

JBJ. It was he who calmed me down when, mid-season, I fretted over the Sox, 2018.

"They're fine," he'd argue. *"Don't worry about it."*

Robby, a Yankee and Giants fan, is a gentleman. He doesn't rub it in when we're fucked and he's generous about a big Boston win. (If I could be so kind.) He can't understand why I'm not a Giants fan given that my Uncle Carl punted for them back in the 1930's.[21]

The kitties flicked and busted one of the bobbles, but JBJ survived and is now out of reach. Love the mid-air leap, the eye focus. I can hear the crack of the bat in my head. One of the best sounds in the world.

---

21 See 'Getting Old Is No Fun' ('The Paragraphs')

Brass Balls

I have not. I am a coward.

I showed up on an off work night at T.T. The Bears. TT's had a horseshoe wrap around bar. If the band on stage was too loud, you could hang on the far side and your ears wouldn't bleed. I forget who was playing that night. I hung on the safe side, away from the blare. Some nut job thought I was staring at his girlfriend. He obviously had no clue about my persuasion. She was leaning against the wall a few feet away. I shrugged him off and then, out of the blue, she flashed me. She popped open her shirt and there they were, two pair, perky and jiggling in the breeze. Knockers up! Her boyfriend gave me a two arm shove. My forever friend, Matt York, punched him in the face three times, knocking the crap out of the him. Kid went down. Jeannie (the awesome bartender who passed away in 2009) asked what happened. Matt told her and she bought us both a round. The Garage Dogs picked the guy up off the floor and dragged him out of the club. When we left later that night and the dude was still sitting on the sidewalk looking dazed and confused. Wrote a song about it.

I may not have the balls, but I have the brass. Leftovers from the house I grew up in. A candlestick (god knows where its mate disappeared) and a bed pan. Not the shit-in-it-when-your-sick kind, but the Revolutionary antique that maids filled with boiling water or coals and slithered under the sheets to invite a frozen body into the happy warmth.

Over the years I've tried to polish them up with Brasso. The stink of chemicals made me dizzy and the fear that poison absorbed into un-gloved skin could induce leprosy. I loathed the rubbity rub-a-dub-dub. You have to leave the scum sauce on long enough to crack fissures on the surface like a facial. You put off the rubbings as long as possible and then go at it until you give up (sooner rather than later). No one noticed. Even I would avert my eyes given the no gleam finish. Unpolished, they looked ashamed, shy about being on display, wall or table.

"I'm not as pretty as I could be. Please hide me in the pantry. I don't deserve the scrutiny."

So I chickened out. I gave up. I let 'em dull out. At the new house, however, I changed it up. I Googled a *"we polish brass and silver 'til it looks like new"* garage in Needham. A buck fifty for both. A two day wait. The candlestick came home, astonished, proud and luminous, as if inspiring a congregation on a cathedral altar. The bed pan blazes in the hallway. Everyone notices. They're fabulous. The candlestick, an Agatha Christie murder weapon. The bed pan, an Aztec sun.

"You did this, Rick?! What a good job!"
— my sister, Janie

I almost wanted to lie and take credit, but I hadn't the balls.

Can't Beat The Mother

for beauty. Musicians, architects, poets, film makers, designers, painters, writers approach the flame, emulate Mom Nature, but let's face it, in the end it's an almost-but-not-quite.

My sister, Janie, has that wise appreciation, reverence, in her world view and in her heart. Mother Nature holds the cards, the cards that count. The insanity that is an unchecked mankind can't hold a candle to the power and the glory that is She. It is preposterous of us to think we can outsmart, out beautify or out control Lady Nature.

A shell, beach-found, comes home in a sandy pocket and sits on a sill, caught by the afternoon sun and warmed from within. It's snail occupant, MIA, or re-fitted into a new home with a bigger spiral staircase.

I'm pretty sure Janie gave me this one, spotting it amidst the pebbles of a receding wave, winking in the California wet. I need her to remind me that Mom Nature is the key to all that is. Too easily I forget, riding my *fast train to nowhere* that can be another busy day in the art shop.

Every time I open the fridge I see the shell and think of her, of my sister. Of the sky, the sea, the simplicity, the universe.

Caper

Back when *Green St* was Green St. When it was The Afterhours Hang in the hood, where there seemed to live at least fifteen people, primarily musicians and artists. Where booze and weed gushed out of the spigot day and night. Where, in the basement, a drum/amp/guitar set up was in constant use. Where 'Mittens' (the band) was born. Where god knows who was fucking whom. Where my friend, Jeila[22] and I would wind up after Doyle's. It was there (before they got evicted after not paying rent for six months) that I went to set up the caper.

I was living at the Piano Factory. I'd stride up to Berklee College of Music to have lunch most afternoons with my unrequited boyfriend, constant companion and band mate (The Shelley Winters Project), David Berndt, who had the unpleasant job of class scheduler for all professors, each of whom wanted priority consideration. The fought for their spots like kids on Ritalin, or like the elderly pouting at dinner and complaining: *"she got her soup, where's mine!?"*.

From a window on the 5th floor, I spotted the erector set scaffold. Perched on a horizonal bar was the owl. His job: scarecrow away any uninvited creature – pigeon, hawk, rat, human. I wanted it. I wanted those big golden eyes and hard plastic feathers in my house. I didn't want to buy one. I wanted *this* one.

2 AM. Pull up to the Green St compound. Fill the Grand Am[23] with three boys, two girls and set sail. Park in the shadows and slither down a dark

---

22　See 'The Mouth That Roared'

23　See 'Carwashed' (*The Paragraphs*)

alley to the scaffold. Boys: scale the jungle gym and grab the bird. Girls: look for cops.

"If the fuzz tries to stop us, I'll say my girlfriend had to pee and couldn't wait."

Embarrass them off with the yellow river threat.

We scored the bird, the Maltese Owl, shrieking and running back to the car like naughty children.

Cat Attack

Plants I own, unless innately strong, die agonizing deaths, green fingers in absentia. I do have one or two that survived over the years. The one above, a case in point. I don't know what you call it, what plant denomination. It was on loan from Noah 'I Am The Buddah' Scanlon (bassist with The Shelley Winters Project) and his at-the-time girlfriend. I propped it up on a high stool in the kitchen at our former apartment. It thrived there, vigorous and unperturbed. I watered it every Monday (unless I forgot).

In those days, when Robby was hard drinking, he and Ricky would go nuts late at night and wrestle in the kitchen. Ricky overhead twirled and hurled Robby's busted up leather jacket in no particular direction. It exploded on my poor plant, knocked it off the stool, cracked the pot, spilled dirt and ouch-bent the leaves and branches.

It had more than Ricky as an opponent. The cats. I'd turn the stool to keep the leaves out of bite-and-eat reach. Even so, my guys laid into it, leaning in from the kitchen table, chewing on the leafy green. It looked like it was attacked by locusts. Leaf bumps pumped up kitty lungs like an addiction. One hit was never enough. Still, for the most part, the miniscule stool turns kept her safe.

At the new house, with a proper back porch, I kept it outside in the open air, cheerfully rained on, cat free. Same with my lesser plant, one that's tough as nails and sufficiently out of kitty destruct-o-thon. Unfortunately, the porch was plant secure for eight, nine months. In winter they'd freeze and die. I had to move them back into the kitchen. The wee plant perched safely on a shelf above the sink, but my long time survivor wound up in the highest place I could find– the top of the fridge. Not good. The delinquents jumped up like Cheetahs and gnawed away.

"NO, Wasabi. NO NO NO! NO! Carlotta, get down *from there!"*

I'd pick them up by the scruff and lower them onto the floor, an ineffectual cease fire, because once we're outa the house, or asleep, they're back up there eviscerating.

Can't wait for spring.

Circumsized

I've always fought for my position in my apartments as The Secretary Of Interior Decoration. The arbiter of what's pretty and belongs in the common rooms and what does not. I'm not a total dick, but come close. On the other hand, most of the crap in the house is mine. Years of collecting furniture from dead parents.

Prime suspect: the kitchen island that came with the new place. I hated it. Unrelenting, obsessive poofter hatred. I already had The Perfect Kitchen Table. In no way was I going to allow that despicable island monstrosity to replace it. That beast was greasy. The doors underneath hung open like torn pockets and bumped against your knees when you sat on the equally hideous stools that came with that grotesque artifact.

Ace realtor, Charlene Carter, instrumental in finding us our fabulous new home, didn't give us much hope. The island was not a deal breaker, but it did wig me out and I wouldn't shut up about it.

"If, and that's a big if, we can move it into the basement, then it'll be history. But we won't know that until the movers get here," she explained.

The Grandfather Clock had nearly been impossible to break down. The fab, handsome Eastern Euro dude, solved[24] that problem as he would this one. He took one look at vile island, cracked open the bulkhead and pulled off a mover miracle, giving the odious island a Nantucket sleigh ride into the bowels of the basement.

---

24   See 'The Noble Clock'

THE UGLY UNDERSTUDY

Alex Gang: poet, humorist, memorizer of songs, Satyr, thief, prankster, flag half-master, volunteer, manager of fancy restaurants, eggplant deliveries and a wise man on a ship of fools, contributed two principle items. His Step Dad's couch[25] (magnificent) and two mushroom cap table lamps (horrendous). I took one look and pouted. No way would these dickhead lamps make the cut. Alex would keep one for himself, the other would sit on the kitchen floor until I got around to moving it to the basement. Plenty of space on top of The Island Of Ugly.

Until I plugged it in.

Oh. My. God! This stubby, kitsch cock, cleanly circumcised, is one of The Coolest Things Ever. The light it throws – as soft as an e e cummings poem. We leave it lit day and night. The cats toothpick their teeth on the edge. This fussy fairy couldn't be happier and he could not have been more wrong. It has me wanting to watch *Europa, Europa* (Agnieszka Holland) all over again. Like the mushroom lamp, *E,E* is funny, sexy and terrifying.

---

25   See 'Curl Up'

Clocked Out

To a fault. I open one eye, then the other, peeking to see if my meditation is twenty minutes cooked, like an overdone egg. The eyelid gets stuck. It feels like I'm trying to lift open a garage door that's fighting back.

It's internal, my clock. It's like that for most of us I guess. I know when the time's up and I need to head out the door. I check the sundial, approve of the aesthetics, but I don't need clocks to know what time it is. An alarm, proof positive. I'll set it when I need to get up at some god forsaken hour. I hate early, but I'll do it in fear of missing a critical airplane departure, the start of the JP Music Festival or a doc appointment. I fireman slide the greasy pole into waiting rubber, don't-be-late boots. Although, nine times out of ten, I wake up before the alarm starts barking. I plan the drive to work specifically so that I leave in time in order to arrive on time. The hour appointed to feed Wasabi and Carlotta clicks boot heels to attention with goose-step precision. Those two know this about me. They count on it even as they worry that I'll screw up.

"Berlin's on time so he can make people wrong who are late."
– Anonymous

Not really. It's not a competition. What it *is* is, I never want to be the person who holds up a meeting, a rendezvous, a band gig, so I show up early. That way I'm able to text updates, herd late arrivals and calm nerves and feel fabulous about myself.

I forget about daylight savings. Someone else has to reset for me. Tech help from the tech wise. On the old-fashioned Grandpa, I correct the skeletal hour hands with a respectful index finger. On the orange beauty above, a tease rotation of the clitoral knob in back. I smile at it, my Betty Crocker kitchenaire orange. So would my never late Mom.

"Put down the funny papers, Rick. Your ride is here."

Cow

Or steer? I always thought it was a cow, but now, looking straight at it? That yellow thing on its head? It could be a horn. Fuck it. For me, it's an udder less cow. It belonged to my boyfriend Steven Perry's Grandma. She lived in the sticks. A shack. A vegetable garden. A goat. One tough, independent, self-sufficient woman. Hair in a Gibson Girl bun. I think she might have churned her own butter. She definitely made her own ice cream. She loved her grandson. Perked up when he came to visit. I'd stand quietly in the shadows and listen to them talk. She lived with a lady friend. Speculation had it that they were lovers. Who cares? She was just a person who never stopped being true to herself, without fanfare.

I'm not sure how we came by the cow. It might have been left to Steven after she died. Thankfully, I wound up with it. I've balanced it above windows, on a shelf, by a door, but always in the kitchen where, like a ghostly calico aproned Auntie pulling a cookie sheet of brownies out of a warm oven, Bessie seemed to belong.

I never really knew Steve's Grandma, but her cow, her wonderful brown and white, touches me heart.

Fire Escape

Bought this white bomb after the Creighton Street fire on New Year's Eve. Four apartment units and eleven tenants had to be evacuated. The building was owned by our intrepid landlady, Aida Lopez, who, in bathrobe and slippers, rushing to the scene in a panic, tripped on a firehose and landed on her face. Swollen black eyes and a setback for an unsteady heartbeat. No one was hurt. No cats lost. Rumor had it that Aida's daughter was barbecuing on an hibachi on the third floor back porch. It overturned, the coals ignited the porch wood and the contagious flames took the house along with it.

Defensive maneuver; buy the white bomb.

A.   I have never used it.
B.   I don't know how to use it if I have to.
C.   Would there be time in a fiery frenzy to actually read the instructions, decipher and utilize?

Not even close.

After the Granada movie debacle[26], Frank (Height) thought we should start a band. There were bags of drug money left over. He bought a house beside a creek in Western Mass. I moved there with *Franny*. Janie, Frank's Sad-Eyed Lady muse, would visit. We painted the interior in wild colors tripping on lysergic acid. The colors smelled like the fruit they resembled. Orange, cantaloupe. Red, watermelon. Green, asparagus. We hadn't rehearsed or played a note, but were living the dream. An easy life, paid for. A hippie's lay-it-on-me adventure, Part 2.

---

26   See 'Busted In Grenada' (*The Paragraphs*)

I set up a tent near the creek; befriended a kid, floating downstream on an inner tube. We were gonna get a dog and hang a hammock. An ideal, lazy afternoon summer, living for free and forming a band. A lot less challenging than making a movie on a Caribbean island. No cops, no jail, no nudity. Good karma, however, was not our friend.

I dropped Janie off at her house in Hadley and was heading home when I saw the flames; a blood orange torch screaming a mile high into the firmament. I didn't realize until I got there, that it was our house, our very fine house that caught fire. The stink, afterwards, was putrid. It lingered in our clothes, our hair. The destruction was full on. A pair of Franny's boots, poking up through the embers, were melted like a candy bar. A guitar, charred and broken at the neck lay under an overturned couch. The fanciful LSD colors, blackened. All that was left was my tent.

We disbanded. The Height highs evaporated. Franny and I went back to New Haven and then on to Cambridge, moving into the same apartment on Pleasant St. It was there, on a downstairs neighbor's piano, at the far end of a living room dotted with their child's we-won't-house-train-our-kid turds, I began to write a lot of songs.

It takes a fire.

Four Outa Five

Discmakers manufactures CDs for the indigent. I know. Nobody has the proper playing device or collects them anymore. Hipsters want too-expensive-for-us vinyl. Spotify handles singles. But me, old school Berlin, wants hard copy disc evidence of work done. So what if expensive promotional packaging gets the heave at radio stations or is ignored by publications that can no longer afford music critics or where they only write up the already huge. Like I said, I spring for this shit. Boxes of inventory in the basement, rotting away.

About the framed discs.

When the first one arrived I thought we'd won something, like a miniature Grammy. But it was just a thank you from the company, hoping we'd come back. Not like they had anything to worry about. Discmakers is the only game in town. They're hooked up with CD Baby, the company that gets you streamed all over the world in a 'bundle'. You get both when you sign up. Print those damn discs. Who wouldn't?

I like the company. They do pro work, moderately priced. I'll keep using them as long as I make records I'm proud of. That's where I spend my money. The studio, the hard copies, the legacy. Bandcamp streams my catalogue. The weirdo demos, Nickel & Dime, Berlin Airlift, The Shelly Winters Project, Luna, Rome Is Burning, The Kingdom, LIVE@ JACQUES, solo projects and music going all the way back to Orchestra Luna I and II. Therein lies the legacy. (Berlin continues to live in the margins of the main stream.)

I feel good seeing those ducks in a row. The great graphics that Nick

Kent[27] did for us. The turnstile of come and go band members. Discmakers has stopped doing the congratulatory frames, the weeding out of a former business model. The acceptance of the reality that no one gives a fuck anymore about albums, or CDs.

Four will do. Proud warriors in the kitchen. Special Forces once fierce that graze, like old man rock stars, out to pasture.

---

27   See 'Put Your Glasses On'

Friends, Enemies

Sofi and Mao: furry gladiators.[28] My girl was nearing the end of her days. Travis Kern's girlfriend and online obsessive, Danielle Hollingsworth (now his wife) was a Petco manager. She picked up this irresistible kitten and brought him home. A ball of fur and a tiny meow that sounded like 'Mao' as in Tse Tung. Thus the name.

Sof was petrified. She hid behind a book on the highest shelf in my closet. I bought an electric aromatic incense device that was supposed to kitty Xanax her into get-over-yourself, to flatline her fear. Didn't work. Mao continued to freak her out. He'd scamper down the hallway and she'd run and hide. The older he got, the bigger and fluffier. He blew up like a blowfish, larger than life, but was skin-and-bones scrawny when wet. Sofi, of course, never put two-and-two together. In her eyes, Mao was Goliath. For him, Sofi was sport. His aggression was never malicious, just play. For her, it was a war with no roses.

On a rare occasion, they were almost friendly. He'd lick her ears. She'd purr. They'd lie side-by-side on my bed and sleep. That's when I took the picture.

Travis and Danielle moved to DC in a snowstorm. Their truck was loaded to the tits, Mao in front on Danielle's lap. That was the last we saw him. Mao and Sofi – both dead. All I have is that picture in the tiny, refrigerator magnet frame. I hope someday to be so enshrined, lost in an ocean of children's drawings, news clippings and memorabilia. A memento that falls off when you're looking for butter or milk.

---

28   See 'Kitty Projection' (*The Paragraphs*)

Life. It's over before ya know it.

Glory Bowls

Both were Sofi's. One for water. One for food. She died. Kept the bowls. Now they belong to the new guys. Their water bowl is different, a dog ceramic, deep and hefty, separate from the chrome. Wasabi likes to flick the water out of it like a cat taking a bird bath.

I wash the double receptacles once in the morning, but not at night. Scrub, wipe, dry. Carlotta and Wasabi jump up on the dishwasher to be sure I'm on point. They skitter around the table. Run in and out of the kitchen. Watch me rake out their shit boxes ahead of the feed, impatiently patient. I talk to them.

"You go over there. I'll go over here. Breakfast is on the way. Don't worry about it."

First the turkey wet which I dice up like Mom for a child. I want them to eat all of it. The squish and cut makes for gorge bites with no spit back. I divvy up fair portions. One 2.7 ounce can per meal sliced down the center with a tablespoon as I hack away, moving bits from one bowl to the other until I'm satisfied that the scale has not been thumb tipped. Then into the pantry for the oven baked chicken pellets. Only the best kitty cuisine for my two. Dry food is supposed to provide abrasive for kitty fangs, wet is kind to the kidneys.

Wasabi gets his under the mushroom lamp in the kitchen. He does a little clown cat trick by curling around my ankles twice, before I settle the bowl onto the floor. He reaches up the wall with both arms and makes pigeon coos. I'd hoped for panther, but get pigeon. So not cat. If he only knew how silly he sounds. Carlotta gets dosed in my bedroom with the door shut. Wasabi's a Hoover. His dinner disappears in under three minutes. Carlotta is demure, dainty and particular. Appetizer, first. Main course, second. Dessert, third. It's all the same crap, but she compartmentalizes. A trip to the radiator for a look out the window after the first course. Back to the bowl. A pellet or two in a petite mouth. Clean herself, visit me meditating on the bed. Jump down and finish the remains. Once she's done, I open the door and her brother shoots in like an arrow and licks the bowl 'til it gleams.

Same thing, day in, night out. I feel badly. This is their only food. Their only din din other than the plant leaves on top of the fridge or an occasional chomp through a loaf of bread we forgot to hide. If they could run around outdoors, they'd kill a rabbit or a squirrel or a bird with a broken wing, followed by fabulous rabies. Fuck that. Indoor cats, period. No kitty froth-at-mouth.

Green Mansions

Ed Sullivan, hard riding member of The Red Emeralds biker gang and stoned owner of Tuesday's Ice Cream, painted this imaginary glade. I hung it in the get-air-in-here window above the shower. A stiff breeze crashed it into the tub and obliterated the frame, but the loosely stretched canvas still holds. Honestly, I prefer the wavy edges as if painted on a still-wet yesterday.

As a Red Emerald, Ed dealt with bad dudes, Emerald enemies. Some dirt-bag raped the friend of a gang member. They kidnapped the bastard, dangled and dropped him like a screaming sack of rats from a railroad bridge onto a moving train. You don't fuck with The Emeralds. Ed promised that if I ever wound up in prison he'd have his boys guarantee my safety. No gang rape of the Ricky fish. No ass jobs by the fat and sweaty. Protected by a biker gang phalanx. Someday I'll ink up a prison tattoo.

"No Fishing Allowed"

Ed's gone. Cancer. He'd visit Billie and Chet at their Crazy Wife Farm after Chet got the big C. With both of them under the gun they figured, screw it. They snorted an Everest of coke in one non-stop, middle finger to Lady Death, revelry. Why the fuck not?

A RELEVENT DIVERSION

"When something precious and irretrievable is lost, we have the feeling of having awakened from a dream."
– Hermann Hesse

"Love, Proust insists, can only co-exist with a state of dissatisfaction, whether born of jealousy or its predecessor – desire. It represents our demand for a whole. Its inception and its continuance imply the consciousness that something is lacking. One only loves that which one does not possess entirely."
– S. Beckett

Youth

An odor like an acid sword made

of plum branches along the road,

the kisses like sugar in the teeth,

the drops of life slipping on the fingertips,

the sweet sexual fruit,

the yards, the haystacks, the inviting

rooms hidden in the deep houses,

the mattresses sleeping in the past,

the savage green valley

seen from above, from the hidden window:

adolescence all sputtering and burning

like a lamp turned over in the rain.
– Naruda

After I gave up chronic shop lifting, I got a job driving Red Cab – a jet pilot breaking sound barriers all over the midnight city. Cabbies were masters of the terrain, dangerously over-confident. I ate up Southie accents, the cigarette tenors of rude dispatchers, the decent money if you stayed in the cab until you made quota, the tense fear of picking up a lethal fare. One time, at Quincy Market, a handsome black dude in a suit-with-briefcase needed to be driven to Worcester. A big ticket. Quiet and polite, not unlike Gus Fring from *Breaking Bad*, a gentleman who would slit your throat. When we got to Worcester he pulled a gun.

"I'll be getting out here," he said, gentle baritone.

"Sure. Ok. No problem."

I was not going to test the threat.

On late afternoon breaks from driving, I'd stop by Tuesday's, a few storefronts up from Brookline Village on Route 9. Red Cab fired me after a head-on, bad-for-cab-insurance collision, so I moved up in the world scooping vanilla and chocolate at Tuesdays.

Truth be told, it wasn't about the ice cream. It was about Finn. I memorized his scoop schedule and made a point of showing up. I wanted to be around that kid. The way he looked at me beyond the parameters of whatever it was that we were talking about. A starry-eyed universe that floated me off the linoleum. We were full-on shortly thereafter, as close as I'd ever come to romantic reciprocity. I wrote *Over The Hill* about him. A local radio hit. Jocks played it on 'BCN in drive time. Finn would be riding in a car with friends, knowing it was about him, about us and would wear the secret like a cloaked badge of honor. No one knew. They figured *Hill* was about Ed's gossip-streamlined affair with one of his *teen girl* employees.

This is the first time I've written about him overtly.[29] Those singular emotions, his gift of 'knowing'[30] me, a True-Love Benchmark paral-

---

29   See 'Pool Hopping' and 'The Switch' in 'The Paragraphs'.

30   See 'Epilogue'

leled only one other time – winter, the Brendan Behan, a biology lab at Children's Hospital, a drag bar, a fig tree – 2020.

Back to the past:

Ed MC'd Berlin Airlift shitfaced the night we opened for J. Geils at the New Haven Coliseum (Geil's last tour before they split up).

"Laaaaadies and gentlemen! let's hear it for Handshahk recawding ahtist Berlin Aiiiiiircraft!"

It was Hand*shake,* but seemed more shark when you thought about it, to say nothing about Air*lift* vs Air*craft,* but ya gotta love it. That was how we rolled back then. The band broke up because we were dealing/snorting suitcases full of dope; a death knell for any project or relationship, but par for the course in our filthy rock n roll wheelhouse.

At one performance, a scull shack on the Charles, as we were winding up, Ed sauntered in. I introduced him to a friend.

"Nice t' meet all three of yous," he said.

There ya go.

Happy Warrior

This guy is my sign off tag for the bulk of my videos, music or otherwise, a windup key poking out of his side like a burst appendix. He plays cymbals like the Energizer Bunny, but runs outa gas in seconds. I approve. No need to run that wee circus into the ground. He's Mr. Coda and should rightfully stop in his tracks.

He reminds me of a pair of windup nuns, similarly constructed, two inch high figures. I set them up on table #9 in the front room at Doyle's to entertain a couple of non-habit Sisters, terrific ladies and favorites at work. They had Faith for real, but never shoved it in your face. Salt of the earth, straight up women who went to their nephew's baseball games, drank beer with our Savior beaming sweetly out of non-*proselytizing* eyes. They got a big bang out of the windups. Starting and re-starting them over and over again.

They bought my CD *LIVE@JACQUES* in solidarity.

"This is how we listen," they explained, patting their ears with open hands, pat, pat, pat *"so we don't hear the bad words"*.

There are a lot of nasty nuns out there. Ask anyone who went to Catholic school. These two, like my plastic monkey, are spectacular.

Hung Like A Horse

This big dick statuette magically appeared in my fifteen year apartment above La Casa del Regalos and stood proudly atop the fridge like an icon, a voo doo cockswain with massive fertility powers. When friends came over they'd glance at him sideways, but, unless shit-faced, made no comment.

Dude speaks for himself. The gravity of his member is a where-is-there-a-hole-big-enough-to-put-it-in divining rod. It looks like it would be painful just walking that monster across the street. Elephantiasis of the penis (like those pictures we stared at in high school biology of watermelon-sized testicles in wheelbarrows). Achingly heavy and painful.

When I tilt him forward and check from behind I see that he has no balls. He's been castrated! How weird is that? What does it mean? Did the ritual for which this guy was carved imply punishment? Did he have a high voice? He looks tough. The double fists make muscle and perk his pecks with a self-assured implacable face and rock hard nipples, but maybe they cut off his nuts to punish an over confident phallus.

I've always thought he looked like President Obama, whom I'm certain has a big one. Barack isn't a pissing contest dude, the opposite of Mr. Tiny Hands. If I thought Barack would get a Kenyan laugh out of this dude, I'd send it to him, but Michelle would give it the heave.

I Think He's Constipated

No question. Look at that face. He's trying so hard. It has to hurt, the retention.

This totem is what my nephew, Sammy Dudley, gave me one Christmas. He finds the oddest objects. Maybe he's in a hurry – find, buy, wrap, give? Who knows? Sammy has, like his best friend Will Hofstadter puts it,

"...a lotta can't waits".

So yeah, either the Aztec constipate was a rush job or there was a 'can't wait' waiting around the corner. Or not. This might have been a well thought out Dudley deliberation. I mean, so what? Berlin does not need a SD3 fucking Christmas present and it's fair to point out that Uncle Ricky slams through *his* Christmas shopping spree in one accelerating hour: Boing!, On Centre, Kitchenwitch. Finito!

The kid has been Uncle Ricky's go-to friend since the day he was born[31] and vice versa. We've always been mad close. From the early days on Long Island armpit farting in the movie theater (boring, age appropriate kid flicks) to the Boy With The *Badville* Tattoo; ink wallpaper all over his skin. I buy him a Pumpkin Tatt gift certificate as my combo birthday/Christmas present every year. He gets to choose for himself; ever the preferred option.

Sam's pretty. He was born pretty. He just is. Blonde, tall, lean, a come-n-

---

31 His Dad had his tubes tied exactly one day after Lisa became pregnant. Sammy was supposed to show up. It was in the stars. Fierce fate.

go beer belly, blue eyes and as many riffs on his hair-do as Bowie. Even so, it took him awhile to make it happen with the ladies. Always a gentleman. Better to hang over an afternoon coffee as a potential friend than a drunken, see ya later, forced entry. I did spot him, late one night, legless, shove a girl up against a wall on Centre St and smack her with a long hard kiss. She seemed to be okay with it and no way was Uncle Ricky going to butt in. There's a decent chance I misread the encounter.[32] These days he's found his mojo and rides into town, Handsome Cowboy Sam, stud guns blazing. A dance bar. An online hookup. A concert. He's rarely afraid to man up and find out where the night might lead. It helps that he's upbeat and happy. For a time I wondered whether he wore a good mood mask, disguising his true being even from himself. But now I'd say it's for real. He's sparkplug sunshine, ask anybody. Exuberant hand gestures and superlatives color every anecdote. In full-on Loveland, murky water. Could be he prefers *not* having a longtime girlfriend. I doubt he'd settle for the sake of it. He's too much the adventurer, wise enough to see through any too-good-to-be-true love smog.

He's a performance junkie. When he was in 2nd grade he was singing in a chorus with a ton of other kids, his face bright red and The Loudest Kid up there. Ask his Mom. He lives for this shit. He's performed with me, or without, too many times to count. When he was eleven he played a trombone version of *New York, New York* to a full house of Red Sox fans at a Shelley Winter's Project show. After he finished, he went outside and fell asleep in the car. If I had a solo gig in Rensselaerville, he'd sit in. He read 'Miss Zablocki's Tits' at the Lizard Lounge. A friend of mine told him he'd be excellent at reading porn. Off to a great start, kiddo.

---

32   When I was a first year student at the Yale Drama School I overheard an altercation in the alley outside my apartment. A man and a woman were screaming at each other. He pushed her up against the wall and she slapped him back, hard enough to hear. I shouted down without going down (coward) telling the dude to cut it out or I'd call the cops. The girl yelled back: 'Shut the fuck up and leave us the fuck alone!' I guess I had no idea what was really going on, my part in it or theirs.

His 10 years with The Nickel & Dime Band? Lucky us. The boy. The
bone. The voice parallel to mine and his Mom's. The flamboyant one.
The dancer. The guy who, like Ricky McLean, knows all the words to
my songs when I forget and mouths them at me in a stage whisper.
Lately he's moved on. New Orleans. My text/song on his departure:

> *"Ok, Sammy. There are no final notes, only false endings. Had*
> *I been a Proper Queen or a First Lady and not an Old Lady I would*
> *take a cheap bottle of champagne and crush it on the fender of your wee*
> *Suzuki chicklet and wish you bon voyage in a warbling British contralto.*
> *But none of that, although there's nothing proper about either of us. Like*
> *Eliot and ET we will always be connected ('under a blanket') regardless*
> *of distance. God knows what the fuck our Karma is. Never mind band,*
> *place or family. All part of the fluctuating wild ride map of life. All the*
> *best forever and ever, amen.*
> **MLA, UR"**

With the server DNA that pockmarks his Mom and Uncle, he scored a job
in The Industry, waiting tables at Café Amelie. That ended with the
lockdown. He ricocheted back to the hood, landscaping for his friend
and boss, Marc Arsenault. Fingers in the soil, grass stains on his ass,
body once again losing baby fat and tightening the fuck up.

He's his Mom and Dad's composite. He has his Father's correctoid
impatience with another's slow-on-the-draw moves, the why aren't you
doing it my way disorder. He'll take a back seat driver dig at me, but
apologize seconds later. He and his Dad share a sincere appreciation
of all music, musicians, music history, archives, LP's and shows. Big
Sam educated Little and it stuck. He has his Mom's sweetness and
easy-to-forgive empathy. Her innocent creativity. Her love of work and
quickly made friendships. Her choice of what to wear (Sam has a big
closet). But, like all of us, he's his own dude. The farty boy in the movie
theater is now confidently out in the world and on his own, calling the
shots, making lifelong connections. A spinning top skittering across
an uneven, excitable, improvisational landscape.

There's not much we don't know about each other. Some secrets deferred out of loyalty to friends and family, but, in general, everything's out on the table. Best about he and I? We're totally onto each other's idiosyncratic, Kinscherf humor of the ludicrous. A behavioral tic. An oddball phrase. Overly crossed legs. A haircut. A bald spot. One of us points it out and we lose it, repeating the riff until it dies a miserable death. Ask him about *"un huh"* – impossible to explain to the uninitiated. One of those you-had-to-be-there in jokes, audio required.

I've always thought of him as The Fool (Tarot card). Ready to step blindly off the cliff. The Way: unknown. The happy dog: impatient to hit the road; addicted to 'newness'. The knapsack: not much in it. The sun: bright in a weirdly yellow sky. (He'll show you the tatt.)

THE ACCIDENT

Sammy was twelve. Visiting a friend in New Hampshire. Big snow. Big snowmobile. He drove it into a barn, flew out of the cockpit, hit his head, suffered a concussion and was helicoptered to the Dartmouth-Hitchcock Medical Center. I got the call from Lisa at the end of my shift at Doyle's. Max Frevert drove me home. I was sobbing. How the fuck could this have happened to this kid? To this non-stop twelve year old?

They plugged tubes into every orifice, socked him into an induced coma, vitals on every computer screen. He looked fragile. There are pictures. When you saw him like that, you wept. So young, so small in the bed, so knocked out, the ticking heart beats on the monitor. It was excruciating to see.

After he returned home, to Rensselaerville, he was, in a few short weeks, his old self. Running all over the place. Yelling and laughing with his sisters and friends. The life of the family party. I was there that Christmas; not my favorite thing. The holiday ritual at Grandma Barbara's was behavior specific. This one carves. That one does dishes. This one removes the plates. That one makes the gravy. Take turns talking and sound like you know what you're talking about. Be pertinent. Make it interesting. Chime in only when you have something relevant to add. No bad words. Don't fart or burp. Wait until you have permission before you leave the table. Compliment the din-din. Be excited about desert. A bit of a stuffed shirt show, albeit well-meaning with an old fashioned, New England propriety. Barbara was one fine, resilient woman. Hickory Hill, her domain. When you visit, you operate under her purview. If you do, you earn her respect. If you do not, you feel the chill. What endeared me to her most was her inability to control her flatulence; a late-in-life condition. At the sink there'd be an involuntary emission; an increased rush of tap water the inadequate disguise. One never made comment, but we Kinscherfs loved her for it.

That Christmas, well past the accident, Sammy and I were being our reckless idiot selves, running all over the property, indoors and out, laughing and making fun of each other. At one point we wound up in the library. Comfy armchairs, shelves filled with books, a fireplace. The activity cyclone came to an abrupt halt and he looked at me straight up and asked:

"Do you still love me, Uncle Ricky?"

As if he was damaged goods? Really? What a brave fucking question. Who wants to ask that? Who wants an honest answer? But ask he did and I answered with the obvious. Hence, the song: *Do You Still Love Me?* which I wrote as soon as I got home.

The following Christmas we stayed back at the Dudley house while the rest of the family had gone early to Barbara's. I played him the song.

"I never said that."

"Yes, you did. I could never have made it up."

We drove to Hickory Hill. After dinner, all hung out in the living room, opening presents and trying our earnest best to be grateful. There was a spinet piano between the couch and the tree.

"Should I play the song, Sammy?"

"Go ahead. It's ok."

So I did. Tears rolled quietly down everyone's face.

Near the end of his time with *Nickel & Dime*, Sam asked if he could sing *Do You Still?* himself, instead of me. The band had learned the song. Robby made it rock. We were playing The Midway and Lisa and Sam were going to be there. He knew they'd be moved to hear him sing it. They were. He was. We all were. Ricky McLean calls it *The Sammy Song*. That it has become.

The totem, I'm pretty sure, hasn't taken a proper dump in centuries. Sam and his Uncle do not have that problem.

Juju

If not from New Orleans, then Mexico or a Caribbean island. Steel drums, drugs, twitchy dancing, pins in dolls. There's something comical, even cheerful about this marionette, the dancing skeleton in party clothes, but I get a shiver up my spine just looking at him, telling myself:

"Don't throw it out or it'll come back and do scary shit while you're asleep."

Like the dangling leftover Christmas decorations that have sparkle spots here and there around the house, I leave Juju up. Loose arms, heavy pants, bright red cummerbund smiling and full of secrets. Maybe the point is:

Death is coming, baby. Laugh in its face. Might be easier with a little doll with a black lipstick grin as a reminder. Death will become mundane or suggest that after you're gone, a party awaits. Trombones and limousines. Boys on parade. Conch shells brimming with potent booze poisons. Spliffs a mile long. A Juju in a tutu.

So up you stay, Mr. Death. I salute you as I avert my scaredy-cat eyes.

Miniature Manger

is a present I got at one of our Christmas parties. I never plucked the figurines out of the box, preferring the green plastic shine-through silhouettes; bas relief in a kitchen window.

Look, I like the holiday, I do, but from a distracted distance. Salvation Army bell ringers in the Harvard Square snow and sour caroling – cool. Decorating a pretty tree and smelling the pine – Joyeux Noel, pansy perfection. The race horse shopping – not so much.

I made a (selfish?) decision a few years ago. I buy my sister's families one decent present per family member per Christmas. I keep notes on what I give to whom and who's turn it is. Instead of shooting my load on a full Santa bag of Christmas crap, I buy one relative something expensive and actually useful. I get their kids quantity over quality, an acceptable handful of offerings wrapped in newspaper and marked up friendly with a sharpie. Uncle Ricky's presents are quick-scan identifiable. But kids need the pile, packaging be damned. Ask my Mom.

Christmas is suicide sad. Depressives fall backwards into the holidays struggling to fend off the dark. Friends have jumped. Others hide at home in an alcoholic stupor. Others tie on a happy face, but you can tell it's a facade. No Star of Bethlehem at the end of that bleak tunnel. One is chastened by their pain during happy season.

Here and there, I keep the trinkets up. They pry a thin smile as I wander the house. They cheer me up like a beauty spot on a pretty girl or a fake diamond earring winking in the middle of a soft Latino lobe.

Monkey Trapeze

I bought this baby blue n brown coat rack built by Tom Lutz at Art For Music: a JP Music Festival fundraiser. He donated it. No one else was interested, thank god, so I bought it. Now it's mine all mine. I don't use it as designed. I just wanted more art on the wall.

The wooden knobs aren't strong. If you thrum them, they sing, a lo-end Theremin sine curve until they pop off. I already lost one, the soccer cats flicked it under a radiator. I won't hang coats. I don't want to. This ain't utility art. It's too cool to hide under a cloth pelt. I imagine that when we're asleep, it makes ethereal music. The monkey, a left-behind Christmas toy I stole from Doyle's, does backflips and laughs. Maybe he plays an accordion and gets the inanimate to dance, chez *Toy Story*. They belong together, these two, monkey and rack.

Tom got a job at a M.I.T. lab when he was a teenager. I don't think he'd graduated from high school, but once in the lab he became indispensable. A place where impossible problems are attacked and sometimes solved. Structures built, robots revved, students and teachers in creative collaboration, a science and art bridge meeting in the middle.

Tom's sister, Nora, a fine musician, teacher and a knockout woman, persuaded her brother (on my behalf) to dress up like a giant lady for the music video: *7' Woman*. A reluctant debutant in drag, who, after a fatty, a six pack and Nora's wig and skirt, went for it whole hog. A killer performance that keeps me laughing every time I watch it.

Hats off to this dude for finding his own way through the vocational maze and to the professors who recognized his talent. Would more of us could be so lucky and could look that sexy in a skirt.

Muckball

I'm not sure why it's called muckball. An amalgam of mud wrestling and softball? Boogers rolled and flicked? A meatball fiasco? I do know that my fired-up friend and boss at Doyle's, Mickey O'Connell Sholes, raised the muckball flag on high these the last three years. Local JP bars competing. Money donated to a worthy cause.

Two years ago she asked me to 'Presidential' the first pitch. I owed her. She and her gal pals made it all the way out to Brighton for a CD release for The Nickel & Dime Band's second record, *When We Were Kids*. An out of the way spot, but Mickey promised and showed up. Girl is as good as her word. No way could I turn her down even though it meant a nasty early morning wake up.

I wanted to refuse. I am a god awful athlete. My Uncle Carl, my sister Janie, my Mom and Dad, my nephew Naren all have jock cred. Me, I throw like a girl. In middle school I played first base. When I tried to catch a ball in that Venus Flytrap mitt, I bent my left thumb back, sprained it and missed the catch. It still smarts. In soccer I yelled a lot, but would scurry up to a rolling ball, fling a leg and miss it entirely as it trickled towards the fed up goalie. Came in dead last in the 440 after a starting gun mis-fire. Humiliation upon humiliation. Good to know later on that I could at least write songs. I don't think gay has anything to do with being a wuss at sports, witness The Caitlyn or the closeted. I just plain suck at 'em, period.

Even so, I'd agreed and that morning, on a dirty diamond in Roslindale, I hurled the first fucking pitch. Mickey's Dad caught at home plate. Dude, I crushed it! A steamer boiled down front and center smack into his glove! I squealed like a stuck pig, wildly proud and happy. My reward: the chartreuse ball itself and a well-earned Muckball T.

PS

The glove. The baby baseball glove was a present from this kid, Ben. We played catch in his backyard in the South End after I picked him and his sister up from school out in the burbs. He was the boy who scribbled his fingers on my open palm and asked me to guess what it meant.

"A thatched roof?" I tried.

"Nope"

"A sea urchin?"

"No."

"The legs of a Centipede?"' (grasping.)

"Rick. It's chaos."

He was nine years old. I kept the glove even as it's too small for my hand. Chaos is how I play the game.

My Filthy Footprint

I mix up without separating trash, garbage and not so sure renewables. I use air conditioning, not fans. I expend a lot of electricity on a space heater and my car gobbles gas. I rationalize that I'm just this one environmentally challenged asshole so what the fuck?! But I know that's bullshit. I'm just lazy and addicted to my comfort zone.

I always hated hearing Michelle Obama talk about us having to *"get out of our comfort zones"*.

I could at least try to use fewer paper bags, so I bought the Whole Foods tote; ugly and girly gay. When I need groceries, I wad the thing into a ball and shove it into a pocket, not wanting to be outed. Somedays I picture myself carrying it like a purse, crooked at the elbow, wrist on high, forearm spangled with noisy bracelets as I sashay to market like a bitch queen.

No Exit

"Hell is other people."
— Jean Paul Sartre

Or numbskull customers at Doyle's.

This 5x5 inch miniature by my first boss at Doyle's, Bonnie Miller, is my fav visual of that joint. The exit sign in the weave is backwards. The bar should be on the left. Maybe the loom mirrored the image falsely. I don't care. I love it. Bonnie gave it to me. Fuck accuracy.

I was given the heave from Davio's following a pathetic a half day on the job:

"Maybe this is the wrong occupation for you," they told me.

The wine list was as thick as the Britannica. The cork broke when I tried to pull it. The dessert menu was ten pages deep. Good riddance.

Jane Mangini, Berlin Airlift's piano lady at the time, lived ten houses down from Doyle's. She bartended. This during her coke period, cutting lines with the back of her hand on the ladies' room toilet and losing half the stash. She'd walk home and wonder where her tips had gone. *"What the fuck!?"* she'd shout at the night sky on the way home only to realize that her bag strap had busted and was following her like a Dachshund on a leash. Crumpled bills dotted the sidewalk behind her like dogshit.

"Talk to Bonnie," she said. *"Come in and talk to Bonnie."*

I did.

"Take those three tables," said Ms. Miller, without blinking.

I'd never waited. Only washed dishes. Back then, there were no computer terminals. Paper pages handed to the backline in the kitchen. You punched the clock. That was thirty-one years ago. Now, instead of being called 'waitresses'...

"Are you our waitress?" I'd be asked, out of habit because *all* the waitresses at Doyle's were women.

"I am she," I'd reply, all pleased with myself.

'Waitress' got PC converted to 'waitrons' (the robotic worst) and evolved to 'servers' (left wing neutrality). Newly minted, I jumped into the Doyle's white water and in minutes I was working it. Making tips, clanging platefuls on brown tables and farting safely in the din.

Bonnie's side gig was the loom. She built it herself and made super large tapestries and sold them to corporate offices for big bucks. Only one of those hung at Doyle's, in the middle room. A sepia rendition of the dark booths, the afternoon light poetically angled. I knew the construct. I knew what those piss yellow lines represented.

"What is that?!" a customer would ask.

"Afternoon sun rays," I told him, suppressing disdain.

"Oh."

Unconvinced.

Those 'light lines' arrow the booths at thirty degrees. One had to interpret. Any leap of imagination seemed impossible for the never-artist and gave me a false sense of superiority. The hooked rug-like 'painting' collected dust and grime. It could use a stiff S&M beating in the parking lot. A vertical hand vacuum never got the job done. Who knows what sort of vile restaurant germs inhabited that thing, wafting down on the unsuspecting customer. But it was too heavy to take down and put back up, so the germaphobes were fucked.

The exit sign? A misnomer. You were not supposed to leave through that door. You'd be directed go out the front. This was the emergency exit. No alarm went off if opened, but if you went outside, it would auto-lock and all the banging in the world would not guarantee re-entry. The sadists at the end of the bar would laugh at you out in the cold with your gesticulating Marlboro. After a few minutes of torture they'd relent and let you back in. It was funny to watch.

Now the place is gone.[33] No entrance. No exit. Hell hath no fury for what happened. I refuse to convict myself by telling the truth and getting sued. People know the truth anyhow.

---

33 See 'Pull Hard'

Our Lady Of The Lamp

was picked up on a Mexico honeymoon by Mom n Dad before we were born. A quiet Geisha who might dance for you in the night, or whisper a provocative sexual position into a tilted ear. She presides over the kitchen in solemn sanctity, as if she knows your secret thoughts, but will never hold them against you. She's made of plaster, chipped white in spots and wears robes the color of dried blood. She was initially crowned with an oversized lamp shade, but the stem above her head that held it in place was busted and bent. For years I suspended it with rope, a gentle noose, not a neck snap.

When we moved, my friend, all-things-fixer, Jay Menekse (The Turk), patched up the stem once and for all. Her elegant neck and perfect posture restored. Replacing the shade are two bulbs, one red, one black light. If I leave them on at night before I head to the bar, they cast a spell that my gummy/Miller Lite eyes find transcendentally beautiful.

Colored lights, like falling snow, incur romantic illusion – the tip-top of my preferred view.

Paddlewheel Savior

My sister Lisa's best and longtime friend, Ellen Wineberg, gave me this tin toy *boat*, rusted and bent, afloat on the radiator and ready to tugboat nudge you to a safe harbor in a distant galaxy far, far away.

Mystery, childhood and fantasy populate Ellen's lifetime of work as a serious, productive, brilliant artist. I'm lucky to have any of her work at all (I have four). She's a tireless original. If she's not doing so tangibly, she's thinking about it. Multiple mediums, variety of approach, world class achievement. She's run galleries and had her own, Room. She's been reviewed by the best and sold work her entire life. When her studio caught fire, little was saved. She just kept going. Started over. Did more work. Of late her eyesight has taken a hit, but she uses the infirmity to see things afresh. Cockeyed, the new normal.

She's a committed, albeit sceptic and realist, of The Spiritual. She has a fabulous laugh and wears crayon colored glasses. Her eyes pierce whatever walls you might have put up.

She and Lisa met (their boyfriends were brothers) in Cambridge in the 60's. They shared an apartment, stories, friends, a view of the weird world and extracurricular trial and errors. Ellen designed the first ever Orchestra Luna T-shirt – two palm trees framing a beach. She brought them to us at a show at The Orson Wells. We put 'em on pronto, our very first merch.

She had her heart broken – a long grief. Anger. Self-questioning. I have other friends who, after that singular, intense pain, just give up. They won't reconsider a romantic encounter, avidly avoiding the evolution from honeymoon to infidelity, jealousy and break up. Fear of loss can numb an inquisitive heart. Ellen might have been like that for a time, but she got over it. Dated here and there, but ultimately, became solid in solitude. Set in her ways. Focused on friends, family and art.

"A friend told me that I'd never meet anybody if I didn't go out. If I didn't go to parties. So I did. I went. I tried. But you know what? The only time I felt happy was when I was driving alone in my car from one party to the next."

I've read that past a certain age, those without a particular someone earn a new liberty. Loving life and themselves with or without partner intimacy. Rejoicing in the unencumbered free time to make art, to be useful to others, to sustain friendships, to be fully awake.

Ellen is like that. She looks after many friends and family. She lives to give. She's quiet about it. She doesn't belabor her part in sharing what she can by scanning for payback. She gives just because she wants to.

"I invest in people," is how she put it.

Ellen, like my sister, is surrounded by love. And Light.

Pandemic Portions

What had been a dude fridge – beer, wine, a water pitcher, cereal fruit – is now full up. Robby and Alex make trips to the store. Stay-at-home geriatric Berlin is lucky to have his friends ask if he needs anything. I do, but I feel guilty about it, but I have to be old man smart. I have to let others look after me and relax the control grip of trying to do everything myself. So I let it happen. I let my fabulous friends shop and deliver as I await the lifting of the joyless viral cloud.

Thank you, Andrea Juan. Thank you, Mickey O'Connell Sholes. Thank you, Erin, Emily and Kathleen Keane. Thank you, Sarah Davey. Thank you Kelly Ransom. Thank you, Dana Brocious. Thank you Maggie Newell and Jill Higgins. Thank you, dude friends: Herb Smith, Mike Condon, Miles Coleman and Shamus Moynihan. Thank you, room-mates: Robby Manochio and Alex Gang. Thank you everyone who's out there looking after those who can't look after themselves. Here's to *your* full fridge and an ongoing, outstanding life.

I've had a great time of it, this weird-assed trip of mine. Wounds and bruises, but all-in-all I've loved every second. I've had a good run. I'll be okay if I buy the farm as long as it doesn't hurt, as long as hospice drugs float me sweetly into painless pink cloud oblivion.

Regardless, I take precautions. I stay inside. I wash my hands until they bleed raw. I keep a tight art-for-the-day schedule. I'm *"regimented"*, as Robby puts it, a diligent, non-practicing monk. The last thing in the world I'd want is to infect another. To spread the virus. Especially to someone younger. They will inherit this screwed up planet, the one my generation has laid waste. We need them healthy, determined, courageous, strong, inventive and powerful. It is they who deserve my pandemic portions.

Paper Dragon

Joey Frechette crashed at 370B. Busted up with his wife, he needed a place apart. Good friends with all of us, no problem.

Joey is many things: African drummer. Shit and fart queen (he texts photos of a pretzel curled turd-in-toilet). Trombonist (had horn, can't play). Believer in *ghosts*. Once so terrified by one he saw in our house he ran out the door in his underwear and holed up at the Behan until he calmed down.

What's wonderful about him is that he's like a seven year old kid. A playground compadre who'd flick his boogers at you. Who'd point at your solar plexus when you looked down and flip your face, gotcha! Who'd chase you with a water balloon. A never-a-dull-moment dude. Also an easy target. Some sad-sack vagabond needed a temporary pad. Joey offered him his room in our apartment, taking the couch for himself. This guy was an asshole. He was playing Joey. Playing us. A freeloader who could and should have taken care of himself without suckering his friend. After a couple of days with this fuck, I forced Joey to get rid of him. A home needs to be an oasis. The outside world is messy enough without bringing some cesspool cunt into the quiet. I don't often get like that, but I was adamant and Joey got it done, no remorse.

The best thing he ever did was give Robby the dragon head. During my stint with David Berndt, booking Marlene Loses It At The Lizard Lounge (a crazy variety show), Joey turned up with his drum circle and the dragon. The full monte. Head, body, scales, tail – a solo Chinatown parade that bucked, undulated and weaved through the crowd. All that was missing were bang-bang Chinese firecrackers.

He gave Robby the head as a present. As cool a paper sculpture as anything in our house. It's fragile. One tooth is about to fall out. The fringe hair is gnawed by the cats. It hangs by a string and, being light weight, is easily bumped off his hook. Hanging next to the fridge it's secure, or so we hope. When someone new shows up, they eye-lock onto the dragon with how-can-I-steal-this envy.

After he moved out, Robby, back when he was on the sauce, threatened to sell it to some bloke he invited over after the Behan shut down for the night. He did that a lot. Sometimes one, sometimes six or seven. A *'party comin' up the stairs'* I called it, just as I was falling asleep. Loud voices, big laughs. I didn't want to kill the vibe, so I ear-plugged and let the party rage.

"$400 bucks", I heard Robby offer through my bedroom door. *"$400 bucks and it's yours. The dragon is yours."*

No fucking way! I lurched into the hallway in my underwear to put a stop to this.

"It's my dragon. Joey gave it to me. We can use the money to pay for studio time for the next record. It's mine and I'm selling it."

I talked him down, thank god. That dragon is priceless. It's still Robby's, but he's sober now. Has been for years and would never part with it. That orange-headed monster is the best thing in the world. It keeps us safe from douchebags who want to take advantage and shit-faced idiots who might walk it out the door and throw it in a dumpster.

FROM ONE FART QUEEN TO ANOTHER

1.

Janie and I couldn't fit into a table at Ann Wigmore's so we opted for Sanae, a health food emporium on Newbury St. We'd finished eating and were reading. I looked up and saw this pert, middle-aged man with a Clark Gable mustache shuffle by, presumably on his way to the loo. Seconds later I barked one out. Soft at first and then developing into a long, sustained rrrrrip! I looked over to check Janie's reaction. She was trying, unsuccessfully, to stifle a laugh, biting her lip and popping her eyeballs. Then she exploded. Apparently the tidy little professor had bent down behind my back to leaf through a newspaper lying on the bench directly behind my ass, his nose six inches from my butt when I cut loose. Janie said he froze for a startled second, a still life, stood up with feigned dignity and returned to his seat, incredulous. Ah tofu.

2.

Lisa laid into me in the Cortina when we were driving back from Litchfield. She was treating me like I had this very separate and serious problem.

"It's really disgusting," she was saying. *"You fart too much. It's not funny to me anymore. It's repulsive. It really is."*

She went on and on about it, saying that the least I could do was to not fart when people were eating.

The next day it began. She was releasing horrific, world class, silent bombs. She was unable to control herself and they smelled so bad she was in tears. They were incessant. I remember going into her room for something an hour after she'd fallen asleep and being knocked over by the smell. It was so dense I literally had to squint in order to navigate my way through her room. This went on for three long days. It was so intense you couldn't get used to it. During meditation. During breakfast. In the shower. At one point she thought it would be nice to visit my room, just sit there and listen to me practice the piano. She lay on my bed with her eyes closed and a pale concerned expression on her face. I shut my eyes trying to concentrate. The entire time the air was thick with the blackest, foulest fumes. I wanted to vomit, but I kept playing because I didn't want to hurt her feelings. When neither of us could stand it any longer we left the room.

I can't remember how to play my songs. I can't remember my own lyrics, but I remember this stuff. I am, in this regard, as truly a ridiculous a person as Monsieur Frechette.

Potassium In A Yellow Condom

I know, a pathetic metaphor, but I think about it every time I peel. It is a very close replica of a sheathed boner. Andy Warhol approved.

> *"Is that a banana in your pants or are you just glad to see me?"*
> **— Mae West**

After a night of Lites, I eat a breakfast banana. Potassium cleanses the system of hangover blues, buzzing your body with a fish school of positive ions. It is a rare breakfast without these guys in my habitual cereal. I'll eat the unripe if I have to, dusty tasting, but the potassium does the hat trick. I'll munch down the rotten ones as well, cutting away the brown bruises.

"Last one in's a rotten banana!"

I hear that shout in my head from a swimming hole sing-song every time I see the bruises. Why a banana? Why not a grape? These silly references kill me. I am a collector of clogging absurdities.

Red Is The New Black

I resisted for years, resisted getting a microwave. My argument had always been that one of the cats would get in there and explode. Cat fur and brains finger painting the innards. Where I got that idea from I have no clue, but I moved past it and bought this baby a few months ago. Picked out the red after clicking through page after page. I got it because I wasn't sure that I'd have time to eat at my new job at The Squealing Pig. You aren't supposed to chow down during your shift and based on how I schedule my day, there wouldn't be time for me to both drive to work and eat. So I picked up frozen dinners from Whole Foods and microwaved them toasty just before I left the house. They all tasted alike. Like bean pudding, but made the protein grade until I realized that I could still have time at The Pig to order a salad and get away with it. But no regrets. I'm pleased I purchased Hot Lips Red. I like that it doesn't look modern. It has a *Lost In Space* sci-fi quality and hums along like a bitch. Who knows if the electricity it soaks up costs more or less than it would to heat the oven, but as an impatient, the speed factor is a plus. And, unlike Doyle's, it never gets spattered with marinara lava or hot fudge. I haven't needed to clean it but once.

I did spring for the proper receptacle to heat things up in. I did it because I've been yelled at. I've come close to making dangerous mistakes with tinfoil or metal bowls. With my perfect Pyrex I'm able to properly re-heat spaghetti and have it last four nights in a row, a big deal given the shut-in. It also is a kitchen cousin to my Nord piano. Red and red. I figure they gossip when we're asleep.

"You play a song. I'll blow something up."

Routine Caffeine

On my 60th I got a lotta great presents from my pals at Doyle's. Plus a surprise party[34] from which I bolted early. Got a bunch of Red Sox swag because they'd won in '04 and everybody made fun of my girly squeal whenever something good happened at Fenway.

Nova Benway, the one and only female roommate we ever had at 370B, broke my Sox cup washing it in the sink, Carolyn Burke's present to me at the party. Nova felt terribly and got me a new one, the one I use every morning, filled to the brim with Bustelo laxative. It's interior is stained with dark brown smears like a Turkish cup at an Istanbul steam bath. I can't seem to scrape it off properly, but figure it adds to the rush and has me feeling 'continental'.

The routine:

Put on kettle. Drink chalky vegetable protein shake. Read online news. Return. Boiling water poured into coffee sieve. Cereal in bowl. Add milk, grapes, apples, pitted dates, raisins, cantaloupe, nuts. More water in funnel. Slice bananas. Lug mess into my room, watch MSNBC and intermittently edit *The Big Balloon*. Once that's done, the caffeine speeds up my brain and I answer emails, texts, pay bills, check snail mail, etc. Every single fucking morning.

I am robot. "*Klaatu Barada Nikto*" is the lieder I sing. Skeleton fingers tickle the ivories, West World style.

---

34   See 'Killing The Birthday Balloon' ('The Paragraphs')

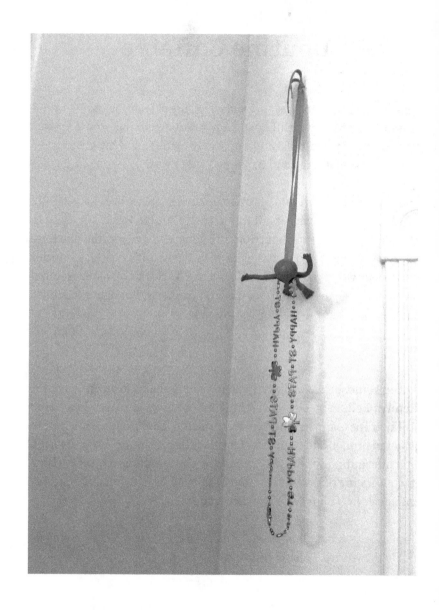

Space Boy

My friend Max Perez, Colombian, was moving back home after graduating from Mass Art in fashion. I met him at The Behan long before I'd moved back to JP. He was half way down the length of the bar. I told the bartender to buy him a drink on me. I've never done so overt a move. Seemed like something Frank Sinatra might have tried on a romantic bender, but for this invert, *so* obvious.

"Make it one for my baby, and one more for the road."

He saluted after he got it, bemused smile. We sat outside on a grassy knoll just up Sheridan St and wandered into the conversational labyrinth, the vast skirt view of the glittering city below.

Best thing about Max – his singing voice. A mellifluous, spell-binding, seductive tenor. He told me about 'boleros', not the Miles Davis/Ravel kind, but love songs a Mexican Romeo suitor who, too shy to speak to the girl he had a crush on, parks under her window with a guitar and sings a self-composed endearment. I saw Max work bolero magic in real time one night at a party. He told me something nasty about her later.

Like all top of the mountain friendships, they seem most vital with a definitive, unavoidable departure. Max was heading south, clearing out his apartment. I coveted the green rubber alien boy with the bright orange parachute shoelace he'd strung up above his desk. He didn't want to let it go, but I coaxed it out of him. That was twenty years ago and it's as cool as ever, defying gravity and walking the wall. Around his neck, Irish, St Patrick's Day plastic jewelry, a green-on-green contradiction.

What is truly awesome is that, as I was writing this up, I couldn't remember the name of the genre, bolero, so I messaged Max. He got back pronto and we ricocheted hilarious ping pong texts about then and now, still friends, two weirdos being weird.

I remember one odd night we slept together (emphasis on sleep). I touched him, felt him up like a perv.

"Is that ok?" I asked.

"Good for you," he said, implying *"not good for me"*.

Squirt That Shit

Colin Burns and his pal, Spenser, graphic art partners at Hi*Con, made two unforgettable Drags, Dicks & Dykes 4 Life posters for benefits I fired up at Jacques one year and 1270 Boylston another. Raising money for the AIDS ACTION COMMITTEE back in the 90's.

I met Colin back when he and Joan Wasser (Joanaspolicewoman) were dating. Joan of *Don't Talk About Joan*. I met her via Eddy deSyon[35]. Both were studying music at BU. Joan hit me like a RPG. I stuttered around her. Fierce, gorgeous, hair-color changer and a Picasso of Song. As if *Nude Descending The Staircase* wound up on stage or record. Piano, fiddle, vox, all Joan. I first saw her in The Dambuilders (part of DD&D II). She worked a double-stack bass rig, one leg forward, one back, like an Olympic fencer.

The song about her happened this way:

Eddy and I were invited to smoke down the hall from his apartment by two punkette dykes – super cute, super direct. We were passing the joint and Joan came up in the conversation. As soon as they heard her name, one of them stood up, hand out front like a cop, like the Supremes choreography for *Stop In The Name Of Love*.

"Don't talk about Joan! I'm in love with her!"

That night, running into Wasser on Landsdowne where she bartended, I told her the story.

---

35   See 'Picture Bats A Thousand'

"Tell me who they are. You have to tell me," she said.

One of them was standing right next to me, but I shut it. I couldn't tell. Wasn't my place to out them, even though Joan liked boys *and* girls.

I was babysitting Eddy's tarantula while he was in France. I hadn't written a new tune in years. With piano and furry legs side-by-side, it felt auspicious. I took a crack at it, writing my first new song in months. (Colin had a dream about hearing it on prime time radio and making us famous.)

Later on, with Chet and Chris Mehl recording a new record with me, *Half In The Bag,* I dragged Joan out to the house so she could play violin on her song. Her fiddle was acoustic. Chet had to mic her up close. She made hilarious snorting sounds we were forced to delete when we worked up the mix. Pull bow, snort. Pull again, snort, snort. Honestly, I wished we'd left 'em in. Thus began my affection for stringed instruments. I utilized a full quartet (Brendan Cooney – composer) for *Old Stag* and found a fiddler for The Shelley Winters Project (first Marnie Hall, then Meredith Cooper).

Colin, cousin of Documentary Ken who, at a family gathering, chided him for not amounting to anything (cunt), had a band of his own. Thick distortion, low growling vocals. But his primary art was visual. His numero uno collaborator, Spenser. They gave me the cum-squirter as a present once DD&D was over and done. It isn't photoshop generated. It's colored by hand, layers of roll-on ink added one-at-a-time. Old school. I love the disturbing images, the red, black and gold, the superimposition of Henry Rollins' face on the cock-squirting torso. They're both straight, but fagged it up for art. As if to say:

"Take that, 'normals'."

Art can mess with your head and butt fuck your complacency.

The Cocksicle

"Rick! Come upstairs! Hurry! You have to see this!"
— Silvio Neef

who, at fourteen in East Germany, was interrogated by the Stasi police
after he marked up a communist poster with a sharpie. All this before
the wall came down.

We clambered up a circular steel staircase to his roof and there it
was, the stalactite, glistening in the winter sun. An ice dildo rising
like a hard Phoenix towards the overhead drip. A miracle dick waiting
to be applauded by a gaggle of ecstatic homos. It's size queen huge and
could only be received by a client familiar with The Cambridge Fister.
Sir David Minehan (friend, musician, record producer extraordinaire)
and I figured that The Fister had his office at The Hotel Commander.
We'd riff on the riff, slowing progress in the studio and embarrassing
anyone within earshot.

The Fister had two requirements if you wanted an appointment.

1.   Douche your rectum.
2.   Allow him to video the session.

I'd consider the first, but the second was a deal breaker. There would
never be documentation of a rubber suited dude with his arm up to
his elbow in my ass. The procedure is not a fantasy. No problem for
those for whom it might be a preferred option. Far be it for me to pass
judgement, although I always do.

I do have a friend who'd been a patron. He told me that once up in there, The Fister could trigger multiple orgasms with tiny flexes of his little finger on the prostate. One after another after another.

"The best sex I've ever had. It ruined the real thing. Nothing can replace it."

The curious from all over the planet fly in and get serviced. Doc F. deserves a print of the cocksicle, but I will never make an appointment.

The God Of Love

A crucifix. Brass. Heavy in the hand.

I'm not a god guy. Never have been, even though my family gave first Protestant, then Episcopalian a try. None of us felt it. Bored to tears as we saw through the phony pontifications and the endless up and down kneel-and-pray. I did like being in the school choir. Blue robes, early morning wood and the rank odor of smothered farts. Initially soprano.[36] Then alto. Then baritone. There's something to be said about choral singing. It stirs the soul and the repertoire, religious music of any denomination, is uplifting, and although singing that stuff never sold me on The Lord, I did feel something, something universal as the hair curled on my forearm.

I nailed the nailed Jesus to the window frame. A reminder of the central, non-Catholic but catholic tenet that puts love front and center. The one undisputed truth that, like Om, links humanity together as one and teaches what to most trust when we feel lost or uncertain about which faith to follow, which person to give it all ya got. A reminder that sacrifice can sometimes be brother or sister to the heart's lifetime schoolroom.

Everybody Hurts
R.E.M

Everyone feels pain
Berlin

---

36   See 'C R Y' (*The Paragraphs*)

Jesus. Paramahansa Yogananda. Jalāl ad-Dīn Muhammad Rūmī – the gay Persian poet: all love stories when ya get right down to it.

Jesu, Joy Of Man's Desiring.

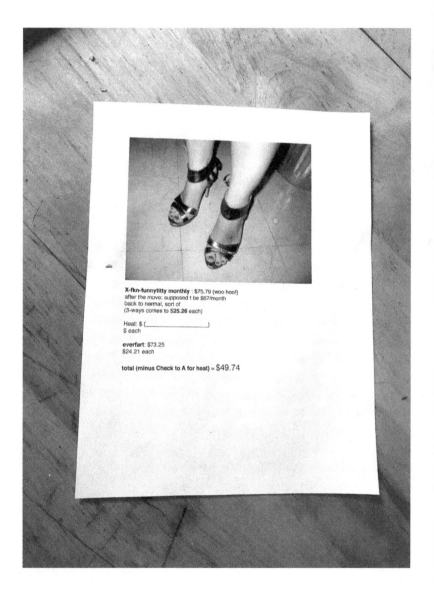

X-fkn-funnytitty monthly : $75.79 (woo hoo!)
after the move: supposed t be $67/month
back to normal, sort of
(3-ways comes to **$25.26** each)

Heat: $ (_____)
$ each

everfart: $73.25
$24.21 each

total (minus Check to A for heat) = $49.74

The Tally

I am the no-manjana Mama in the apartment. I collect and pay the bills. All but the gas are in my name. Same for rent. I don't stall. I refuse to be in debt. I would eliminate a need if it got too dear. I never want to be beholden, to live beyond my means. Just enough is enough, although there are non-essential essentials – Netflix, HBO, Hulu, Amazon Prime, Disney. I'll hang onto those 'til this old mule stops watching the tube. Also, the annual hits for Bandcamp, Soundcloud and my website: up-in-the-attic evidence that I showed up for a few years and did shit.

The photo is of my former roommate and obsessive, online smart shopper, Danielle Hollingsworth-Kern. Those are her kickass, Christmas party shoes. I haven't changed the picture since I started using it for the tally back at 370B. A talisman icon which, floated obscenely onto the kitchen table, reminds Robby and Alex that it's time to pay the poofty piper.

Money[37], a conjecture, an infinite blank check for us to accumulate without bartering. A bunch of numbers on paper that separate haves from have nots. The fat cat acquirers who have more rooms, houses and cars than anyone could need. The measure of failure or success in a capitalistic, industrialized economy. Even in a dystopia, there will always be some version of tit-for-tat. We're stuck with it. The numbers add up or subtract down. We suck them out of the bank and make note of the debit, the numerical measure of our 'value'.

I print up the tally. I pay the bills. Would I have sat hunched over

---

37   See 'Money' (*The Paragraphs*)

at a high top desk in Dicken's London? Ink stains on long sleeves? Scrooge or Cratchit?

Both.

These Guys

Justin McCarthy came up with it, the albino squirrel as the JP Music Festival mascot. The Perfect Choice. His Whiteness has been spotted all over JP, especially in trees along Jamaica Pond, which makes him all the more relevant given that the Festival tent goes up close by at Pinebank. Shamus Moynihan[38] (co-producer of JPMF) thought he looks like Justin, thought we should glue cotton balls all over Justin's body and parade him around the field on the day of. (One of our best kept secrets now cracked open.)

The little guy wears a pork pie hat making him an off-beat hipster and suitably un-self-important as we are not some fat-assed hot-shot Coachella. We are, as I've been spinning from the start, *"a Mom-n-Pop, Corner Store Festival"*. Sprung lifelike from the oddball JP community womb. Unpretentious and real. A day of respite from circling rain clouds or political nightmare echo chamber harangues. A day of families, kids, dogs, horses, food trucks and music. Mr/Mrs Albino Squirrel sit on their acorn thrones like cheeky royalty. I keep them in my house. I am their custodian. Reason being: I had the ridiculous idea that at the 1st Annual (2011) we should include a stirring, albeit preposterous, 'moment': The Ceremony Of The Albino Squirrel.

Before Ferris (Mueller) and Margie (Nicoll)[39] sing *America The Beautiful* (now a tradition) there would be, in front of the stage, a popcorn bucket with a circus of helium balloons attached. Like Pixar's *Up* they would lift the bucket into the cloudless blue. In the basket, Hizzhonor, the squirrel. Children and parents would cheer. Drew (Chasse), daugh-

---

38   See 'The Blue Ox'

39   See 'The House That Margie Built'

ter of longtime friend, Jeff, would approach, cradling the squirrel in endearing arms. A trumpet would play a solemn march as she walked. The plan went swimmingly until The Moment Of Release. When the cord, holding basket to earth, was cut, bucket and squirrel sank sadly to the ground. Hizzhonor remained farcically in basket and the balloons dead floated in front of the stage. No lift off, no illustrious JP as NASA. It was one of my absolute favorite things that ever happened, ever. There's a video.

I will be endlessly fond the 1st Annual for all the things that went wrong. The back line gear that we got for zip was so fucked up we had to tie, duct tape and band-aid drum hardware throughout day. There was only one big stage. The second, a low boy, swaybacked plywood job, was an embarrassment. One of the soundmen plugged the wrong cables into the wrong holes and the wrong instruments and voices were outsized, imbalanced loud. The big banner on the big stage gave sponsorship credit to one sponsor, unfairly over others. Shamus[40] and Bill Brown had to manhandle the generator, which nearly got away from them like a bucking bronco on the Jamaica Way. During what was a not very loud African drum circle, someone from the Ugly Uppity Apartment Tower called to complain about the noise, even though it had been safely kept within the legal limit. This forced us to move the staging to the opposite side of the field the following year; ultimately a good thing. All these mishaps made me love that damn day so much. But it was, first and foremost, the listless, no-blast-off of squirrel-in-basket that won my heart.

Two, three years later we decided to present Hizzonor to an Unsung Hero of the Festival; an acknowledgement of a volunteer who always, always shows up and makes it happen. There are many. We could never do it without them.

---

40   See 'The Blue Ox'

Tin Man Is Heart Broken (3/21/20)

This is Robby's robot. I think it came from home, from New Jersey. I think he has a British accent, or Scot. He would, if he could, start moving, make everything in your life better. But he can't. He can't fire up his motor. But if you close your eyes, when you're sad? When the tears won't quit, when your heart is about to burst with feeling, he might start singing, a song he wrote just for you. The exact one you need. You need only to open your heart and let it in.

I can hear his song, because I really need to now. I don't know how long this missing of you is going to last. I know you're there and here too. I know it so big. You hold my heart like a puppy in your arms wherever the fuck you are. 14 Mark, the lab or 3,000 miles away on the left coast.

We were not supposed to hug at the airport, but we did. You did. I can still feel it. That gentle parenthesis. Your forehead on my shoulder. Mine, yours. You have located me, Michael. I had never thought I could be found in this way again, but it happened. We found each other, a thunderbolt. Same time, same station.

This crying is not sad. It is a sincere, deep sense of being alive. Awakened. I see you smiling with your Santa Barbara pals. With Olivia. Boogey. Beaming with happiness. Which only adds harmony to the robot song and sustains me.

Netflix

THE DIRTBIKE DIARIES:

Season1, Episode 8

Press Send

(3/15/20)

Michael Dirtbike:
So some developments in the story here. Think I'm going back to Santa Barbara until the Harvard lab reopens

I'm actually really torn up about the whole thing honestly

I will not know all the details until tomorrow, but I'm hoping Yang will invite me back when the dust clears. I'm sure he will

Maybe just in time to attend the festival

Rick Berlin:
Oh man. big news, Likely makes good sense. is this based on Yang emails or a hunch? Either way, I agree. he'll have you back. But it will be a long summer with you not here, my dear one, tho for the best. You must let me drive you to the airport, no argument.

Rick Berlin:
Please don't take this the wrong way, Michael, because, in essence, it's beautiful. like you. But I can't stop crying. Typing or watching the tube or in the shower or feeding cats. I'm such a baby. And then, Thru the waterfall, I laugh at myself for being like this and thank fucking god we had these few out-of-this-world weeks. Honestly, tho there's no scientific measure of the strings of the heart and how they resonate or compare (string theory, right?) and who needs comparisons? I've been hugely loved. I loved hugely. What's different, what's new is that no one, truly, has loved me back as deeply, as

clear-eyed as you. In the way you get me, know me, catch me before I fall. Your bow down Wasabi laugh, like his, a nod of the heart. Mountain top in my whole ridiculous life. And so I'm blessed. At this late moment on life's schedule. That this could really happen, ya know? You had absolutely everything to do with it. With us. At least we didn't have time to get sick of each other or wear each other down (like that could happen).

From the start, Dirtbike.

I'm happy y'll be home in SB. With Olivia and your dear friends and the beach and dog and maybe cat.

I close my eyes and I see yours. Can't be helped. Would never want it to. There will be no further deliberation. my heart belongs to you. I suspect it did before I met you. Berlin Babylon

Michael Dirtbike:

Sobbing as I'm reading this. You are an amazing man, a once in a lifetime friend and I will not let our relationship slip away. Your energy has changed the way I act, even when you're not around. Being around you has helped me transform into the man my mother wants me to be, and that is the most beautiful gift I have ever received. I will never be sick of you riggy, but I may be sick without our Behan/dipper/movie night escapades during this break. The antidote will be my return, and it will be glorious to reunite. I love you man. Love always MD

This sucks so much because you kept mentioning me having to leave due to unforeseen circumstances, and I thought you were crazy. Now you turned out to be right and I feel like my heart is being ripped in 3

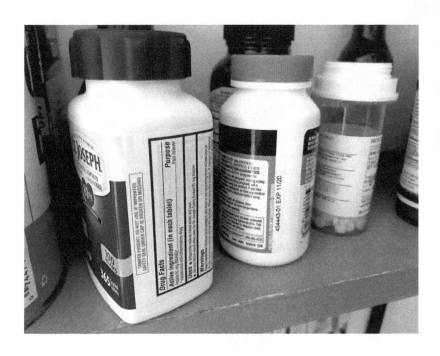

Too Many Pills

At least it used to be. An army of vitamins long ago prescribed by Billie Best in the basement of Toad during an Awful Truth gig. I bought the plan and have been hosing expensive piss into the morning toilet for years. To this I attribute my fabulous good health.

> *"You'll outlive all of us."*
> **– Shamus Moynihan**

God knows I don't want that. I so miss my friends who are gone. Who left this life before I did, who knew 'the old me'.

> *"Nobody knows my life from the beginning anymore. Most of them are dead."*
> **– Jane Friedman**

And I have too many today friends whose loss would be unfathomable. Please let me expire before that happens, that I not last longer than my dear comrades in and out of arms.

I ate the V's for decades, until, a few weeks ago when my face bloated up. I felt my skin heat up during my morning meditation, a bumble bee buzz on cheeks. In the mirror the lines on either side of my mouth – crevasses. Under my eyes, purply red bags. My primary doc told me to look up the specific amounts of each vitamin to find out if I was developing a reaction. She had me grab a bottle of Benadryl (fucking drug spellings) so my throat wouldn't close or have me swallow my tongue. All this because of one too many vitamins?

We whittled and diddled my intake down to L-Lysine, Acidophilus, baby aspirin and Amlodipine. L-Lysine lessens the Rudolph red-nose mouth-zit Herpes sore. It works. Nobody wants to see that shit, or scare off a kiss. Acidophilus restores the happy flowers in your intestine, the ones that get destroyed when you overdo it with antibiotics. They're fabulous protectors of the immune system. Baby aspirin, as everyone in the world recommends, sustains a tireless heart. Amlodipine keeps the heart and blood pressure copasetic. An earlier primary care doc, a tiny woman with tiny hands (awkward and short of the mark during the digital prostate exam) told me that she just *"loves this little pill"*.

These are the Final Four. I will keep my elbow in and shoot a trey into the vitamin basket.

Toy Rabbit

Lisa water colored and stitched this isolated fragment from the portrait of Mum. The held-in-arms stuffed rabbit, a talisman for our sense of the girl we never knew before she married Dick and we kids showed up. The artwork is dwarfed by the frame, enhancing the held breath I have looking at it. Lisa has a way of teasing essence out of the ethereal. A poetic abbreviation, a sigh of the heart, a truth that dare not speak out loud. It hangs at a poked-out angle, the eye-screws protrude it away from the wall, leaning it towards you as if two lovers face-butt forehead-to-forehead, eyes closed. Past to present to future. Mum, rabbit, sister.

Wooden Bowl

A long time back, when I lived in that enormous house next to Doyle's, Billie and Chet gave Steven and I two wooden bowls for Christmas. After we broke up, I kept mine. Used it for everything. Gruel dinners, Oriental de Cuba take out, bird seed breakfasts. Eggs only on Sunday at the Little Dipper, The Haven or The Frogmore and the one day I actually read a book. It can take months to finish, but always good to get lost in brunch land.

> *"Eat only 2 visible eggs a week."*
> **– Rene Ricard,**

who said that the way to stay young was to *"break the hearts of young boys"* – an odd advocacy.

I've stuck with it, a habit unbroken. After years of wear and tear and a leaky split in the Billie Bowl, I continued to use it until my sister, Janie, gave me a brand new one. Bigger, uncut. I waited before using. It felt like I was cheating on the broken fav-for-years. I do that. I anthropomorphize inanimate objects. Talk to them out loud.

"Sorry KIA Soul. Sorry I parked so poorly that I dinged your back fender. All apologies big new broom. I prefer the one that was left behind, but I'll hang onto you nevertheless. You will remain dirt free and I will admire you as you quietly lean against the pantry wall like an unpopular whore. Sorry, vacuum cleaner. Sorry for yanking your hose and banging your nose into the stove."

I am now attached to the new. I use it over and over and over again. Wash it perfunctorily with the hottest out-of-spigot water, no soap.

It is my friend, my *guten morgan, meine freunde* bowl of lathed wood.
I wonder when I'm gone, who will want or replace it. A Pilgrim?

Livingroom

A Pen In Hand

Composing or practicing for a new song demo I need attempted lyrics in front of my face. They need to be copasetic with new music.
They need to be remembered as I replay old songs. Taped to the piano
doesn't cut it. I've tried gently applied masking tape so that it won't
leave a sticky thumbprint on the Nord, but the paper gets in the way of
my left hand, or falls to the floor. Same with the pencil or pen. Hence,
the music stand.

Working up a new tune is a frenetic activity. Each new idea is recorded
and re-recorded on my phone as the song struggles to emerge. Once
close, with intro, chorus, verse and a sometime bridge, I mark down
and abbreviate the form and record a more professional mp3 on my
special (often frustratingly out of battery juice) device. I scratch it out:

Intro

Chorus

Verse

Chorus

Verse

Chorus

Bridge

Chorus

Chorus

Outro

and follow the hieroglyphs as I lay down the track.

Piano, pen and stand, piano, pen and stand back and forth until I have the confidence to transfer the result and jack it up full throated on Garageband.

Part of me doesn't like to see these two, piano and stand, glaring at me, waiting to be used. Waiting for a new song. Blank page pieces of musical furniture. They're sociopaths. They don't care how I feel or if I'm inspired or not. They want to be activated and love/hate me like the conniving human robots in *Westworld*. If I fail, they'll shoot me in the head without compassion and find another composer.

Write or die, motherfucker!

Aida's Rocker

Our Cuban landlady at 370B, Aida Lopez, is one fine woman. When I first looked at the place, I was blown away.

"Why hasn't this been taken?" I asked.

"It was waiting for you," she said.

"$1,500, right?"

"No. $1,400."

I would have paid the $1,500, she didn't have to correct me, but she did. That's how she rolled. As I settled in, a new fridge was hauled up the stairs, replacing the corroded former. When the kitchen linoleum began to peel up, threatening to slice a bare foot, she had the floor re-tiled. When the bathroom sink fell off the wall (ass support for a quickee at a Christmas party), she installed a new one. Same for the bathtub. Same for the broken windows on the sun porch.

She gave us presents. Candy (which I never ate). Tin foiled Cuban things you were supposed to boil and eat, but were bland tasting and peculiar. I left them in the freezer for weeks until I threw them out. Cookies. A card on a birthday. A fireplace paper fan. I miss her musical laugh. I miss dancing[41] with her in her nick-knack 'office'. I miss the presents.

Best of all, the rocker. An indestructible hunk of furniture; a last blown kiss from Lady Lopez. Carlotta appropriated it. She'll stretch herself

---

41   See 'Dancing With Cuba (*The Paragraphs*)

up the back and make it rock. I worry she might slide a tail or paw under a wooden eyebrow and break a kitty bone, but so far so good. Cats are more wary than I give them credit for.

In her late eighties, Aida has, as she freely admits, numerous psycho-somatic heart attacks. I can't count how many times 911 was called and she was whisked to the emergency room just to be on the safe side. I hope she stays strong. She's weathered the loss of her husband at an early age. The death of her son. Of her longtime friend, L'uba. Of a tenant whose body lay undiscovered for days and had to be carried out of her apartment by a dude in a hazmat suit. Another kid who od'd and exited in a death bag.

If nothing else, she is the proud,

"I am the KING! Not Queen! King!"

survivor at La Casa del Regalos and a rebel. She raised her huge family single-handedly after her husband died. Her favorite toilet paper had Fidel's face on each square. During the 2016 election she sat in a rocker wearing a Trump mask. I loved seeing her through the glass door, busy at her desk, glue gunning tchotchkes for Latino coming out parties, her day job for years, hair in a loose bun, shoes crushed at the heel. Things ended with us being evicted after a fifteen year, under market run. I'd never hold it against her.

One last cha-cha, Aida?

Angel Vs Id & Being
In A Cover Band

My friend, Chris Nash[42], gave me this object as a good-bye present when he left for CA. They are, I believe, replicas of lover's held hands excavated from Pompeii. Love imagined.

"First I look at him this way and I think he's beautiful. Then he turns a little and I think he's not so beautiful," says Peter Barrett.

"When you can find someone who's 360 degrees beautiful 365 days of the year, then you've found God," I reply.

"I want God," says Pete.

Angel
There really are angels out there. They exist because they don't know it; the opposite of narcissism.

Walking up Green Street, Lucas was hauling a hunk of painted up cardboard, part of a science project. The thing was as big as he was. He couldn't have been more than twelve. He passed by, walking faster, stopped, turned around and waited for me to catch up.

"Hi."

"Hi."

---

42   See 'Ariel'

We walked the rest of the block until he took off.

"When you grow up you'll be...?"

"A scientist!"

Very definite.

I put it together. I remembered Lucas and his Dad were Doyle's regulars. They played a self-invented game with a paper puck which they skittered back-n-forth, keeping score, earnest expressions. A sparkler kid, blonde hair down to his shoulders, serious for his age. I asked if he played drums. He did not. I asked because he looked so much like my friend, Jason, a drummer. I dialed up his photo and showed them. They saw the likeness. His Dad laughed. Lucas was nonplussed.

I run into him at the JP Music Festival, throwing frisbees or playing catch with kids around the baseball diamond. He's all grown up, seventeen and a high-powered cyclist, logging miles all over New England. He's six feet tall, hair cut short and no longer looks like Jason. He rides to raise money for the Y.E.S. program *'offering young people paths to S.T.E.M. (Science, Technology, Engineering and Math) careers.'* – in line with the twelve year old I ran into on the Green St. sidewalk. Full circle.

Boy has wings.

ID

Jason bartended at Jonathan Swift's, a downstairs pub and music venue half a block from Harvard Square. Early twenties, Icelandic features, an ironic, don't-fuck-with-me ball buster. And he was hot. The sight of him sent a shiver. I wasn't sure which side of the tracks he played, but he sparred with me. Back-n-forth humor that ridiculed and accepted at the same time. A wink and a nod. When some asshole gave him shit he cupped his hand on his crotch.

"Eat this," he said.

I would have.

During the eclipse of my relationship with Steven, we stopped living together. He was fucking anyone remotely interested. My duplicitous eyes wandered as well. Glad of it. I needed to be distracted. I used his infidelities to indulge my own. I moved into a top floor flat on Beacon Hill. Patty found me the place to keep me close by. She had hopes of roping me into a conversion (a story for another day). Whatever, I loved the new spot, a dollhouse garret. I wall-papered my bedroom. Had visitors.

It was late. Jason got out of work and came by. I had coke. I always did in those days. We snorted line after line, not saying much. Mad horny. We knew where this was headed. Pants to ankles. Shirt uplifted. I went down on him up against the wall with the lights blazing. Any fool on the Hill could have seen us. We didn't give a fuck. We were too far gone in the cocaine heat. Hot bullets down my throat. The sound of him getting off, gasp music. He left in a hurry.

We did repeat a few times. Coke triggered until the thrill wore off. He was barely bi. Liked women. Like to fuck. Whatever. I ran into him on a summer afternoon on Newbury St. He had that look in his eyes we all know that says *"we are both aware of what we're both not saying"*. He was living in a rehearsal room and losing his brain down a crack pipe. We gave it one more try in the shower. That was the last time I saw him. He's off the pipe, lives in PA and is still drumming.

A chasm of difference between these two. Lucas, Jason. Angel, Id-boy. Those old fashioned flip cards that purr like flash movies in your hand? I run one of those in my head remembering. Both would be appalled.

AN ALMOST BUT NOT QUITE FIRST TIME CHEAT
(I regret to this day not following through.)

The Luna Band learned cover songs so we could make money as musicians. The idea was to fold in our 'originals' as they were called, as if they were unworthy, bastard children. Every time we'd play an 'original' the crowd would exit the dance floor until we played something they knew. It was humiliating, but we made ok money and drank a lot. At one gig, Chet choked down at least four Long Island Ice Teas and drove the truck into a river.

At one club, after the show, I'd been invited to a party by this kid, Bill. I kept it under my hat. I wanted to check this out on my own recognizance. We'd been scarfing eggs, bacon and pancakes at a nearby diner and would soon head back to the motel and crash. Instead, I left the diner and decided to walk to Bill's house alone and anxious.

Bill was great looking, Luke Skywalker without the light sabre. I hadn't a definitive clue about what he had in mind, but instinct held promise. His house was a three mile walk up Route 9. I decided to check it out, show my haggard face and be cordial to the fans at the party. Have a look and report back to the band if it was worth going.

Liar.

It was ridiculously late. 4 AM. I walked and walked and walked. I told myself that if I actually found his house, then I was supposed to. Lady Fate. I wandered up a road that looked right, a light was on and I heard the thin buzz of TV static. I tip toed to the window and peered in. Bill was asleep on the couch in Bermuda shorts, plain white T, one arm stretched above his head. I went to the front door. It was open. It seemed as if he was waiting for me. I walked into the living room and he woke up.

He was glad to see me. Wasn't drunk. Everyone had left. I apologized for being late. He was amazed that I'd walked. I said that he must be tired, that I should head back, but he asked me to stick around. We sat on the couch, a respectable distance between us. The house was immaculate, everything in place. He went out to the kitchen to get some wine and brought back a sickly sweet claret which I drank without complaint.

I asked to see his room and he said sure, but had to run upstairs to find out if his brother was home. His parents were away for the weekend and it turned out that his brother was in absentia. The coast was clear so he led me downstairs. The room was also immaculate, as if made ready. He showed me where he'd put his Luna sticker (to patch a cracked window) and he clicked on his stereo softly enough to talk. He showed me his paintings. He showed me a driftwood mobile that an *"older man"* had given to him up in Maine. Somebody he met on the beach. Ah ha! Mind working overtime. He is. He isn't. He will. He won't. I could. I shouldn't.

I can't.

He got up to get me a glass of water. I sat on his perfectly made bed. He told me I could spend the night, that it would be foolish of me to walk all the way back to the motel. I protested. I felt badly. I missed my boyfriend, but Bill was fucking sexy. I felt like the boy-chaser of the old days, thrilled with the possibility, but horrified. What about fidelity? What about my relationship? Mad at myself for having to once again pass up so obvious an opportunity. Or not.

His foot, in a white athletic sock, was precariously close to my knee. He said he was real nervous. That he had to take an aspirin. That his hand was shaking. He held it out for me to see. I wanted to hold it, to kiss his dark red cupid's bow lips, to take his body in my arms, to see him naked, to run my fingers through his hair.

"I'm eighteen, but I still get carded. I look young for my age. I guess it gets things for me. I always have friends, but I change them every couple of months. I hate my parents. I want to move to Texas. I want to be out on my own. They are too possessive of me. No. I have never been in love. I don't think I want to be. You know, this may sound selfish to you, but I'm out for Number One. I always think of myself first. Yeah. I lost my virginity when I was fourteen. You know a lot of kids are hung up about sex. Kids my age who still haven't lost their virginity. I've got all that together. I still feel nervous. I got strung out on aspirin for two years when I was a kid."

Aspirin? Really?

Every so often he would look right at me and his eyes would soften.
I noticed him catch me checking out his body. I told him he had a handsome face. I told him I should go. That I had to wake up early in the
morning, that I was thirty-seven years old. He said I looked twenty.
I didn't tell him about anything else. My mind was screaming about
the cheat. I thought Steven might have begun to worry. Of course all
that changed big time in a few short years.

Bill promised to drive me back to the motel, even though the clutch was
fucked up on his car. I couldn't imagine staying any longer. Something
would have happened. Maybe I was afraid it would. I was unable to
justify any part of this. And if it had happened, Steven and I would have
had to reevaluate the whole business all over again and then *he'd* be on
the prowl and the vicious cycle of who does what when, with whom
and how did we'd feel about an open relationship would rain down
the drama. Steven would for shit sure turn into a skank. As would I.

Does fidelity constitute a healthy relationship, or is an open relationship the only honest horse to ride? Does any of that matter if the center
of how two people are together is an immutable absolute? I mean
what the fuck difference does it make? Here I was in the presence
of this unbelievably great looking, willing, young boy/man and I was
frozen. Was it because I had been witness to how Dad screwed Ma
over? I began to hate the word relationship as if it came from a dead
culture and that, in the end, in the last analysis, I am the only one who
can fuck myself up. And so I am not so different from Bill who is out
for Number One, who has never been in love. But I convinced myself
that I *am* in love and so I leave. I get the fuck out of there. No naked.
No head. Nada. FUCK!

A COVER CLUB REGULAR
Towards the end of soundcheck a stooped-over, hunch-backed ste-
reotypical little old lady tip-toes across the dance floor in front of the

stage, her tiny head wobbling like a rear-window bobbly dog. She's tossing cornmeal like Lady Appleseed onto the stinking Lysol floor.

"What's that?" someone asks.

"Cornmeal!" she replies in a high reedy squawk.

Her name is Katie and she's worked at Asheulot Ridge since it opened up on the cover circuit seven years ago. She's sixty-five and loves to mother the bands that come in. Her eyes are black brown and one drifts to the left under a permanently lowered lid. She takes you by the upper arm in a firm squeeze, leans into your ear and shouts. Her voice sounds like feedback.

"I love *music!"* she screams.

She's been a waitress since she was seventeen. She collects broken drum sticks and makes belts out of them. One kid gave her a guitar pick.

"Keep that, Katie, it'll be worth a lot of money to you someday because I'm going to be famous."

She took it home and had her husband drill a tiny hole in the tip and she threaded a single-link silver chain through it and

"that's how I started making guitar pick necklaces," she brays.

She has hundreds of lines on her face and practically no lips at all. Her lipstick lasts five minutes and is cherry red. She proscribes Blackberry Brandy for the vocal chords.

"Every singer loses his voice up here," she yells. *"It's the air. They're not used to it."*

Her favorite songs are *Stairway To Heaven* and *Brown Sugar*.

"Now that song's as old as I am, but I love it. And you'll notice that they always get up and dance to it. Last week this band played 'Stairway' and it was so bad I sat down and cried. I'm a very emotional person, you know. They collected money from all the people in the club the other night. They passed a little bowl and then they gave it to me. The band asked me to come up to the stage and they presented it to me and boy, the tears flowed. I couldn't even say thank you. I couldn't say anything at all even though I thought they were a terrible band. I felt sorry for them. And you know, last night I was mad when they wanted an encore from you guys. All night long they wouldn't even clap and then they wanted an encore. I say bullshit!"

Katie is retiring in one week because the doctor said they she had to either get off her feet or go into the hospital and have her legs operated on.

"They're not gonna touch 'em," she says. "But Saturday night, a week from now, is gonna be awful. My last night. I hope the band is good. You know what I believe is that what we have is Hell right down here on earth. There's no Hell later on, and if there is that's where I'll be goin'? Downstairs. I'm gonna have some fun. Now I been married for forty years. Faithful the whole damn time. I do exactly what I want and my husband does exactly what he wants. I'm a terrible cook and I hate housework. Fact is he does that stuff. I'd much rather come up here and sweep the floor of the club and throw cornmeal."

AN ENCOUNTER WITH A PHILOSOPHER KING

We were out late for breakfast at Joe's Diner after a cover gig in western Mass.. The place was packed. There was one seat available at the end of the counter so we asked the people next to us to slide down. They explained that someone else was already sitting there. We heard a disturbance down the counter and there stood Bob Reynolds, raising an enormous oak tree arm.

"You need a seat? Go ahead. What the Hell."

He was shattered. The kid who was washing dishes behind the counter was staring at him. He had thin lips and an angular build not unlike the boy leaning out the barn door in one of those Andrew Wyeth north country paintings. He was taking it in. Staring at Bob and laughing under his breath. Maybe Bob made a nuisance of himself every Friday. We sat down and turned in our order.

Bob maneuvered onto the stool next to mine. He volunteered that he was *"definitely hhhetrassessual"* and was married twice. He told me he was six feet five. He had a serious paunch that hung over his belt. His face was thick and round and heavy from the booze. His jowls hung low and he had to lean forward to concentrate. One hand was bunched up on the edge of the Formica. It was the biggest hand I'd ever seen. It looked like raw steak. He'd been in a lot of fights. That hand had

"pushed in a lot of faces...but that don't matter. I was a big basketball star in college. And a teacher. Math. Got fired because of personal problems. But that don't matter. Basketball...math. There's only one thing that counts, and I want you to remember this one thing..."

(pointing a threatening torpedo finger in my face)

"A man is only as good as he is to the man sittin' next to him."

He said this with practiced enunciation.

"A man is only as good as... Now I ain't a religious man. Christianity or whatsoever. I don't know about that...but one thing I know...A man is only as good as he is to the man sittin' next to him. Now when you came in I saw right away, I liked your face. You have a good face. How old are you? I'm almost forty. I may not know much, but I do know that a man is only as good as...Hell. My brother, he's a Baptist and he says that unless you're a Baptist you won't go to Heaven. And I said what about Mahatma Ghandi? Won't he get to Heaven? And he said that he was really sorry, but that was the way it was and I think that's bullshit. You have good eyes. I can see that. You say you're thirty-five? That must explain it. You musta seen somethin' of life. No. You don't have to love your enemies. You just need

to understand their point of view. If you're good to him, to the man sittin' next to you, then you're worthwhile. And nothin' else matters besides that. Basketball. Math..."

"I got a little campsite up north, near the Canadian border. I coach a football team of sixteen year-olds. I been married twice. But all that don't mean nothin' unless I'm good. You must think I'm an old drunk. That's not true. I only do this once a week. On Fridays. Believe me you don't have to believe me and if you can't it don't matter. The only thing that matters is that you're good to the man sittin'...I don't care who he is. You in a group or somethin'? Glitter on your face. Don't matter, you have a good face. There's love in your eyes. I can see it. You have something to give people and you better do it. You better do it. Do you hear what I'm sayin'? I don't care who he is, the guy sitting next to you. I don't care if he's a fag or what. A hummasessual. My best buddy is a h-h-hummasessual. Me, I'm definitely as hhheetrasessule as you can get. Don't matter. You gotta remember..."

He dug his forefinger into my shoulder.

"You're only as good as you are to the man sittin' next to you. I been smoking pot for twenty-five years. Way back. Years ago. Taught school. Played ball. Don't matter. Now I been detaining you long enough. I'll go. I'll vanish. Not that quickly, because it will take me awhile to get to the door. I'm bombed. But I'm going. Just you remember, you got a good face. I like your face. You got something to give people. And you remember Joe's. You remember Bob Reynolds. You remember that a man is only as good as the man...no... as good as he is to the man sittin' next to him. Goodbye. Remember now. Goodbye. I'm going."

POST SCRIPTUM
I saw that tall black-haired Somerville kid riding his bike, hair disturbed in the wind, a smile of skin at the small of his back where his shirt lifted above his belt. Last I'd seen him was at the Music Inn. He was working as a crew/actor in some atrocious rock musical. He was paired up, I was told, with an older member of the cast. They were constant companions. I remember running into him once, on the Red

Line, riding out of Cambridge. We talked about nothing even as my mind was working overtime.

The second time I saw him was outside that upscale progressive school on Marlboro St. He was playing stickball with his friends. He was laughing, pushing around and leaning against the other boys. Looking long into their faces. Taking glances 'down there' when they leaped up to catch the ball. I was going crazy.

How do I remember these details? He was of little consequence in my life. A snapshot of beauty out of the corner of my eye. It has me feeling emotionally nauseas. Or starved. How can I waste so much of my time day dreaming about someone I don't know? I surrender to it so easily. I surrender to my thoughts of this unknown boy as if it were enough for us all to thrive on fantasy.

Bent Elbow

This lamp, like a stick character from Tim Burton's *Nightmare Before Christmas*, came without a lampshade. I found that floor tom behemoth at Boomerang's. It fit the bill. The pin stalk showed up when my first roommate, Joost Rosenbaum, moved in. When he moved out, he left spoons. Big stainless steel beauties, the perfect size to lift a hard-boiled egg.

"It's Joost like toast" his friend, Sam Pierce, pronounced. *"Wait 'til you meet him. He's so beautiful."*

That he is. If Tom Brady was blonde. Like that. He'd grown up on Clive Street in a layer cake house his parents bought when red lining made owning a home in JP affordable. It had a Peter Pan attic where kids from all over the hood could hide and play. Their Moms would knock on the door and ask Femke (Joost's Mom, Dutch) where their son's sneakers disappeared.

"Buy him a new pair," she'd laugh.

I have a picture of Joost mopping the living room floor, a mirrored sheen under foot.

"I like to work," he said, swirling the gray wig across the slick caramel floor.

One night we sat outside his house in my Mom's Grand Am and he talked about life, his Dad, Slug, his Swede girlfriend whom he'd moved to Sweden to be with and who dumped him. One of those intimate talks that bring you within range of another. The nod of recognition from across a crowded bar. The confessional as an opening salvo to a meaningful friendship.

In '04 he borrowed a projector from his Mom's non-profit, Spontaneous Celebrations, so we could project the World Series on the living room wall. When Hell Froze Over In New York we hit the streets, screamed ourselves hoarse, jumping up and down in front of the Brendan Behan like thunderstorm rain dancers. One New Year's Eve he was jonesing for a coke bump. It was the last time I did that shit. I was paranoid. Joost kept me on beam. I couldn't wait 'til it was over. Time's up for me and the nose candy.

Joost powders his balls with Monkey Butt Powder, I kid you not. I couldn't lay a glove on him about it, though. I tried to publicly embarrass him, but he waved me off.

"Dude! You don't powder your balls?! You don't know what you're missing!"

Turns out that what was hygienically unknown to me is ubiquitous. Joost ain't the only nut fluffer. He still powders. I do not.

My other first time roommate (the first family of 370B) and dear friend, Dru Toews, got tight with Joost once in. Camped out in The Study, an almost-but-not-quite 3rd bedroom snuck in under the rent wire. He built a loft bed so he had space to work out beats and tunes. When he fucked his girlfriend up there (bang, bang, *slam!* against the Study wall) they rocked the house. Joost and I shrugged, kept watching The Wire.

I found Dru one morning, asleep in a bathtub full of water. A cereal bowl floated like a toy boat in a sea of Corn Flakes. I averted my eyes. When his girlfriend, Alissa, moved to Brooklyn (don't they all?) he snapped a selfie of himself naked in a snow field with the words '*I Love You*' in hurried magic marker across his chest. I envy the move.

Both were taller than me. Both their girlfriends were taller too. A Redwood Forest of tall. I came home late from work, a monster blizzard raging, snow dizzy in the street lights. Joost, Mary (his eventual wife) Dru and Alissa had dropped Molly. As high as they were tall, feeling the MDA love, snow piling up softly in the back yard. I went to bed.

The three of us were the perfect initiates at 370B. I can picture them commiserating, talking about life at the kitchen table, a pyramid of PBR cans stacked between them. What do they call 'em – The Halcyon Days?

Left behind? A crooked lamp and a drawer full of spoons.

Curl Up

Something there is about a couch. Take a seat. Feel a couch-y hug as warm as the boobs of an Auntie embrace. That's what our off white elephant promises and delivers. Two of these belonged to Alex's Step Dad, Step Dad Gang. He was replacing them with brand new. Did we want them? Duh. Our former couch, pilfered from the street and covered in don't-tread-on-me clear plastic, was on its last legs. It had a good twenty year run. Cat scratched and disgusting when you looked closely. Coins, pencils, earrings, guitar picks and food mold collected under the cushions. The underpinnings were tattered and torn.

Alex, Miles Coleman and Dana Brocious (recently married) drove a pickup truck to the Cape and loaded up these two ass huggers, the Couches of Dreams. So fat, so puffy. Arm rests like shoulder pad epaulettes. Pillow generous. Long enough to fit a tall friend for an overnight. Just the right color to inhibit dirt so you can't see it and need a pro clean. A snug fit under the bay windows.

Mike's first visit sat him on the left. I perched like a parrot on the arm of the right. I can see us now. The rapid fire talk. That moonshot first connection exploding like a grenade. Long legs outstretched or crossed. Trying not to look at each other too directly. Laughter like sunlight ricocheted around the room. The first few paragraphs of the personal buzzing in the air like hummingbirds. The impatient wait 'til midnight to head back to the Behan, to beer euphoria.

Seems to me that this house, these walls, that couch arrived just in time for him to show up. An unforced miracle following a mirage and changing my sense of who I am, again. I cannot overstate this as illusory as it might sound to others. I don't give a fuck what anyone might think or denigrate. I know the before and after difference. We both do. Ask the couch.

Dark Chocolate

The cedar chest my Grandma bought in Italy after her camel riding honeymoon in Egypt sits like a dark sarcophagus in the corner of the living room, heavy as lead. It's carved like a cowboy belt with mysterious hieroglyphics. I store sleepover blankets in there. The cedar chips have their own inner closet to keep the moths at bay, but the cats, especially Wasabi, love the soft clay candy and claw at it as if on a sugar high.

"Wasabi, no!"

He ignores me. He's in kitty drug Heaven. I sweep up the shavings and I wonder. Will the clawing's wither the chocolate into a nub? A melting, half-eaten Mars bar? An antique eviscerated by my rabid Noir Chat?

The big heavy used to live on the sun porch at 370B, sat upon by the stoned and drunk, creaking under their fat-assed weight, but it survived. I'd prefer it artfully located under Uncle Carl's water color of the spook house, but the Nord piano had to be put somewhere and there's no way to accommodate it in my bedroom, a held nose for Lady Interior Decorator who had to cradle his tiny doggy in one arm and stomp out the front door in a huff.

It is nice that it lives like a dark dot under the exclamation point that is the Jeila painting[43]. An anchor for the disturbed, for the-Duchess-will-blow-you-now lipstick mouth.

---

43   See 'The Mouth That Roared'

Dinner Is Served

Needlepoint. My Mom's Mom was way into it. The piano stool that the cats pluck and scratch and where sits my piano amp is all her. As is the doorjamb brick, needlepointed, covered and soft. All Granny. Same for the above. Immaculate miniature flowers microscope needle-fingered into the dark forest green. God knows how long it took her. Using your hands quiets the mind. Maybe she needed the respite. Needlepoint your tits off or drink 'til you drop. She was an alcoholic. When my parents were away and she looked after us, they'd lock the liquor cabinet. Duplicitous, given the booze hound my Dad was. Granny did offer one major gift: piano. She played. Read music. Left hand just so. Right tickling ivories in a saucy here-a-miss, there-a-hit blur. Got me started on the keys.

The pull chord? Can't be for sure, sure, but I suspect it's designed to be used as a bother alert to the kitchen maid, *Downton Abbey* style.

"Bring my soup, Geneva. I'm at table. Do hurry."

I don't recall servants in my family, although we did have 'help' in Weatogue. A couple that looked after us and lived on the third floor. An overweight mother and daughter and a broomstick thin dad. In Wayne we shared an Irish cook with the Voorhees family from across the street.

"You're a beautiful boy, Ricky." I remember her cooing in her musical Irish brogue. Took it to heart that I might be someday handsome. The other side of that coin was spit at me by a socialist faggot at Doyle's:

"Were you ever good-looking?"

(One of my all-time favorite questions.)

But servants, really? Starched aprons, stiff postures, dirty secrets? Sur-reptitious backrubs in cloaked drawing rooms by liveried personnel? First blood sheets whisked into hand washed laundries to prevent clues of a young girl's that-time-of-the-month first human stain? Steamed open letters from undeclared lovers? Fairy farts camouflaged under white tie and tails? None of that happened.

I think, had we highbrow help, I would have befriended the kind ones, appropriating silent wisdom and good will onto surrogate Aunts and Uncles. Children need the non-parental bandwidth.

Granny fell down the stairs at the Rogers summer house on Prouts Neck, alone at the bottom until she expired. No one was home. At her funeral I can still see my Mom's eyes, normally a dull blue-green. That afternoon they were bright emerald, radiant. At a cynical, acned fourteen, I was blown away.

Fenway Park

speaks for itself. I appreciate the roof tops of Wrigley and the Babe Ruth boast of Yankee Stadium. I've never been to either. Someday I might, but Fenway has it in spades, especially at night. Sliding into the slipstream like a salmon in the crowd, the smell of sausage and onions, beer, peanuts and hot dogs as I try not to be overtly looking at boys. I constantly check my ticket stub[44] to be sure I know where I'm going and then, at the lucky moment, I walk through the archway into the park and my chest swells up with Red Sox Nation pride. The flood lights exaggerate the so green field as if photoshop enhanced. The crowd leans forward with expectation. The barkers hurl bags of peanuts I'm too spastic to order or catch. The red seats are tight-fitted and not new enough to accommodate the obese 21st Century asses the cushiony couches they provide at Yankee Stadium. The dug outs empty with warmup athletes and rock star famous favorites who humbly ignore the crowd. The first pitch, the first crack of the bat, the first base hit, home run or hotshot out – there's nothing like it.

This wide screen, framed poster, the start of the first World Series the Sox won since 1918, the giant flag on the Green Monster, was a birthday present to me from Johnny Mulcahy, a Doyle's line cook who went on to take a top job in the Fenway kitchen. I can still see him marching it into the back room at D's, unwrapped on his shoulder, knowing how much I'd love it. Me, the fan who knows the least about sports, but who, like all of New England went crazy in '04 and the three parades after that. How perfect that it hangs above my Uncle Carl's painting,

---

44 Thank you John and Nancy Hanifin who give me awesome seats on my birthday.

the guy who pro punted for the New York Giants[45]. The consummate athlete/artist. Twin stars in jock Heaven.

---

45   See 'Getting Old Is No Fun' (*'The Paragraphs'*)

House Abandoned

My Uncle Carl[46] was a great artist, a Steinbeck master of water color. After he died, his work proliferated among his family, honored and revered. He never made it to famous, but I doubt he cared. This is the one I've got. My cousins made sure I did. Carl made the frame. I'd say it's spooky, a ghost house, except that it isn't. It's abandoned, empty. A place to be found by strays, by kids on the lam or just looking to hide, drink and get laid. Or maybe no one ever found it. He painted from the actual, not from photos. He had to be standing right there, in real time, in front of his subject. His house portraits have a simple affection, a nod to beauty and deterioration. The wood worn out, the trees waiting for Spring, the windows without curtains. I can smell the tall grass where he stood to paint. I can smell his cigar, or pipe, the wizard smoke curling around his head. I know this house because I've lived with it for so long. It cannot be entered, although I do. It will not collapse, although it must. It will never be inhabited, although it's filled with tears.

---

46 Getting Old Is No Fun' (*The Paragraphs*)

Kitty Hot Tubs

Easily the best thing I ever got the kids. (Thank you, Shamus Moynihan[47].) I think they had advanced knowledge.

"Hey, Shamus. Tell Berlin about the tubs. We read about 'em in a cat-alogue. He's way behind on that shit."

A perfect curl up fit, day or night, warm or cold. Their weight turns on the heat and they're back in kitten-land nestled against Mommies' belly.

I don't wash them. I'm worried I'd mess up the electronics, the hot tub becoming a frigid sink. I don't want to take away any of the familiar smells or pinch out tufts of Wasabi, Carlotta fur. They drift apart. One mauve lily pad south of the couch, the other at the foot of the Grandfather clock. I'll nick a stray nearer it's nephew. I don't want them stuck under a chilly winter window.

My guys don't like being disturbed when settled in. No chin scratch, no ear pull. If they're dead tired, they let me say goodnight. Wasabi, first to finish his dinner and unable to jump Carlotta's bowl, has, of late, spent lap time purring away as I stream *Babylon Berlin* or *Ozark*. With his ears back he looks like a baby Yoda. He's good for ten minutes, then he hits the tub. Conked out in a furry coma, one eye at a squint, he lets me say bye-bye.

"Love you, 'Sab. See ya in the morning."

---

47   See 'The Blue Ox'

Just under his head and chest I can feel it, the hot tub warmth keeping him cozy.

Lady Liberty

I was invited (and paid) to take the train to Manhattan for a series of dances inspired by my solo record *LIVE@JACQUES*. Clint White, instigator and benefactor. Honestly, I was nervous about it. Those ten years of Mondays at Jacques Cabaret were as unparalleled as they were unpredictable. It was a stretch for me to re-imagine them as choreographed dances.

Back story.

My roommate, Charlie Isenberg, had been a manager at the Loews theater next door to the drag bar. Needing change for the ticket window, he'd stop in for a pop at Jacques. Got to know Kris Turelli, manager and bartender at the oldest drag bar with some of the oldest drag queens in the country (Sylvia Sydney), and booked me in.

The initial set up: I play my songs and 'accompany' Vaunassa Vale on piano. I pretend to play as she pretends to sing or tap dance. It was fun at first, but as the year wore on, I ached for a change. Vaunassa was on a drag sabbatical so I took a chance and fired her. I booked a litter-box full of opening acts and the night became a clubhouse, a hang for years. The crowd would turn over periodically. One particular group of friends and fans losing interest and replaced by others. It was my only live gig for a decade. You want to hear Berlin? Show up at Jacques. This forced me to come up with new material each week and challenged my repertoire. It brought new life and the curious into this are-we-in-Isherwood-Deutschland?, Bay Village, underbelly venue.

The queens were not happy. I'd stolen their Monday stage time and dressing room, but Kris and the club dug it and Monday night was

Shitcity dead no matter who was on the bill. The sound system was unreliable, the stage lights now-they-do-now-they-don't work, the men's room stank of piss and disinfectant. The dressing room on the other hand was the tits; crammed to the gills with wigs, make-up, big foot stilettos, trashy jewelry, falsies and fake nails. The spotlight caught stardust in its unblinking gaze. The queens at the pool table were quint-essentially fabulous. The world outside disappeared for a brief couple of hours and a miniature 'scene' emerged. All this before I had a car to lug my piano back and forth. Taxis hated me. Some refused to let me shove my keyboard ass-ended into their trunks.

"Call somebody else!"

All-in-all that crazy decade was mad, irreplaceable fun.

I recorded, five nights of Mondays, *LIVE@JACQUES*. It took forever to mix. The producer (Dan Cantor) was doing this for me pro bono, so patience was a critical necessity. We mic-ed the room, the dressing room and the pool table where Les Girlz would bang and crack balls, yack about this cute number and that closeted trucker, firing ass-in-the-air bank shots with $5,000 tittie jobs spilling out of skimpy halter tops. Those girls and I did have one thing in common. We liked straight guys. They gave me a wider berth once they heard my song about that not-as-rare-as-you-might-think predilection.

Back to the Big Apple.

Like I said, I was apprehensive about the choreography, about the interpretation of that singular record, about hearing those songs after years of absence. But once the evening got underway, in a cool, beau-tifully lit Manhattan loft and I heard those songs again, I was moved. It all came back. That decade of Mondays. This performance in the big city surprised and brought me to tears.

I invited Brad Zygala, my friend and co-worker from Doyle's, to come with me. He'd never been to New York. We were given a hotel room to ourselves and a spectacular after-show dinner paid for by Clint. Zygala was the right guy to do this with me. He was fine with the homo songs and homo dances/dancers. We had an brilliant night of it. Got to know each other better than we had before or since.

After dinner we decided to head back to the hotel. Brad lit up a joint on the sidewalk; not the brightest idea in a city that criminalized weed and prosecuted fiercely, especially out-of-towners. But fuck it, we smoked, laughed and decided we wanted to elevator to the tourist top of the Empire State Building. But at midnight it was too long a wait, so we kept walking. I was so out of it on THC that it was a) hard to talk, b) hard to walk and c) impossible to know where the fuck the hotel was. Brad had his head on straight. He GPS'd the hotel and shepherded us home. I watched him sleep, the rise and fall of breath, high on perv. Told him later. He laughed it off, said I should have taken pictures.

Next morning, before we caught the train home, we walked around the cluttered Great White Way, hitting up buy-this-buy-that bodegas. Brad picked out presents for his Mom and Grandma. I got the miniature Lady Liberty, gold torch on high.

Here's the thing. The Statue was, for real, (maybe)[48] designed by my Great, Great, Great Uncle, Frederic Auguste Bartholdi from Alsace Loraine, my tiny eyebrow country of origin. I was uncertain about the veracity of all this until my brother-in-law, Chris Clark, did the deep dive research and proved it true. Frederic designed Lady Liberty and he was my god-damned GGGU. I'm a waiter who plays songs in a lady bar, the perfect counterpoint, right?

Jane Friedman (who was part-time managing my performance trips to New York) told me to stage an event. If I did, she promised, my profile in the Boston Music Community would rise. I already knew

---

[48] Grain of salt: Mary Bartholdi was my great grandmother. Not directly related to The Statue of Liberty designer, although it's likely we Kinscherfs are connected to Auguste through a distant Batoldi cousin. Therefore I stake my (false?) claim.

what I'd call it. Jack Reilly, of Jack's (where OL played) and later his jazz club, Ryles (where OL had its reunion)[49] told me that if he ever put on a benefit he'd call it:

DRAGS, DICKS & DYKES

Which I stole and added (4 LIFE) and thus my benefit night to raise money for the Aids Action Committee debuted, of course, at Jacques. Upstairs and down. Ten queens, Ten bands; a total Babylon blast. It was so busy that night that those who couldn't get in were happy to party in the line outside. Girls were pissing between parked cars. We raised a grand.

Hence, the beginning of Berlin putting on events. Watch what you wish for, kiddo.

RETURN TO THE SOURCE

Before Mike flew home to Santa Barbara, we hit up Jacques on a Saturday night. He'd been dying to go; the Berlin stories ad infinitum. Johnny met us at the door and let us in for free. Made me feel special, cool to impress the boy. It was packed, mostly women, another bachelorette party – Jacque's weekend bread and butter. The queens were at the top of their game dishing the crowd lovingly and being hilarious and cartoon sexy.

Mike was soaking it up. Got a tongue-in-ear from one of the girlz dancing on the bar. When I went for a piss (in the ladies room as advised) a much-younger-then-me dude took my seat. He vanished as soon as I returned, glowering at him.

"Jealous?"

"No," I lied.

"I am so happy. This will be on my lifetime highlight reel."

---

49   See 'Picture Bats A Thousand'

My fav moment, however, caught me off guard. I nearly fell off the stool at our best seat in the house at the corner of the horseshoe bar. A fabulous queen with an exaggerated ass and tits out-to-here was lip synching *Let It Go* from *Frozen* (a movie I loathe). She was immaculate in her delivery until it was apparent that she was *actually* letting it go. Farting at appropriate pauses in the song, sticking her ass out in emphasis, shaking it in the spotlight and rolling her eyes, fanning the gas blowing out her ass. It was brilliant, drag genius. Especially for a fart queen like myself. How the fuck did she do this? Did she have an accomplice backstage feeding recorded farts into a mic? None were repeated, each had its own farty personality, sound and length. I totally lost it. I wished there'd been time to ask how she pulled it off. I haven't laughed that hard in months. Walking around town, at work, in the house I picture her performance all over again and lose it. I had a hunch that there must be something pre-recorded that let this happen so effectively in the club that night.

A few days later I wrote a song, *Carnival*, about Jacques, about that night. Took me that long after my heyday of Mondays. Took Mike to get me there, to compose a song that would remind both of us of that wild scene.

He'd be gone in two weeks.

Pastel Ricky

You've seen 'em, the easel-propped street artists on tourist trap sidewalks, egging on the vanity of portraiture. Mine? Tuscon, 1948. Three years old. The predictable profile. I think it's easier to render an accurate profile than a front-on. Anxious parents need likeness, not art. They're paying for this. Little Ricky in a white T, big ears, boy's regular with an overbite.

Around then I was selected to be on the cover of Time Magazine. Not just me, but with a pair of actor parents. An outdoor shoot, the cactus background, the smiles of ten thousand teeth. Hot lights to squint against. I hated it. Hated the phony parents. Hated the over-encouraging photographer, the make-up lady fluffing my cheeks, the nervous concern from my Mom. I burst into tears. They dried me off and sent me home. Boy #2 scored the cover. Likely an Aryan blond with a ready smile. Luck was not my lady that day.

SMALL BOY FLICKERINGS OF MEMORY

I shit my pants in Second Grade. I had to go to the infirmary and Mrs. Leonard had to scrape the pudding off my ass.

My Grandmother, Teddy[50], laughed so hard that she bounced out a fart which made her laugh all the harder and fart all over again.

I remember watching Elvis on the Ed Sullivan Show with Ellen who weighed three hundred pounds. She screamed all the way through it. She was so fat she had to roll herself out of the swimming pool like a walrus. She split a toilet bowl in two one day at South School Elementary.

---

50   See 'Me, Dick & A Cactus'

I dreamed about delivering babies. I used an over-sized round cookie-cutter and cut the mothers open with it, peeled back the skin and lifted out the kid. It was a repetitive dream and I wet the bed afterwards. The warm piss woke me up.

Steve McIntyre and I used to studiously watch each other shit out by the chicken coop. We covered it up with leaves.

I could hear the cows bellowing as they were shot to death after the Connecticut River flood.

Ridgemont Street

'All the colors in the air have changed. No. They're still the same...'
— *Doris Dreams*

It's still there, the Orchestra Luna house. Same puke yellow aluminum siding, decrepit porch. In the photo: Peter Barrett, Kenny Gardner, Lisa and Richard Kinscherf, Charlie Isenberg, and Debbie Lehman (invisible behind the screen door). Flo and Solly Hemus (our dogs). Out front on a summer day with no idea where any of us would wind up. This, the petri dish that orchestrated Orchestra Luna. The music, Barry Keating's choreography, the first place we heard the full symphony for our LP (Rupert Holmes, producer/composer). Where we painted backdrops of exquisite corpses, sewed costumes, made ourselves up like clown prostitutes. We rented the entire house. Both halves. Six bedrooms a side. I built a loft bed. Stored music gear underneath it which, when closed, was hidden from view. I had a highboy acoustic piano next to a window and wrote and wrote and wrote.

Doris came out of that room. I lost my voice as I sang in a don't-worry-about-it piercing soprano developing *Doris* in that room (requiring vocal polyp removal surgery). Brick gave me a black eye in that room. Evjan Tupy, who escaped Czechoslovakia as a small child all by himself (his parents whisked him out of the country solo) and who I met at a country and western bar in the South End, came in my mouth in that room. He left me with two drawings, one which I still have in my scrapbook[51] and the other I gave to Patti Smith as a present when she played the Jazz Workshop. I began to type just words in that room. Karla deVito auditioned in that room. I fucked up my hearing in my

---

51   See 'Scrapbooks'

left ear leaning into the horn of my first amplifier when I blasted it for the first time ever in that room. I painted the bed and the woodwork metallic silver in that room. I stripped and urethaned my *RMI Electra piano* in that room.

We set up an outdoor shower behind the house, just because. Turns out the neighbors could see 'everything'. We got busted and had to take it down. Peter painted pink clouds on Lisa's ceiling. Debbie brought home a different black guy from the disco inferno every single night, infuriating Peter who could hear the goings-on from his tiny closet room next door, where he'd built a desk-to-single convertible bed, where he hid his porn mags, wrote poetry and worked on *Moosup, The Musical*[52]. A trumpeter lived in the basement and rehearsed into a cardboard box stuffed with Styrofoam so as to not bother the neighbors. Kenny and Charlie lived across the hall from Debbie and Peter in a split screened room where both saw endless action and *"roaring hard-ons"*. Ridgemont was a sex palace and a music house all at once. That was how we rolled.

Jeremiah's, the restaurant we landed a Saturday night residency and out of which we were signed by Epic, was three blocks down the street. We walked to shows a-tilt in platform shoes and pink silk candy pants. We closed off our end of the dead-end street, hired a square dance caller, dropped acid, danced and played OL songs on a make-shift stage. We watched the sun transmogrify from twilight to starry, starry night – my pet hallucinogen transition. We were carefree, insane, mutually inspired and chasing anything that moved. The house still stands. Same color, same rotting porches, but essentially dead inside without us. Peter, Solly and Flo are no longer here. Neither is our wonderful drummer, Don Mulvaney. Nor the twin brother of the trumpeter. Nor Mike Scopino, Liz Gallagher's boyfriend, who took his life. Also gone, David Sweeney, a handsome redhead from the Vineyard whom everyone was hot for and who crashed his helicopter into the ocean.

---

52   See 'Moosup, The Musical'

It's a blur, those years. A cloud of up-swirling Tinkerbell pixie dust. We were magic. We didn't realize it. Those who saw us did.

LETTER FROM LISA TO *FAYE WRAY* (a former Ridgemont roommate)
"Dear, finally, Lynn (aka 'Faye Wray'),

This morning, 10:15, everything in the house feels a little lonely, a little too grey and quiet for me. Every sound I make, with everyone else asleep, seems to crash into my ears. I just put on Stevie Wonder to better the atmosphere.

Let me tell you. You're a star in this house. Every time a letter comes from Lynn, everyone gathers in the kitchen, crowding around the receiver who reads out loud amidst bursts of laughter, 'on no's' and 'my God's'.

This place becomes more wonderful every day. I love the people here altogether more than I have ever loved just one lover. The other morning I was sitting in the orange bean chair, the full sun pouring through my window, listening to Aretha Franklin. 'All The King's Horses'. I went way out, melting in the warmth and yellow, a sensation of total happiness in contemplation of my friends. Realizing that I could never experience such a feeling of love, satisfaction and security in a man/woman relationship.

We've established some really great routines around here. Especially in the mornings after meditation. Hanging around in the kitchen. Taking two hours on breakfast. Peter making toast. D. I. reading a letter from you, or a letter to a lover or from a book on homosexuality. All laughing, shouting. I haven't laughed so much in my life as I have in the past month. Peter's making a jellyfish out of me. He had me on the floor one night, practically nauseated from laughing.

It seems, as the days pass, things get tighter and tighter around here. We continue to paint walls, move pictures and rearrange furniture.

Wish you were here right now. The more I write to you the more I think of how much a part of all these goings-on you are. How you would be supporting us through concert-itis, unfortunate involvements and mixed-up relationships.

See, outside the house I get pretty lost in my affairs. Six months – no attraction to no one. Nobody. No body. Every performance I look out into the audience for someone. The other night at Lucy In The Sky I found one. Saw him the next night at Oliver's. After much deliberation and pacing's back and forth I approached him and gave him a Valentine's cookie. Told him I thought he was beautiful and walked away.

His name is Michael and after all this he has to turn out to be a twenty-year-old screw-up. Alcoholic. Dope dealer. Saw him several times afterwards at work and told him I didn't want to see him until he was sober. This has been quite a relationship, Lynn. I feel so objective about it now, as though I sat in a cinema watching this movie of me involved again with another person. Total pre-occupation. Total paradox. I can't describe it to you.

It seems to be a compulsion of mine to fall for the fuck-ups. If only I could point out his weakness to him and ask him questions about himself he wasn't ready to answer. Anyway, a single week's relationship knocked me out for two weeks following.

I've painted my room white. Believe it or not, no more dogwood wallpaper. Window and door frames the lightest shade of pink. Ceiling: light turquoise. It looks beautiful and breezy. The plants love it. They have become the objects of my attention and reward me with flowers and new leaves. Except Mickey eats them and shits in my bucket of potting soil.

Really into costumes now. And make-up. Jesus. Look like death-warmed-over in the mornings and like a star at night.

Love,

Lisa"

ABOUT LYNN'S DOG, LAMPCHOP

Lambchop is a miniature poodle. He belongs to Lynn and he is her first dog. He is grey and the fur around his lips is brown. He is constantly humping Solly. Solly has a wing of grey soot on his lower back from Chop's forelegs. Each new visitor gets his toes eaten out, uninvited. His quick little tongue darts between and under and over and upside-down, inside-out, like the Diana Ross song. Sucking and nibbling. He can't get enough. He runs like he is being shot at. When you pat him you have to wash your hands afterwards. Lynn slammed his front paw in a car door and crushed the finger joints. She took him upstairs and fed him her drug of choice, a Vitamin Q, a Quaalude. He shits the bathroom floor after she leaves. Hard black sausages. He has a piercing bark that he cuts loose whenever the front door opens. Lynn screams at him:

"Chawp! Shut up!"

He sucked Rene Ricard off. Rene put honey on it and Chop went down on him. They had a wonderful relationship. He called her *"Michette"*.

Michette was hit by a car and killed. Isenberg put him on a chair in the basement. Later on he and Kenny flipped him into a dumpster. Wouldn't mind if they put *me* in a dumpster when I reach the end of the line.

WHERE *DORIS* CAME FROM

(BEFORE PETER FRANKENSTEINED HER TOGETHER WITH A STORYLINE ARC – 1970)

I'd been standing around the fringes of The Other Side. My mind racing, trying to keep the excuses coming as fast as the disappointments. It was closing time. Few were left. A boy with a dyed white-blond shag was dancing on the stage. He'd taken off his shirt. He was thin. His skin, milk white. He was dancing with an older black guy who's head was shaved. They were getting into it. Dancing like madmen. At one point the boy collapsed on the floor. The weight of his body brought his shoulder up to his ear. The lights were changing colors and altering the tone of his skin. His eyes traveled around the room as if looking to see who might have been watching. I figured he thought he'd put on a pretty hot show. He caught my look, held on and then continued his search for an audience. The black dude was looking at me.

The lights came up and the room stank. My eyes hurt from the glare, the cigarette smoke, the beer and Lysol. I felt ugly and wanted to get the fuck outa there. As I was about to leave I felt a hand on my shoulder. I turned and was nose-to-nose with the black dude. He must have been jacked up on meth, because he was talking a mile-a-minute and there was a tiny, accumulating gob of spittle in the corner of his mouth. I can't remember much of what he said, but he took my hand and put another hand in it. Behind him, the boy.

"Bobby," he says, *"I want you to meet..."*

"Rick."

"I want you to meet Rick. Rick, this heah is Bobby. He likes you. He wants to go home with you."

"Hi, Bobby."

"Now you two have a good time."

I nearly shit my pants. He picked me out. We held hands. Outside on the cobblestones we waited for a taxi. A long black limo pulled up with five suspicious looking Mafiosos inside.

"Hey, Bobby? Where you headed? You and your friend need a ride?"

We climbed into the back, nestled against each other. We drove in silence, except for my directions to Somerville.

He told me his real name is Lorne Chadbourne, Jr. He said that he loved me. He gave me a Crackerjacks ring and a scuffed up paperback. I sucked him off under the covers. He was shy about his body.

I also think, happening upon us one night, that Brick was jealous. Hurt. Angry.[53]

Bobby drew pictures all day. Late at night he'd disappear, calling up later from the South End. On speed. On Quaaludes. Bummed out, threatening suicide. Eventually the cops picked him up outside the Greyhound bus station, the hang for hustlers. Turns out he was a runaway who had, apparently, torched houses. A pryo. At his hearing we met Mr. Danielle of the Ritz-Carleton Beauty Salon. He bailed Bobby out and gave him a job. Gave me one as well, to wall-paper the salon. That's where I noticed all those bottles of hair dye with the crazy names: Chocolate Kiss, Nice Change, Frivolous Fawn, White Mink, Golden Buns... that I appropriated for *Doris Dreams*. Peter's spoken words stitched the whole thing into a coherent narrative.

Lisa and I actually considered adopting Bobby, to get him out of trouble. We went to court for him, alongside Mr. Danielle who had fallen in love with him. They stuck him in Mass Mental. When he got a chance, he ran. The last time I saw him was in Copley Square, years later. His hair had grown out. It was Buster Brown. He had a lot of zits and his body was bigger and more awkward. I'm sure he recognized me, but we just hurried past each other on the way to the bus.

"Dear Lorne,

I just got home from work, got your letter and a weight was lifted off my shoulders. I've been worrying ever since you took off, but you know I kept thinking you'd turn up in Boston. I don't know where that street is, but I suppose it's not far from the Boston Common or Park Sq. I used to live in Dorchester. Lower Mills if you know where that is.

Lorne, it's been about two years and two months since I put you on that plane and I've thought about it a long time. There wasn't much I could do about it at the time. Life had to go on for Debbie and Linda and it still

53   See 'Guns' (*'The Paragraphs'*)

does. Although Mama and I messed up yours and Billy's life, I still had to bring them girls up in the manner that I, in my own humble way, call right. I have succeeded so far and to do this I have had to forsake love or even consider it for myself until they are eighteen years old. This is a hell of a cross for me to bear, but I think it's worth it if they come to some good.

I'm not trying to cry on your shoulder or anything like that, it's too late for that. I just want you to know that I've felt like you are now, many times. I've walked over bridges and felt like a giant magnet was pulling me over the side and you know, I didn't care. But something up in that seven-and-a-half sized head of mine said

'Later, on the Big Trip, Chad.'

So I'm still staggering along with this perpetual bummer of a life and if you have my blood in you, you will follow suit.

Think about it, right?

As for Egbert or Bill, whichever you choose, I gave him the boot three weeks ago. I had gotten him this job near where I work and it paid him $110.00 a week. But the lazy bum didn't like work so he stayed home all day and made believe he had been working. I found out and told him to shove off. He had been out here since April, ever since he got kicked out of the Service, free-loading off me, which I didn't mind except when he didn't want to listen to me. So now I guess he's waiting in the welfare line.

I knew most of what you told me because I have a grapevine to Oxon Hill too.

I haven't lived at Lorna's since May 15th. I live in an apartment similar to the one we lived in on Mercy Ave. Remember? You know. Two bedrooms, two baths, wall-to-wall carpet, air-conditioning, swimming pool, rec room, pool table, ping pong table, etc. So when the chill wind blows in Mass, which it soon will, and you decide that Calif is the only place to be in the winter, you will always be welcome at my house, even though there's an APB out for you. But you've been sweating that for months, haven't you?

A word of advice, maybe if you sheared your locks you would look a lot different than the police think you do.

Hope this letter doesn't bore you but if you notice there are no promises made for me to break. Just straight talk. I know you are a man, Lorne, not a Midnight Cowboy. So shit-can that speed, grass, skag, uppers, downers and don't do that big freak-out, dig?

Love,

Pops."

It don't get sadder than that.

Set Sail In The Wild
Blue Yonder

A kite. A present from Sam, my brother-in-law. It sat around at 370B unopened for couple of years. Not adept or patient with instructions, I didn't want to deal. But with a sweet ceiling hook in our new house it called out:

"Hang the fucking kite!"

So, one afternoon, house empty, I amazed myself and strung it together. As with prior instruction papers and recipes, I made up the how to. This piece seemed to go here, that there. It didn't matter because I was never going to fly it. It is an art object, under full sail, billowing above our heads.

Part of me would like to run it up to Pinebank and see if it would lift, fly and not nosedive crash. But I won't. It will live up there next to the Green Man and collect Tinkerbell dust. I think it's pleased to be out of the box, to sail like Captain Hook across a full moon it will never know.

BLUE SWEATER BOY BULLYS SET
SAIL IN HIGH SCHOOL

I used to walk down City Line Avenue after sports, on my way to the Paoli Local that took me home. Me and my friends in our Episcopal Academy navy blue sweaters with the narrow white stripes on the arms. I felt the breeze in my hair, would take in a long deep breath and my fingertips seemed to glow as I thought about that boy across from me in Chapel. His eyes were deep and rested on mine longer than I would have guessed. His head was slightly large for his body.

His lips were dark red and if I could have kissed him I am certain he would have blushed, but would not have backed away. I was a 'pizza faced' fourteen and thinking about it, but hid all spurious thoughts in a teenage lock box.

The sidewalk was covered with pages of the Philadelphia Inquirer which blew about as the cars rushed by. The Ginkgo trees littered the street with their pink translucent fruit like marshmallows that popped underfoot and discharged their foul odor. The other kids from school would scoop them up and charge one of the fat kids or the effeminate ones and hurl the stinko candies at him until he covered his head with his arms and ran away in tears.

I'd have just gotten out of soccer, out of the steaming showers where young boys seemed to arrange themselves like animated Degas paintings, coming alive in the white mist. Laughing and yelling and snapping towels in the locker room at each other's tight red asses. Poor Andy Lockhart would have a big hard-on that pointed straight out. His face would blush deep red and one of the more playful jocks would slap at it and watch it bob up and down, back and forth. But most of the time we left him alone. Or pretended not to see it at all. We were afraid that the same thing might happen to us.

Every morning in Mr. Balsley's english class we would set up the desk chairs in a semi-circle and almost every boy's legs were either crossed or jack-hammering in place. Everyone it seemed had a morning stiffy. You would have to pull your underwear up tight and center it so that only the zipper would bulge but no one would notice. Each of us thought we were the only one with the problem and hoped we would never succumb to a bully in the shower.

Steampunk Has Big Balls

My sister-in-law's husband, handsome Dave Fowler, made this lamp. A California kid. A triathlon athlete. A landscape artist and metal sculptor. Janie's husband, Chris, gave it to me for Christmas, one of the few pieces that survived the fire that consumed Dave's shop. It was Iron Man heavy. Disparate found objects, machine parts the he soldered together into a lamp. It resembles that skinny robot in *Mandalorian*. I wait for him to speak, but he looks used up and worn out. I suspect Dave left his rusted vocal chords on the workshop floor. Dude feels at home on the iron radiator, which, on another castaway day, might be Fowler converted from scrap into art. Either way, it's rock-solid support for his mechanical, underarm, silver ball epauleted frame. The old timey filament light bulb is a de rigueur requirement. It had to be for this, the prettiest light in our house. The zig-zag wires, when lit, look old fashioned, as if screwed on by Thomas Edison himself. If I light it up when I'm watching the tube, it reflects onto the flat screen, so I have to shut it off which is a good thing. The filament will last for months. I hung the balls at Christmas. They belong. They look like the float bulbs in the flush works of a toilet. They give bicep heft to those toothpick arms, even though they're plastic and weigh next to nothing.

Jay, The Responsible Turk, re-connected and tightened the fixture so that it can't be snapped off with a rash curtain pull, or a hyperkinetic child bouncing off the couch.

"I will not break. I am strong like ox." (Russian accent.)

There is life in the inanimate, but you already know that.

The Big Red

Swedish Nord. Should it have been a blonde? Big lips? Pale blue eyes? Depressive Ingmar Bergman tonality?

For me it's utilitarian. Weighted keys, tough on the road. The full 88 means the lo-end is fat and deep and gets as loud as you want it once plugged in. It can do a lot of tricks and has endless audio options. I use one or sometimes two at most. Real piano. Wurlitzer. I'm stubborn that way. All I want is a piano that doesn't need to be hoisted into an apartment that doesn't have room for it, or require tuning and a humidifier. I want it to last. I'm a banger. I hit those plastic ivories like a demolition dude, no mercy.

I've never been a fan of the electric piano sound. I had to acquire the taste. Acoustic is another story. Those beauties are pie-filled with songs-to-be and have a near human life force. The Big Red, not so much, but serves its purpose and songs eventually shy violet out of the crimson closet. I wonder if, having to set it up, plug cords in holes and fire up the amp retards the creative impulse. Hitting a single note on an upright tips my ears into an immediate, here-comes-a-new-song lucky day. I could be making that up. As busy a workaholic as my friends think I am in the project department, I look what I accomplish and it's never enough. I'm a lazy fuck who could always do more.

Or not. The Berlin Catalogue ain't slight.

Doubt virus. Have I've written my last song? Have I landed on the Hemmingway beachhead? His final apprehension being that he had, for shit sure, nothing left to say, his art license revoked. Blew his brains out with a shotgun, third try. Who knows? Songs continue to fall into my lap. One thing's for sure, I would never kill myself because the composition well dried up.

The stool. The involuntary stool as I sometimes refer to it. I came close to naming one of my bands 'The Involuntary Stools', but let it go. Too scat and no one besides myself would have agreed to it. With an acoustic, I favor the spindly, three-legged wood-carved, old thrones with claw-clutching glass-ball feet. This one, the blackie, I stole from The Midway with Jay Balerna's permission. I'd forgotten to bring mine. This baby is perfect. Sturdy, reliable and a perfect ass-fit. Since I can't break it down and fit it in my car, it never leaves the house; a solid trio – piano, amp, stool.

I am a charlatan piano man who straddles the big red and pries songs out of god knows where. I play adequately, but not well. No piano, no songs. No sublimation, no legacy. I am what I've invented.

The Green Man

I bought this plaster caster dude[54] from an upstairs shop on Newbury St. It was a cool place run by white haired hippies and had a Harry Potter magic about it. Dead leaves on the floor, replicas of gargoyles from the old country, winged creatures, dark rooms, dusty light filtering through venetian blinds. It's gone. I miss it. A great spot to find a something for someone of an object they'd never dreamed existed. Each piece spoke to you as if a reminder of other worlds, other times, other faiths. I keep a lot of these beyond the pale truths in my back pocket as proof against 'reality', letting intuition sing out, a Pavarotti shattering the tinkling chandeliers of accepted religions.

I hung Mr. Green high above a living room window. He needs to survey the landscape, to take it all in even as I forget about him being up there. He shoulders the ceiling, an Atlas Un-shrugged. House, sky, earth on his invisible back. I admire his unblinking stare and soft leaves. I doubt he'll let me fool myself or someone else without a silent objection, his larger vision a truth I need to be reminded of.

The eucalyptus bough is part of the deal. A friend of mine, Larry Owen, had temporarily quit his job as a bar tender at the Bee Hive to landscape in the healthy outdoors. I run into him at odd times in the hood. Most often at the Behan. One afternoon, there he sat, outside Whole Foods, eating an indecipherable salad. We fired up our usual talk about everything in art and love land. He has his own take and doubt about that stuff. Me too. When we wrapped it up, he gave me the eucalyptus.

---

54 The Green Man is primarily interpreted as a symbol of rebirth, represented in the cycle of growth each spring. It is most commonly depicted as a sculpture or other representation of a face surrounded by, or made from, leaves. – Wikipedia

I have no idea if it represents anything in particular or has a relation-ship with Mr. Green, but it seems like the perfect place for it to float.

Two as one. Friendship in the face of a man in a tree.

The Mouth That Roared

Jeila Farzaneh, nick-named Farts-n-eggs in high school, is half Iranian. She is stunningly beautiful, resembles Audrey Tautou (*Amelie*). Black hair. Theda Barrow winged bow mouth. Mirroring eyes. Smart make-up. We were inseparable for a long time. She was one of those rare, exceptional girlfriends who never 'fell'.[55] We looked at the world through a parallel kaleidoscope. I've written and lost countless of songs quoting words she said.

Bermuda Triangle, Jeila, Empathy, Sympathy, Apathy – for three.

Triangle refers to the crappy cement island across from the 7 Eleven. She'd had a fight with an actor earlier, at the Behan. He insulted her, calling her a whining obsessive. She banged out the door, stomped down Centre St and wound up on that cement chunk just as he pulled up in his car. He didn't look over. It was freezing out and he sat there in his warm car, staring resolutely ahead, waiting for the light to change and took off.

"Felt like I was standing in the Bermuda Triangle," she laughed.

Jeila is a song portrait. I was trying to cheer her up. She could be off kilter around dudes she likes. Aren't we all? Spilling drinks, losing a shoe in a drunken chase, wearing a girdle to pull in a belly she was ashamed of. At Man Ray, a bi-sexual dance club in Central Square (now gone), Jeils, her best friend and sister painter, Katie (another knockout) and Chris Hemmeter (whom we all adored) were dancing it up. Bumping and grinding like the fools we were.

---

55 See 'My Girlfriends' – *'The Paragraphs'*

"Oh my God!" she yelled in the middle of a twitchy move. *"My date bra* broke!*"*

Tits bouncing out of her shirt. Hysterical, hilarious, fabulous.

E, S, A is my favorite. Describing a roommate. Someone she cared about. Someone with a drug problem. Someone unable to take care of herself let alone behave responsibly.

"I went through 'em all," she said. *"Empathy, sympathy, apathy."'*

Summing up the frustration we feel when confronted by the friend for whom all the love in the world can't save. We exhaust ourselves in the face of it. I had the song on a cassette. Threw it out. Threw out all those dusty cassettes when we moved. Never listened to them anyway. Down the bloody hatch.

Fair to say, Jeils is an art genius. She studied at Museum School and earned top accolades. Other students were inferior. I saw their work. Atrocious stabs at whatever they thought was 'happening' in New York. Farts-n-eggs' brush strokes, her teacher noted, were old school right on, as sure and as brilliant as the Dutch masters. She won a trip to The Big City to continue to study painting with the best in the field. A short, three week victory, but with no prize money. She had to pay for everything herself. We hung a show at James's Gate where she bartended, with all her paintings on the walls. It sold out. In one night she made over $10,000 bucks. I'd had six at my place, but had to drive them down to The Gate for the exhibit. Made me sad, losing them, but she promised I could keep the mouth girl, ultimately the cover of *The Paragraphs.*

After the three weeks, she decided to stick it out and move to Brooklyn. Snagged a bar tending gig at a mafia joint, landed a well-lit art studio/ apartment and continued to paint. The work changed, became more abstract, but was still astonishing. The girl has it in art spades, but like me, an inveterate romantic, she fell in love with a man she'd chased back in the *Green St.* days. This time, he loved her back. They flew all over the place. London, Italy, Paris. Got married and had their first kid. She moved back to the hood (a fiduciary necessity) and stopped painting. She's a Mom now, but will get back on the art horse, no question.

One time, after hearing an amusing love lost lament, a black woman said to her:

"Honey, I want you to have this."

She placed a single bullet upright on the bar and walked out. Things like that happen to this girl. What I miss most? The two of us at the Behan writing comic book word balloons about the clientele.

"He can't stop looking at himself in the window!"

"She is so into her boobs."

"Long beard? Total chocolate ass paint. Dude don't wipe."

That, and drawing exquisite corpses on napkins at The Lizard Lounge with Katie and laughing like stoned bitches.

Jeils has a knack for music. Could learn a song on guitar she had no idea how to play. Drummed in a band that I booked at Jacques. Very Velvet Underground. I bought her one of those kit-in-a-case drums that Andrew Mazzone strung together. You bring him a suitcase, a snare, a drum stool and an XLR plug and he fits all that gear into the hat box. You open it up, lift out the snare, rack it, attach the mic to the XLR and convert the suitcase into a kick drum, kick pedal unpacked and placed just so. As incredible sounding as it was ingenious. When she moved, she lost it. She does that. Loses shit she was given or loaned. I forgave her. I always will.

Most memorable malaprop in all the world:

"God, Ricky, I am so self-defecating!"

— JF

The Noble Clock

I brought a photo to that fussy GBH *Antique Road Show* to find out what Grandfather was worth. Figured if it was a few grand my sisters and I could use the cash, but I was coldly informed that my fella was a dime a dozen. The cabinet, built in Boston, the works, Deutschland. Common furniture back in the early days of the Republic. The good news: I still have it. The chimes, activated, shake the foundations. I grew up hearing them. Brahms? *"Dah, da-da, dah. Dah, da, daaah"*. Resonant, powerful, time stopping. I've locked them down as neighbors and roommates would freak. You hear 'em, you wake up.

Mom made end-of-life decisions about her furniture. Lisa got the refurbished inlayed desk. Janie, the massive, heavy wood dining room table. Me, the clock. These were good decisions. She knew what she was doing.

The mahogany giant stands like a Centurion, monitoring the comings and goings of visitors, rehearsals, cats, song writing attempts, endless Netflix streams, the pendulum keeping patient tick-tock time. He squeals when I wind him up as if in complaint. But if the weights fall testicularly low, the entire gizmo will stop working, so I keep a ready eye. I'll need to instruct my roommates on what to do if I'm ever away longer than a week.

In the past, moving it was a costly bitch. $350 bucks to slide it a mere fifteen feet from living room to study. I was told when I got it that a professional clocker would need to be hired to get it properly re-set. Too fragile a structure No 1 and No 2 it needed to be perfectly level in order to function. That went out the window when we moved last June. The heavy lifters, Eastern European, just went for it. No clock pro necessary.

"We can do this," they assured.

Their main man took it apart. Lifted the head casing and extracted the face. Then we ran into a problem. I couldn't find the key to open the glass door. If you can't open it, you can't dis-assemble the weights and bells. Now what? We had to get in there, remove the tubulars, mummy wrap the big boy in cellophane and get him the fuck outa the apartment. When we looked at the back, we noticed that the fabric covering was torn. We ripped it off and Main Man went at the lock with tiny surgical tools, removing it and opening the door. Grandad got prepped, loaded onto the truck and lifted into our new house where it proudly stands. Dude replaced the lock in reverse. I found the key later.

His hind quarters were exposed. The cloth covering, disintegrated. I replaced it with a swatch of a water color I'd sketched and painted years ago. I stitched the edge lines with dark thread to sharpen 'em up. There's one of Brick performing his circular arms-in-the-air invented prayers. One of me as a four year old standing next to an Arizona cactus with my Dad, Dick.[56] And one of Lisa as a little girl, staring out to sea. I buried a glass vase full of Christmas lights in the well. Grandpa is lit from within. No one notices any of this. The stitch painting in particular. It hangs in back like a banner from the past, art behind the curtain.

Grandfather is one supreme object, an Ent in The House of The Big Balloon.

---

56   See 'Me, Dick & A Cactus'

The Wire

The toy, not the show, although as captivating. My guys lose interest pronto in kitty swag. Instant catnip gratification followed by an 'is that all there is to a cat toy' reality. The mouse Jesse Adams-Lukowski gave them years ago has survived. It visits every corner of the house. As well, the scratch pad on the floor near the piano, a rare but considered option. But this toy, this present from Jess Murtha (who babysat my guys at the Murtha Kitty Hostel during our big move last June) takes the kitty cake. I find it, like the mouse, in new places, deliberately nudged around all rooms by the pushy beasties. I think that's how the butterfly lost its perch banging against a radiator until it went missing. It used to bounce irresistibly on the tip, inviting a boxer's jab from the cliché curious. In the end, though, it's all about the wire, the wire version of dental floss for cats, an ecstatic tooth cleaning ensemble.

This is not their first rodeo. Back when they were kittens, back at 370B, they'd find Robby's discarded guitar strings and flick them all over the apartment. They never got sick of it. We'd rescue a pointed piece from a kitty mouth fearing puncture, but they knew what they're doing. They were not going to opt for kitty piercings.

Note the dust mouse under the piano stand. These guys wheel and deal as they bite the wild wire, a feline frenzy making light weight pussy dust sculpture collect like packrat presents in every nook and cranny.

When You're Old, You're Cold

That's what my boss's dad, Gerry, Sr. says is a universal truth. He's right. Even when it's fifty degrees out I wear my Armadillo armor coat, the one my sister, Janie, gave me for Christmas. It's impenetrable. With the hood up my sidewalk shadow looks like Fran Lebowitz, the zipper tucked under a dripping nose. The three minute walk to the Behan, stoked on a gummy, is a wonder, exposed legs feel the freeze, upper body warm as a kitten. I lower the hood entering the pub as I can only tolerate so much ridiculousness in my presentation (as if anyone notices).

Same goes for watching TV from the couch, the fab white elephant my roommate Alex larded into our living room last August and an inarguably aesthetic improvement. The 'throws'? They're the blankets I layer up on myself times three. Over and under feet, up along the full body and tucked under chin. Carlotta or Wasabi purr in my lap. Even when it's warm out, it can be cool in the house so I utilize the blankets, an Igloo of warmth. When insufficient, I pull on the Armadillo. I do not need tits shivering like minnows in my T-shirt when I'm trying to focus on a thriller.

The big three.

1. The Native American blanket. Mum wanted to know what I wanted for Christmas. She sent me a catalogue (before there was Al Gore's internet). I picked out the knock off. Love the colors, the loose edges, the never dry-cleaned, summer porch aroma.
2. The green and yellow was crocheted by my sister, Janie, and given to Mum. I inherited it after she died. Something about the

holes keeping body heat in. It smells like Scotland although I've never been there.

3. The fluffy soft brown, Janie again. A miracle of warmth. I sent similar versions to both sisters who know all about Old Is Cold.

Altogether they cocoon warm blood into a quivering body. No butterfly has more successfully metamorphized.

To fold or not to fold, that is the question. Weary and about to crash, I fling the blankets off like a wet shirt and leave them on the couch in disarray. But in the morning my sense of pretty is affronted, so I fold them up and place them aesthetically, a family trio. A part of me wants to appeal to my visiting friend. If he's on his way over, I rush to fold and place. I doubt he'll notice, but I notice and that re-sets the Berlin romance gyroscope in chiming balance.

Bathroom

Crosby Frills And Stash

Was Rene Ricard's abbreviation of CSN and sometimes Y. He was regular at Warhol's Factory and a friend of Peter Barrett's who said of me:

"You're just like Andy. You have no personality."

He was also famous for a perfect imitation of Joan Baez singing *Diamonds and Rust*. He sang it in my ear one night at The Rat.

I noticed this little pot picnic on a bathroom shelf. Weed, pipe, grinder, papers, what's left of 'em, given to me as tips at Doyle's. I never turn that shit down. These days, with pot being medicinal and legal, I'm all about edibles. I've narrowed it down to gummies and chocolate, Indica-style. I stopped smoking (my preferred high), because I'd wake up with a cough and it fucked up my vocal chords. I miss the instant rush. The higher high. The passing of a lit joint. The touch of fingertips to fingertips. The shotgun near kiss. Edibles take longer to get you off. The high is more subtle. Thing is, nothing is more nightmarish for a singer than losing his voice. Why make that a threat when you can eat THC?

I keep the dried out, leafy ganja around because, well, ya never know who might want an old fashioned hit. Some dude with whom it might be cool to lose my good boy, no cough ruse, set aside the gummy and get ripped. When I get that high I say really dumb shit. Everything, every word, look, object gets over-the-top high marks. I can't help it. I'm over being embarrassed and, weird as I sound, it feels right at the time.

"You have a Calvin haircut. Calvin and Hobbes. Spiky cool. You must be a poet. Or a writer? Your eyes. It's in your eyes. And the sound of your

voice. *The way you cross your legs. The hair on the nape of your neck. Your forearms..."*

I can't shut up, but fuck it. It's now or never. Take your best Mary Jane shot, Berlin, and external speaker exactly what's in your stoned head.

MD suggests, wondering if whatever text he'd drunk tapped into his phone in the wee hours could be poorly worded or inappropriate:

"Just

press

send."

Exactly. And if I can't find a publisher for THE BIG BALLOON, I'll call my company Press Send Press.

THE BROWNIE

First thing we notice at Gene Amoroso's pot luck farewell Lisa party is a plate of pot brownies.

"Oooooooo," squeals Peter. *"Let's start with one of* these*!"*

Soft and chocolatey. Pop in mouth. One bite. Two. I thought it was a joke, more flavoring than high. Forty minutes later the kitchen began to tilt and I ate and ate and ate. Turkey and stuffing and shrimp and peanuts and broccoli and cauliflower and raisins and corn bread and pineapple juice and jello mold and cheese pie with strawberries and tapioca and curried eggplant. I swelled up like a tick. I'd worn my too-small sports coat and had buttoned the middle button because my favorite shirt (the teen-sized Bruins) failed for the first time at trussing my bloated paunch. I puffed up my chest and strutted about in slo-mo while the tiniest details captured my undivided attention. Too much is too fucking much.

Fat Lady Fearful

I didn't buy this flying saucer. Robby did. I've used it once or twice. Kinda don't want to know, although I think I'm ok in the weight department. A buck eighty give or take.

"You can never be too rich or too thin."
— **Diana Vreeland**

She should know. She was emaciated. Thing is, I like it when I'm slender. I want to be able to see my gear in the shower without my gut getting in the way. Life is short. Eat up or be pretty. Or eat up and don't give a fuck. Sophia Loren married an overweight Carlo Ponti. Paunchy Alfred Hitchcock won over his slender had-to-be-blonde leading ladies. Big women become fanatical pen pals with the incarcerated. The old masters painted the voluptuous. Thin can be gross. Fat can be gorgeous.

Back in the day, Orchestra Luna time, I would fast one day a week and a full weekend once a month. Boys are thin. Boys are hot. Thin is hot. Or so my reasoning went. With the fasting and the fruit smoothies I was rarely a buck over 140. Tight sweaters. Tight T's. Tight, tight, tight. Not only that, I felt great. Feather light was healthy. I liked it like that. Float away, Berlin, into the pretty pink sky like a feather boa.

At seventy-five, does it matter? Could I lard up and eat like Henry VIII with slobbery fingers? Roll into bed following my belly? I don't have a weight problem, but I can't help but notice those who do and I worry about them from a distance. You don't want to say anything. It's hard enough for those experimenting with lose-it-regain-it shit diets or meth pills.

AT THIRTY-FIVE

I spent quite a bit of time staring at my face in the mirror at Tiffany Hair Design. It was a full-length mirror with a faint but flattering rose tint. The rest of the place was done up in Fanueil Hall exposed brick and grey granite. Blow-up nylon-stockinged fuzz portraits of exhausted looking models decorated the walls and everywhere else: mirrors, mirrors, mirrors. Usually they intimidate me, but this time I decided to stare them down.

To my amazement I liked what I saw. I liked my slightly slanted, Ghengis Kahn eyes. They looked like they'd seen a lot and they looked kind. My good bone structcha? A definite plus. No visible under chin ropey sag as yet. I even accepted my lips. They almost looked full at certain angles. I made faces and tried sincerity smiles and screwball expressions. I did look young after all. It was not a desperate face melting into a thirty-five year old slump. I tried to puffy cheek punch out the smile lines and crow's feet. Then I tried to accelerate the aging process and affect William Burroughs' furrowed face. The dried apple boy-junkie.

At that Footstock south shore festival the other day, just by raising my fist and jumping up in the air and sharing the *Ugliest Man In The World's* bottle of whiskey, I pretty much knocked them out. The kids. All those teenagers with their shirts off, cross-eyed high from weed and heat and life. It was an awesome and confusing moment. I loved it, of course. That I could excite them vicariously. But I felt like an asshole because it was so easy. To see *"awe in their eyes"* as Ian Hunter described it. The energy synapse. Us and them. The rock-n-roll conflagration of the performer with his audience. What really mattered was that split-second moment of forgetting, of transcending, when the vanity of the performer's seduction of the crowd melts into an innocent unification. I felt ageless. I didn't feel *'young for my age'*, just happy. Transformed. Strong emotions. Shining eyes.

Most likely it will be a shock when I *do* look older than I feel. Or worse, I'll start to feel as old as I look. Hopefully I'll be able to seize the advantages: a wider scope, deeper ongoing friendships, true-love understood and downplay the disadvantages: senile narrowness, cranky impatience and an inappropriate, bad surgery face-lift.

I just might be able to look forward to the rest of my life.

Loofah-Waffen

If I'd seen a V-formation of these in the sky during the Battle Of Britain, I'd have snuck out of the underground shelter just to watch the Red Baron nose dive on a sponge. Pushing the metaphor, I know. The pairing of those two words after a long day at the desk.

A floppy face cloth in the shower has never done it for me. Hand, soap and fingers preferred. Face, body perfunctorily swiped. I've had loofahs come and go, lost in moves or appropriated by former roommates. I finally found one at Whole Foods that wasn't attached to a stick of wood, the ones you're supposed to use to reach the hard-to-reach on your back. I hate them. I wanted a simple, ocean grown coral weed, easily held in one hand, no popsicle stick.

I know. They should be cleaned, sterilized, picked though for dirt boogers and made fresh. I don't do it. I figure hot water and Dr. Bronner's should take care of business. Fair to say I'm washing myself with my own accumulated filth. The loofah scuds along like a bumper car, not keeping any promise of a respectable wash.

Then again, how many promises are ever kept? Especially my own.

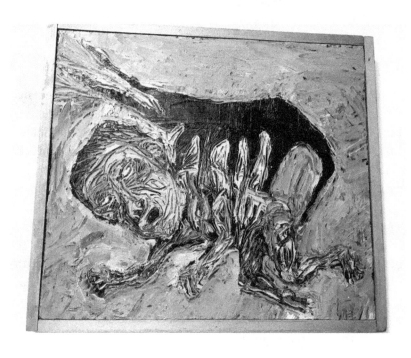

On Your Back

This guy is feeling it. The screaming victim owning up to the daemon on his back even as his weak grip fist is trying to fight the power. I hung it in the bathroom where I'm apt to notice it on a daily basis. This man fetus is yelling at me to hurry the fuck up, to get back on the discipline horse and kill the habits I am loathe to change.

> *"Discipline should never feel like a yoke."*
> **— my sister, Janie**

In my twenties and through my thirties, it was cigarettes. Lilian told me, early on, that she thought I'd look hip lighting up. So I did, choosing lung melting Kools, two packs a day. A bent and glowing ember and a terrific rush on speed or acid. My approach to giving them up? Never buy, just ask friends for a butt until they hate your guts and you have to quit. So I ended it. I threw the nicotine nails in the trash. That monkey let go of my back and my lungs are pink and celebrate regeneration. In a way, I miss the smokes. The comradery of lighting up on the sidewalk, butts not allowed in the bar. Striking up a quickee with a stranger can instigate a conversation that's less apt to occur without the entree of a cupped hand light up.

Up through my forties, it was hard liquor. I hit it the sauce with a vengeance. At Yale in particular. The triumvirate: singing, boredom, booze. Bourbon-n-ginger. A tad girly, but it had me acting out, encouraging the drunken spew of insults. I woke up in the infirmary after a blackout. I told off a Marine who'd returned from Nam. He picked me up by my wrist and ankle and spun me head first into a brick wall. I deserved it. A decade later, I was still suckin' 'em down, lesson unlearned. I'd wake up in the morning and remember all the insults I'd laid on my friends.

I'd call them up, one after another, and apologize; hangover guilt. At long last, hard booze has been crossed off the alky list, although I'd politely accept a shot of hipster Fernet at the Behan. (Thank you, Jess Murtha.) An occasional bottoms up never shuttles me to the nasties. That monkey – poof!

Hardest-to-break habit of all? Jealousy. I never see it coming. It overtakes me like a seizure. I do think of it as a habit, more lethal than then cigs or booze, absorbed from some long ago ontological drama, a devil's tail that loops around new love, choking it off and trying to destroy it. When I fail to control the uncontrollable. When I fail to remember, deep down, that the person I adore is going to and should love others and to expect someone to be my One And Only is an ownership charade. That it will inevitably pour jealousy cyanide into the love cocktail. Throw a sex log onto that fire and I'm ready for a strait jacket. I forget that this jaws-of-death grip on my heart has history. The history that flexes the jealousy bicep, forcing it to punch in the gut the carefree geography that is brand new love. If I can bear witness before I'm pissed off at myself, before I say something cruel, unfair or untrue to my new friend, jealousy retreats from the battlefield. It might still have its talons in my neck, but noticing it ahead of time assuages the impulse. Maybe. If I'm lucky. On a good day. Then again...

> *"Unless you're jealous, you're not in love."*
> **– Mary Dudley**

She has a point. No jealousy, no love story. It's all over art, literature, film, plays, songs, symphonies. The dark dart that hits a fanatical heart. It's a good thing that monkey-on-your-back painting is a daily mantra. A prayer to myself. I can't be reminded often enough as I continue to be ravaged. Best I've done is to keep it close to the vest. Nevertheless, I'm a transparent, jealous cunt.

You catch it, Michael. You're quick that way. Maybe you're familiar with the scourge in yourself. Maybe that's how you can intercept the line drive jealousy hardball with a mid-air catch, with a smile. When you see el destructo roil up on my face, you forgive me with a laugh, a long look, trapping that Luna moth in an offhand net.

I remember two.

1. I was home, waiting for the Captain Midnight hour to hurry me to the Behan. You'd texted about Connie, the woman you'd met with the Southie accent who'd been through hard times with her daughter. You'd been drinking with her. I pictured her hot, horny and after my boy. I yelled at myself on the sidewalk to keep cool. To not anticipate a scene and bad Berlin behavior. When I showed up, you introduced me to Connie and...

    "I can sit over there. I don't want to interrupt you guys hanging out," I say, hangdog pathetic.

    "Ricky!" you laughed.

    Your extended hand, your lopsided smile, told me to get over myself. You shuffled away, backwards, a sort of comical dance; as simple a gesture as lifting an eyelash from a face with a fingertip. Wordless. I hated having to be reassured and I loved you so much in that moment. For saying my name that way. Same as when we first met.

    "Can I call you Ricky?" This after you entered your last name in my phone: *"Dirtbike"*.

2. We hung out at the front end of the bar, not our usual spot, but the one near the window, near the crow's nest. Jay was butting in in his funny, friendly way. I made a cutting remark. I wanted him leave us alone. Our time, precious. I always want to monopolize my new friend and avoid pass interference. You took my arm in your hand and looked me straight in the eye for a really long time until I got it. That I'd way overreacted. Your eyes normally

dart away when I look there, but this time you held on and made it count.

My karma needle on life's LP still gets stuck playing the jealousy song like a hiccup. I owe it to those I love, to myself, to move past emotional anarchy. I guess it's something that can't be fixed on one's own. It requires forgiveness and an understanding heart. Or, maybe it can never be excised. The human part of a human being. Human. Being. Yin. Yang. The dichotomy.

Finn was the only person I've loved in this way who was able to do the same thing. Able to pick up on and stop jealousy in its venomous tracks.

I am ashamed of myself. Of not trusting you, or remembering the bar stool happiness that we always discover when we hang. There is the truth and the rest is a liar's club. Get that monkey off your back, Berlin and man the fuck up.

"Everyone does the best that they can with the consciousness they have at the time."
— **Isabel Hickey**

Overstock

My fine friend and co-server, Andrea Juan, when I told her that I never run out of necessities explained that this was *"an old person's thing"*. I qualify. I am an old person, but I am not a hoarder. I only stockpile what I use. Just this side of hoarding, but not full tilt.

My former roommate, Travis, warned that since our newest roommate was going to be a woman, Nova Benway, we'd better buy shower shelves for female products. I thought he was making it up, but we punched in at Bed, Bath & Beyond (beyond what?!) and hauled home three stainless steel daddy long leg holders and fitted them snug tight in the porcelain. Nova filled that shit up with a proper girl's inexplicables in a hot minute.

So here I am in our new home, noticing how crammed the bathroom shelves have become with man products: shampoo, shaving cream, toothpaste, hydrogen peroxide, Q-tips (Carlotta's fav as she teases and flicks the Q's off shelf and all over the house), deodorant, tooth guard Efferdent, pill bottles, gummies, sunscreen, generic drugs once bought and since unused, ad infinitum.

Do I need all this crap? Do we? I wonder, when I'm feeble and inca-pacitated, will I cane smack the hapless friend or hired nurse to hurry their ass down to the store, load up on the useless and calm my fevered OCD brain? I worry about that. The nascent tyrant in me.

Reaching for something far back on the cluttered shelf, I knock over or spill the nearer. A squished toothpaste tube hits the floor and deposits a seagull dropping on the tiled floor. Falling floss clicks open like a clam shell. I imagine sliding waxy string through my teeth with god knows what clinging to it. Grabbing a new roll of toilet paper is a long reach and creaky bend over. Hygienic spray bottles to whiten the tub and dispose of whose-are-they piss droplets in front of the toilet line the bottom rung. The other night I came this close to brushing my teeth with sunscreen. My toothpaste tube stood parallel to the 100+. They look identical (an edible distortion). I chose poorly and squeezed a pea shot onto my toothbrush. Who knows, maybe fat-ass can promote it as a C-19 cure. Thank god I caught it in time as I frantically scrubbed off the poison.

Somehow though, in our all dude house, these toiletries are (vaguely) organized. Put another way, we aren't pigs. We share shelf space but most of this junk is mine.

Nova? We dudes just like you, girl.

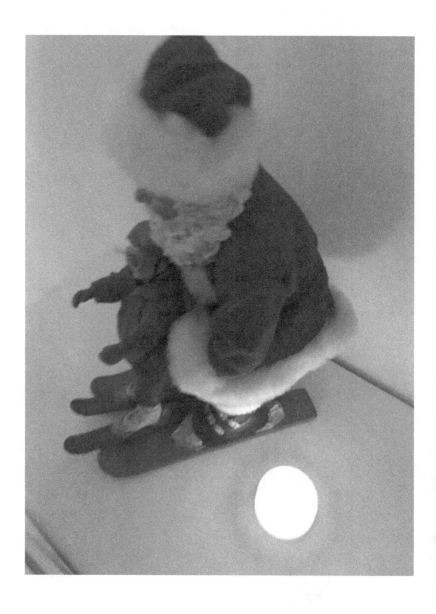

Pedophile Santa

We have one party a year. Just one. Christmas. Get a tree. Over decorate. Pretty lights in every nook and cranny. Invite everyone we can think of.

Then there's Pedo Santa. Encouraging the little boy to hit the slopes with a Ho, Ho, Ho hardon under his fluffy red. The Worst Sort of priest in Santa drag, but darkly hilarious. I spotted him hiding on a shelf at Boomerangs. Brought him home. I usually set him up on the toilet. Pissing, you can't miss him. No one made comment, but ya gotta love the perv.

"And what do you want for Christmas my little ski bunny?"

Slingshot

I'd been cracking jokes with my room mates (Robby and Alex) about losing a crown and needing an emergency visit to the dentist to enjoy The Worst Exposure Possible – an open mouth. Spit and spray dotting face, throat and baby blue dental bib. I should have been careful what I wished for, because, two nights ago, flossing incorrectly with typical Berlin vengeance, I plucked a fat hunk of dentistry gold out of my choppers and watched it plop down the drain before I could save it. Before I could even react. I slung the shot like David, fired it out of my mouth and down the Goliath hole.

Testing with the tip of my tongue, it felt like the Grand Canyon back there. Thin stalks of what was left of my real tooth and a miniature inner tube of rubbery gum. This at one in the morning, too late to call the dentist. No way was I going to an emergency room and sit on my ass for ten hours, especially with way more critical patients fighting C-19. Thank god there was no pain. I'd saved one single Oxy from the hernia surgery, just in case, but left it in the pill jar.

Like the sore throat you hope is subsiding, swallow checking every two minutes, I tip-toed my tongue into the canyon like a lizard until I fell asleep. Indica helped quiet the mind even as I worried if I slept on the wrong side I'd crack off what little was left, shards knifing into gums and cheek.

I decided that I shouldn't eat anything. Food could make it worse. Chewing could instigate contamination, rot and decay. I made up my own rules until I was able to call Longwood Dental and get professional advice. Next day, on the dot of nine, I reached the secretary on duty and explained the emergency. She told me that no doc was working that day, but she'd have the on-call dude ring me up within the hour.

Fifty minutes later I got the call. Dr. Brett; nice voice, good bedside. He told me:

A.   He was free the next day, although I could wait 'til next week if I wanted to. No way. I was going to get this shit done and over with. I didn't want splinters of ivory stabbing my tongue, his physician's opinion notwithstanding.

B.   He said we'd do the entire procedure in one session. He'd have no assistant and would do everything himself and that I'd walk out of there with a new crown. Normally, that requires a rubber/plastic impression, mailed out and returned days later, but I didn't second guess him. I overly trust the guys in white. Until I don't.

C.   He said to please eat. Anything I want. Chew on the ok side, but eat. Especially the morning of the appointment, because if I don't, the Novocain won't take. Hearing that made it a no brainer. One skimpy omelet, toast, coffee. Berlin loves the 'caine.

D.   Even if I'd been able to retrieve the crown from the drain, it wouldn't have mattered. He'd need to dig a new trench and build a new tooth basement before I got new royalty.

We set it for noon. I showed up early. The secretary had me read, initial and sign papers that exonerated the dentist if, somehow, I contracted the virus. Or he from me; no fault assurance. Just the way things have to be these days. Doc Brett was on the money. I wanted to ask if he spelled it the same as Kavanaugh, but didn't want to jump that engine. He bossed me around as I kept asking annoying questions.

"Why are you doing this? Why are you doing that? What is that neon blue hook you put in my mouth?"

"Stop talking and keep your mouth open!"

I liked being bossed. I think he liked bossing. We joked about it later.

He was right to do so. He was juggling a lot of tasks at the same time, banging around the room, starting and re-starting the drill. I could hear his heavy breathing against mask and shield, his hyper focused, intense energy inspired confidence.

He took an x-ray. He wanted to know exactly where the tooth nerves ended so as to not pierce them with the *Marathon Man* drill bit. I needed, as I always do, a thousand grateful gallons of the Big N. Doc Brett obliged. It wouldn't be smart to have me flopping around in a pain spasm or have that drill bore a blood gushing tongue-ring hole.

He went at it like a champ. My mouth smelled like burning flesh, billowing clouds of stinky smoke. He held my jaw down hard, yanked my head left and right and excavated for at least twenty-five minutes. Wearing both shield and mask made his work cumbersome. The shield, blooming with mist, blocked his view. My gums took a beating. I could feel unavoidable divots and slices and the metallic taste of my own blood. Fold in vertigo. I hadn't had to deal with that shit since I lived at the Piano Factory in '02. When he had me move to the x-ray room it took an elderly moment to stand up without keeling over. The merry-go-round swirled the room, but the gyroscope re-set and I was ready for rays under the snazzy lead vest.

The coolest thing, the big surprise, was the creation of the new crown. Brett stuck a large white wand into my mouth. It looked like man-scaping shaver with a blinking purple LED. He poked, pointed and prodded inside my mouth, checking the flat screen to his left. I slanted my eyes like a frightened porpoise trying to see what was on screen, but it was a blur. I did notice that his very long eyelashes were magnified by the face shield. Like I was going to mention *that*. The gizmo was lap dancing around the Grand Canyon. I was gagging on my own spit. He vacuumed it out periodically, slowing the procedure. I think he'd have preferred to ignore the high gag and be done with it, but my little cough chokes forced him to suck the phlegm out before he could work the wand.

Here's the incredible thing: that rod was digitally charting the empty molar. A precise cartoon illustration of what was in there materialized on the screen. He manipulated the image with his fingertips, like a spaceship pilot in *The Expanse*. Wild, CGI dentistry, Lucasfilm sanctioned. The last step was to print the tooth in 3D. It took fifteen minutes and popped out a purple, not fully operational or solid, first attempt. It needed to be shaved and pruned until precisely fitted. It would then be oven-cooked, hardened and turn a pearly white.

The whole thing took three and a half hours in the chair. Just before I left, he gave me a crash course correction on flossing. I didn't want another crown down the drain. Turns out I'd been doing it wrong for years. Sliding the thread into the fiord, manipulating the up-n-down and then jerking it out. All it had to do was catch the edge of another crown and pry it free; slingshot redux. One needs to floss the part of the tooth that's under the gum. Slide the thread down gently and work it, but don't yank it up and out. This side, that side, all around the town, then slide it free horizontally, no forklifting another crown. Old dog, new trick.

We shared our favorite streaming shows. I thanked him and left. He did a fabulous job. Dr. Brett will be my go-to dentist from now on unless he's worried that I have an interest, which I do not.

Spear Carrier At The Pearly Gates

I skulk around CVS pretending I'm unsure about what I'm looking for. I don't want customers to think I have dentures, as if they'd notice or give a shit. This doesn't rise to the level of paranoid, closer to a fool's vanity. My teeth, braces straightened as a kid, look filed down and caffeine stained. Brighteners singe, I'm told, and promise a phony smile. I like my Brit ugly teeth. The other side of the coin: I grind at night while asleep. My dentist of forty years (retired) told me I needed a tooth guard or they'd whittle down to gums only. It cost a mere $300 bucks. I never got a spare even though I cracked a hunk off the back molar plastic. They still get the job done and I bond with Steph Curry the way he plays with his. In. Out. Back-n-forth like a Python tongue. The teeth cleaning lady at the dentist sanitizes it in a vial of around-the-corner chemicals when I remember to bring it in for a douche. They return, grateful from their beauty bath.

Still, at CVS, I am a shy shopper.

Taking The Plunge

in fear. At the old apartment, there was, too often to count, toilet regurgitation. Too many turds piled under too much toilet paper meant the horror of horrors – surge and overflow. Wet oily brownies on the tile floor and dead bird clots of stained TP littered everywhere. Yuck.

Never has panic been so manifest. Sitting on the throne and then, standing at half squat as the brown tide rises to the rim and threatens to crest and flood. On a lucky day, at the brink, the swell balks and subsides in the nick of time, but you can't count on it. With a false sense of security, you re-flush and fuck, the scum rises, breaches and waterfalls and there you are, ankle deep in an in-house cesspool. It's like losing the battle to not vomit, you pray you won't and then you do. In puke land, you're relieved when you finally disgorge. Not so in shit city. In a save-the-day frenzy you plunge the orange suction cup, a mad masturbatory jerk of the wooden handle, hoping the porcelain will swallow.

"*Please! Take it* back!"

In a lucid moment, my bi-polar landlady's daughter told me about a Cuban remedy: mix baking soda with wine vinegar and pour it into the toilet. It loosens the clog and the porcelain throat surrenders. The panic quiets. All clear. It works, it really does. I don't have the Cuban ingredients in the new house, just rod and rubber. So far, so good. No overflow emergencies. What I *do* do, however, and have been doing ever since Hurricane Turd, is not overload. I do my business, look (in prep for a quantum read of a potential disaster), use first, ten squares of Charmin Extra Strength and flush. Then, twenty squares and flush again. This keeps the throne copasetic and averts catastrophe. Get on your knees and pray, Berlin. Sing that toilet hymn.

A PLUNGE OF A DIFFERENT SORT

Elwood babysat the three of us for years. We loved him. He had big muscles, the kind that grew from his waist up towards his armpits in a superhero 'V'. During the summer Janie, Lisa and Lilian used to sneak down to the Voorhees bathhouse, touch his jockstrap and run away, naughty and giggling. One night he came up to my room on the third floor to read to me aloud from *Gulliver's Travels*, the part where Gulliver pissed on the town to extinguish a fire. He thought I'd like that. Such a big husky man reading to Little Ricky.

He rode over on his new Vespa motor scooter. He taught me how to run it. I fucked up. I threw it into first and it jumped out from under me and putted into the swimming pool. Splash, sink! It was November. The water was black and freezing cold. The surface was covered with leaves. I ran up to my room and locked the door. I was sure El was going to smack me around, but what he did do was hurl an inner tube into the pool, take off his clothes and slip into the water, arms supported by the rubber donut, feet dangling like the tentacles of a Portuguese Man-O'-War. He felt around until he located the scooter. Hooking his feet under the handlebars he was able to drag it up to the shallow end and lift it out. I watched him do it. I peeked out at him from my third floor scaredy cat window.

What would I have done if he had tried to, you know, have his way with me? What if I had had to deal with some older guy chasing after my little boy ass? Wanting to hold me in his big capable arms? Was that you, Elwood? Not a chance.

Bedroom

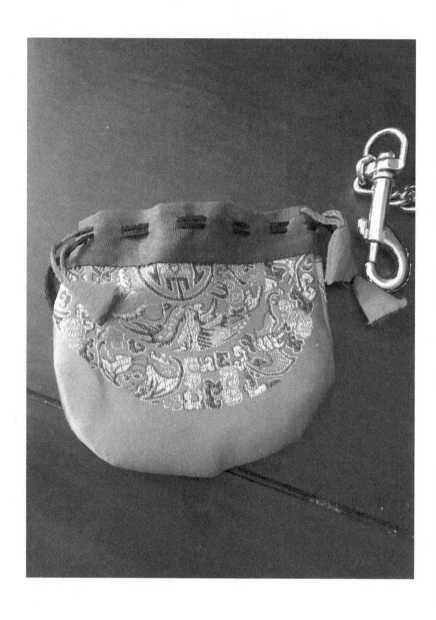

A Secret In A Tiny Purse

Sam Dudley, my brother-in-law, gave sacred wrist beads to me and Sammy for Christmas. They came in an orange India silk purse. The clash of colors (pink, green, orange, gold) appeals. Makes me want to visit that colossal country choking with population, spirituality and conflict. To inhale the wild spices, hear the ding-ding of bicycle bells, the vertiginous music of the Sitar, peer at the wiry limbs of Siddhas, inhale the ubiquitous incense smoke and ride the busses and trains crammed with humanity.

This little pocket is probably the closest I'll get. I wear the beads. They don't fit. They pull on my skin and I expect them to pop and break, but they haven't. I like 'em against my arm. They shine in the shower.

Sammy, as instructed, located the beneficial oils and scents one is supposed to apply, activating their power. All I have is my sweat and the bubbly, endless hand washing asked of us these days. I'd like the magic oils, I would. But I didn't have the patience to shop, let alone sort out which ones would be beneficial.

It's a curious present from a curious man. One with the encircling wasps of ten thousand thoughts, comments and judgements in his head. So many crosses to bear as he soldiers on. Tip of the hat to you, Sam, for your courageous perseverance in the face of onslaughts visible and invisible.

Hope you already know the secrets in the tiny purse.

Ambience

Night lights litter the apartment like fireflies. Glow guides that point the way to the pisser for old man relief. They soften hard edges, keep ghouls out of the cupboard, warm a cold room and suffuse my world with magic. I stock up on replacement bulbs as I refuse to let a night light go dark.

This puppy, a cheerful sun next to the gun, is my all time favorite. I've given the same to friends and family. It's the real shell. The scallop, scalloped by Mom Nature, halved and dried. Shoved into the socket and clicked on before I hit the sack and peer out at my illumined room.

"Goodnight, room."

There was one time, on the Vineyard, out on the bay in a skiff with Toby. The water was shallow, clear as glass. He reached underwater and yanked up a scallop, cracked it open and fed me the salty muscle. He looked like Poseidon, a belt of seaweed stuck to his forearm, a hero's grin. The grandson of the master of the upbeat, P. T. Barnum, he'd disappear when depression cloaked his slumped shoulders and wait for the dark to pass. Sadly, down the cobweb road, Toby took his life. He was one of those sensitive warriors of a truth too painful to bear, more visible to them than to the rest of us. They point the way to a deeper veracity, wrestle the night before the dawn into a takedown pin, or, sadly, leave us and the world forever. I love them for it, for feeling that much, for taking the weight and for letting us in even as they shut us out. I never know how best to support a depressive who's under a cloud. Read this book, the *Noonday Daemon* (Andrew Solomon). Try that new age mind control aromatic. *"You ok?"* is hardly helpful or meaningful.

I have no idea what it's like, treading those whirlpool waters. I don't see them. I see light at the end of every tunnel which, for the depressive, is as endless as it is bleak. The blues is the worst it gets for me and that occurs only when I have my heart broken, or imagine that I do. I've entertained suicide. After Moosup, I told myself that no matter what, love doesn't work, or will never work for me. What did I do? I walked around South Philly in black clothes hoping somebody would shoot me.[57] How candy-assed is that?

It's not straightforwardly manageable, because it's hidden. Your smiling friend, ever ready with a smart remark or a joke, locks the door to his bedroom and cuts his throat from ear-to-ear. The mother of your best friend hooks the vacuum cleaner hose to the exhaust pipe and locks the door of her station wagon just days after you'd gone river skating with her.[58] The boy you loved, abandoned, drowns himself in a bathtub in a mental hospital.[59] Another hangs himself from a tree in his back yard. The man you looked up to for wisdom and guidance jumps from the top level of an airport parking lot screaming at the passing strangers on the sidewalk below to get the fuck out of the way.

We all know these gorgeous, full-hearted, poetic souls. For them a silly night light wouldn't come close to quieting their pain.

---

57   See 'Moosup, The Musical'

58   See 'Best Friends'

59   See 'Rimbaud, Redux' (*The Paragraphs*)

Before I Met You

I always, after a period of adjustment, want to investigate. To find out who The Person Of Interest was before I knew him. When he was walking around, solo, on a sidewalk far from Boston. Having a life, fantasizing, farting, fucking, ebullient or unhappy. When I had no idea he existed. Will he be 'new' to me compared to his biography, or an echoing repetition?

What made him laugh? What did he look like in junior high? Hair, long or short? Zits or clear? Boxers or briefs? What mattered then? When did he first cry or fall in love? On and on they go, the questions. The Berlin Interview. I search out the high school yearbook photo of dude with mullet. The driver's license portrait from a few years back. The family album. The oddball anecdotes, imagined youth, slim boy teen years and body. What his room looked like. Who he thought about when he jerked off.

Hair-brained theory:

We won't kick the bucket until we encounter every single soul on the planet who belong to us, who hold one end of our being's karmic thread. It may be a lifetime relationship, an intense affair or a fiery, short term more-than-friendship star burst. It may be a face in a bus window passing by, who, in a split-second, we 'recognize'. It could be as obscure as a pin prick person in an crowd at a football game on a flat screen in a noisy bar. It is a 'yes, I know you, I see you' connection that educates and enlivens the spirit. So be it. True or false, I buy this crap.

I met Jeff at TC's Lounge (isn't it always a bar?) near Berklee School of Music when I lived at the Piano Factory, a stone's throw. A cramped pub, floors slanted, smelling of beer and disinfectant, clanging pin ball machines, a distorted jukebox, boys and girls of all persuasions and packed with foreigners; a Youth Hostel was parked at the end the street. Musicians, legless, pounded polyrhythms on scummy tables. It's now shuttered. Another dive bar bit the dust.

A skinny guy on the stool next to mine was writing in a journal. Ant droppings of handwritten words. I didn't say anything, but I wrote my number on the top of one of the pages. Too cool for school, right? He called me up the next day. When he buzzed I saw him on the security cam – big Converse All Stars. We hung out a lot after that. His laugh, an extended intake of breath, sounded like a bowed bass fiddle. A dragging, lo-end vocal scrape. He was funny and serious at the same time. Spoke in a monotone. A lot of stories about the gravel pit town he grew up in, thus initiating the before-I-met-you deep dive.

Favorite anecdote:

His brother's girlfriend went out with the dude from the house next door. She dumped him and traded up for Jeff's bro, pissing off her ex; a tiny town soap opera. One night, Jeff and his brother saw, out their living room window, a dude in a ski mask skulking around on elbows and knees, casing out his brother's Pinto and slashing the tires with a kitchen knife. His brother tore down the slope with a baseball bat and clocked the perp over the head. When he pulled off the ski mask, it was the ex's fucking *Mother*!

Jeff laughed his trademark, long form guttural laugh. If this was an audio book I'd demo what I mean.

Favorite quote:

"I was hitch hiking 'cross country and wound up in a bar in St Louis. I sat next to a girl who asked me if I was an artist. I said yes."

"What medium do you work in?"

"I work in drunken conversation", I said. "She was impressed."

(Bass fiddle laugh.)

He turned me onto punk. He'd never go to a show that cost more than $5 bucks. He never liked a song that was longer than two minutes. He was a fanatic. I covered a rad fav of his at Jacques.

He was a personal care assistant for a quadriplegic. He could live with the guy and have his own room for free as long as he'd be on call (a beeper) 24/7 in case the guy needed emergency help. To be turned, preventing bed sores. To take him to the toilet. To get him a drink of water. The guy lived in a seven story apartment building across from The Victory Gardens. Those dirty weeds and deeds near Fenway Park, the gay garden where anonymous action would be in full swing after the bars closed. Where the brute with the claw hammer attacked the furtive in the bushes a few years ago.

If I wound up at Machine after work, or after Jacques, I'd buy six or seven beers and hide them, opened, arm-squeezed tight under my black leather jacket and head over to the quad's apt. Jeff and I would climb to the roof to drink, smoke and hang, the city spread out gloriously below.

It was hanging with him that inspired the song: *I Like Straight Guys,* and, after he left, *City Is Empty.*

We tentatively, awkwardly fooled around, nothing hard core. It was his offbeat reasoning:

"Why should I look further than you, look for a girl, right, when we already have this with each other?"

I loved his body. Dime-sized nipples, porcelain skin, dark black inquisitive eyes-behind-glasses, a teenage boy in a young man's body. You know, my type. But sex was not seriously in the cards. Obliquely desired, but essentially un-acted upon. Ultimately, it didn't matter. Love first, sex later or never.

> *"It's either sex or love, Ricky. You can't have both."*
> **— Danny Fields**

We took a road trip to Montreal. Borrowed his Mom's car. Dropped Molly. Did our college try best to actualize, but mostly walked all over the pretty town. I have pictures.

The last time we hung out we dropped acid. I hadn't done it in years. I was nervous, but it was something he wanted to do. The hits looked like rubber cement-rolled boogers, but worked fast. We tripped our balls off. Gazing from the center point of the Salt & Pepper Bridge, the Charles river bowed, an up-swelling of water, curved as if seen through a fisheye lens, but Jeff was feeling anxious. We flagged a cartoon, bent up LSD clown cab, went back to the Factory and lay on the floor in arms, until quieted.

Last I heard he moved to San Francisco. Another cross-country hitch. Got a job writing for a punk rag, the one he loved most: *Maximum Rock N Roll*.

Where is he today? Who knows? His present is as unclear to me as was his past before I met him. I have the yearbook blow up. I have the pictures I took. I can hear his laugh. None can bring him back.

Part of me thinks each new connection stands on the shoulders of the former. Building a reading room library of heart wisdom upon which we hope to make fewer mistakes. I think I've failed the love exam more than I've passed. Bottom line: we're here on this earth to learn to love properly. To not own another. To want their happiness even when we have nothing to do with it. To love without fear. To love outside the intense, obsessive, do-or-die connection that is one-on-one in hopes that the heart does not implode. To love even when you can see the window closing. Nevertheless, the *"dark forest of the heart"*

(Woody Allen) remains as mystifying and defiant as ever. Could be said that I've learned nothing as I totter along, pogo-sticking the yellow brick road of romance like a fool rushing in.

CABOOSE

My refrain, for at least two decades, when asked about my romantic life:

A weary, dry-needled Christmas tree loaded to the gills with the lights of those countless many who love me and whom I love back. I'd be nowhere without them. Still, there's not been (for years) a tinfoil star on top, a quintessential single heart and soul shining star until you, Mike. You meet me where I stand and have somehow known me before we met, as insane as that sounds. So yeah, Ricky's in love. I never expected it to happen. I thought I'd aged out.

"I'm glad it was me."

– MD

Best Friends

Where did this come from? Yard sale? Sidewalk? Seems like it was taken in the 40's, these two long dead, time frozen in the backyard. I love the ultra-green, the aura around the boys, off to Sunday school or to Grandma's for dinner or a trip to the circus. They could be brothers, but I prefer them as best friends, shoulder to forearm, unforced smiles. About to tell a joke. Maybe the older kid let out a stinker. There's something about that first time realization:

"You're my best friend."

I think when first spoken it is the onset of first love.[60] Of being 'in love'. A secret withheld, then said out loud. When a window on a world other than your immediate family cracks open. When you share the exalted, brave new world intimacy.

---

60   i kept doubt to myself until i met my first best friend. he was the first person i told things to i never told to anybody else and with whom i did things i never did with anybody else. things that were secret. secrecy is a part of love. my first best friend was the first person i ever fell in love with even if i couldn't use those sacred words. i thought about him when he wasn't around. i felt differently when i touched his arm and when he leaned against me. i was hurt when he criticized. my heart leapt when he laughed. it was the secret of how i was with him that changed me, made me feel new, re-invented, bursting with light. which is why, later on, a love affair gets it's charge from secrecy, from a dream world enshrined in a cathedral built, stone by stone, with the person you love. why, early on, i didn't want to use the 'L' word until i was sure. i didn't want to jinx the miracle with a silly verb. i didn't want my friends to be in on what was happening or to break love down into shards of demeaning transparency. (from 'Secrets' – *The Paragraphs*

Stand By Me (Rob Reiner) caught this in one movie. How best friends get born and sadly, how closeness fades. If this is first love, it is also first death. The lesson of letting go. Two boys or two girls, it doesn't matter, although at that age it's often same sex discovered. In some ways I think we hope to re-create that first moment each time we find a new friend, a new lover, a face that rings a bell.

These unknown two say that to me in one old time photo. Would that it was a Civil War Daguerreotype, two exhausted soldiers in front of a tent, a Walt Whitman, poetic proximity as historic evidence that first love, best friends, shy discovery, is a universal constant.

Peter Havens and I were best friends for at least five years during high school. In some ways I was closer to his Mom than I ever was with him. In another way I was best friends with his whole family. His mother's name was Weastie. She was the first woman, besides my mother, that I saw naked. She was an artist, painted a lot. Weird stuff. Huge figures of Alice In Wonderland with a row of tiny black ticks crawling up an elongated neck.[61] She set her house on fire so she could redecorate it with the insurance money. She had five other kids besides Peter. Wick, Peter's older brother, Wendy, identical twin girls, and Janie. Wick used to wash his money and iron it. He had a parrot named Polly. Her previous owner was an opera singer who had taught her snatches of arias. She died when Wick rolled over and crushed her in his sleep. They had a white Newfoundland and a lot of cats that fucked all over the house, howling in the middle of the night. A roomful of musical instruments waiting for Weastie to master them. A cello, a piano, a viola, a flute. She was the sort of person who laughed out loud during performances of the Philadelphia Orchestra. Music made her laugh. One afternoon she ran to her Pontiac station wagon, revved it up, no warning and yelled at the house:

"Those of you in the car in the next five minutes can go to Colorado with me."

---

61   See 'Ambience'

She was gone for two weeks. She returned with a snake that was trained as a belt. It would slither through the loops and bite its tail. She wore it to parties. She loved to fart. I overheard her and Dad trying to out fart each other in the liquor closet. Dad was on the floor he was laughing so hard. At her place in Kennebunkport, she had us construct giant sand sculptures of mermaids to which she would add thumb-sized candy strawberries as nipples, seaweed pubes in the crotch. Her grandmother, Moe, hid herself upstairs in a neighboring apartment, peeping out from behind closed curtains to see if there were any nuns about. She hated nuns. She threw flower pots at them when they came to ask for money.

She got us to try new things. She drove us to a river in the middle of winter that was frozen over for miles. We skated up ice and built a bonfire. She took us inner tubing down a river at her sister's house in Paoli. She introduced us to her sculptor friend, Wharton Esherick, who adored her. She believed in art. She loved artists. She was voraciously alive.

I always wanted to impress her. She was the first person that knew the 'me' that I thought I knew. She praised that kid when he most needed praising and caught him up when he was a jerk. I went over to their house on Louella Ave all the time. I got drunk for the first time there. Went to jail for it with Peter. There were always goings on at that palatial place, jammed with no-holds-barred life.

Running up the stairs at her house, I rushed across the landing, newly carpeted and painted from the insurance money, and, needing a hurry-up piss, pushed open the door to the bathroom. Weastie was standing on the bath mat, elbows over her head, hair damp and dangling in clots at her ears, tits lifted because her arms were raised, splashing powder on her armpits. He mouth dropped open, her eyes popped out, she snatched a towel and screamed. Just like Brigitte Bardot in that movie Peter and I snuck into in Wayne. (We were underage.)

"Eeeek!!"

I backed up and slammed the door. I heard her begin to laugh, but

Jesus Christ, she was my best friend's mother! I went into her enormous bed room and sat down on her king-sized bed and looked at her paintings on the wall and waited for her to come out so I could apologize. There was a jumbo-sized jar of Vaseline on the night table with deep hurried gouges in it. Apparently it was used a lot. Ma and Dad had nothing like that.

One afternoon after school, Wick dropped me off at home. Ma met me at the door. She was crying.

"Weastie's dead. She committed suicide."

I walked to that spot at the end of the croquet court, where that gnarled tree twisted shadows over the lawn and stared down the hill. It was the same place we went when we heard that Tommy Supplee had died of a wasp sting at the age of twelve.[62]

I could not believe she was dead. With her gone nothing would be the same. Peter and I gradually lost touch and their house was sold. They said she did it because she thought she was holding her husband back. She was too odd to be a bank president's wife. He'd be better off with another woman, a more suitable spouse. She did it in the garage. Stuck a vacuum cleaner hose onto the exhaust pipe and started the car.

FOURTH GRADE FRIENDS DO THE DIRTY

Brandy Lee used to invite Henry, Harlow, Teddy and me up to his hayloft in the sheep pen just after we moved into Atlee Road. I was in the Fourth Grade. He had whittled a stick into what he called an *'asshole explorer'*. He came all the way up to my room just to show it to me. It was about sixteen inches long and had two points, one on each end. They had been carved down to the shape of your little finger. One was slightly thicker than the other.

"Jeez, I get a boner just thinking about it," he said.

---

62   See 'Giving Up On God' *(The Paragraphs)*

"Yeah?" I answered in the quietest whisper.

I didn't play with him much after that, but, truth be told, we did go through with it once and I did watch the insertion on my friends. When Brandy said it was my turn, he didn't get the explorer far in. I produced a miniscule caterpillar fart.

Oddly, the name Brandy Lee resurfaced years later when Orchestra Luna played one of the consistently name-changing venues on Landsdowne Street. This Brandy was a hard core drag queen who used to cover Peggy Lee's *Fever* as she lazily snapped her fingers at the end of an outstretched elbow-length gloved arm to suggest a jazzy, 1950's rhythm. *"Ya give me fevah..."* Snap!

I used to wriggle up next to Karl or Rusty on the rolled wrestling mat in the high school gym and watch Goose Clement jump into the air, spread-eagled and grab the rebound, his face screaming with acned, bright red effort. I was only pretending to watch the game. Basketball didn't interest me. I was terrible at it anyway. It was leg-to-leg against my Best Friend of The Week that offered the critical view. Being that close to someone? Touching them without acknowledging it? The subtle exchange of pressures? Yes. Yes. No...Yes. A small forest of pencil erections.

We used to accuse each other of being 'homo', but it was never vicious. I don't think we knew what it meant, but it never stopped any of us from fooling around.

Boxers

Now that Old Navy For The Old Lady is defunct in Watertown, I have to drive to Dedham to upgrade my wardrobe. Cheap and likely made by an Asian slave kid in a fume factory, but that's what I buy. Same for jeans and socks. I like the candy colors and silly designs. I've made mistakes. XL instead of L – lampshades above lily white legs. Even worse, the elastic waist band would relax and stretch out from the heat in the dryer and expose a pair of silly drawers-to-knees. An ass crack poking a vertical nose above my belt at work necessitating a call out from a ridiculing co-worker.

"Yank 'em up, Berlin. Your ass is not something anyone wants to see."

I flap down my t-shirt to cover the damage and try not to bend over.

Which pair to wear? I shoot a brain snapshot forward into the night's imagining, the possibility of sharing sleep with an encounter (as rare an event as unearthing a dinosaur bone). Jodhpur wide and frilly patterns are just not cool. Depending on the projected visitor I pick out the opposite: dark, serious, nice in low light; as if such a decision would make a difference. I laugh at myself. I do that a lot over dream boy fantasies. An old fuck on the prowl is as absurd as it gets.

The no underwear clause.

For me it has always implied a hippie in overalls with a Hershey Highway paint stroke. No undies provoke el stinko even as it promotes the happiness of swinging balls. Have to admit I like it when I've done it.

Like Richie Havens sang at Woodstock – *"Freedom...!"*

And another thing? Hot dudes these days opt for tight, hug-your-sack undies. The ones that snug the upper thighs and emphasize substantial equipment. Which leads me to the horror of man-scaping, the selective shaving or trim of pubic real estate. Apparently the idea is that less hair makes your cock look bigger. Me, I love genuine bush. The unknown rising unsheathed from a sweaty, fleecy jungle. Besides, a shaved bush transforms a dude into a hairless prepubescent (which I thought to the straight world was abhorrent). Girls don't want their guys to look like little boys, do they? Are they as perved out as the predatory priest?

I think not.

Braided For Beauty

This carefully researched and chosen green throw rug was initially for, as Robby christened it, 'The Study', 370B. A perfect Grandma fit, implying cozy and cute in a no fireplace nook. Curl up, kitties in hot tubs and watch *Breaking Bad* to end your day, heels comfy on the green round.

I've always been a fan of the braid. John Adams would have had one in his Quincy farm house, braided by his stoic wife, Abigail, warm in the winter New England freeze and bedding a big dog in front of the hearth while John wrote pamphlet diatribes in the corner by candlelight.

Where should I put it in our new house? Decisions, decisions. At the last minute I frisbeed a third of it under my bed, the remainder poking out like a green wave on wooden floor sand and secured safely with a hefty wooden leg-of-bed.

Like most of the furniture in the house, it isn't mine. It's theirs. The cats. They pluck at the braid like woodpeckers drilling a tree hole, lengthening their claws for a kitty-pedi. Tufts of fur are left behind for me to pinch and toss.

No matter, it's still nice, the rug. It looks appropriately patriotic on the floor, in the company of the Civil War rifle and the gold eagle. If I ever get around to stretching and exercising again, no longer fearful of my hernia repair busting a gut, I shall lie on the braid and cushion the back of my head just so. I will be a yoga patriot, my sun worshipping ass high in the breeze.

During the Revolutionary War, would I have joined up and been instantly shot, or would I have slipped on a Betsy Ross calico, pretended

I was a member of the DAR and patiently braided green upon green like a ferocious closet lesbian?

You know the answer.

By Hand

My sister, Lisa, has a full resume. Mom, wife, carpenter of steps, singer, immaculate painter of walls, upholsterer, lover of plants, animals and people. She is also a terrific writer. An originalist with words.[63] Succinct, poetic and sharp. She humorously denigrates these skills. All three Kinscherfs are guilty of what my father called 'false modesty'. My mom as well. Proud as she was of all three of us, a born Yankee, she frowned upon crowing about success, small or large.

"Mom! They elected me President of my senior class!"

"How nice for you. Have you done your homework?"

Lisa took criticism to heart. Shade on work done would have her slamming the door. But, innately gifted, she'd inevitably return. Her abilities flow out of her even as she complains about having to unravel something she messed up and start over; the Madam LaFarge of Rensselaerville.

With nimble hands her ace in the hole is sewing. She can make just about anything: dresses, button down shirts, curtains, pillow cases, vests, stage costumes; fine stitching, measuring, cutting and imagining. Best of all, for me, is the diamond jubilee quilt. I've had it for years. Sometimes curling over pillows on a made bed, or thrown over the back of a chair. Mostly it's been folded on a shelf, underexposed in a closet. Until now.

What inspires about homo decorating in our new home is that so

---

63   See 'Ridgemont Street'

many objects d'art found prime time location. I have four windows in my bedroom. Full curtains for two (one by Lisa, one from Ricky McLean). Venetian blinds on all four. A half curtain (Lisa again) on another. On top of the middle bay I push-pinned the quilt. It catches sunlight and appears warmed from within, a cloth heart. It is impeccably constructed and seems just right at its lopsided tilt. I smile looking at it and, like many friends and family who inhabit the inanimate, it reminds me of her.

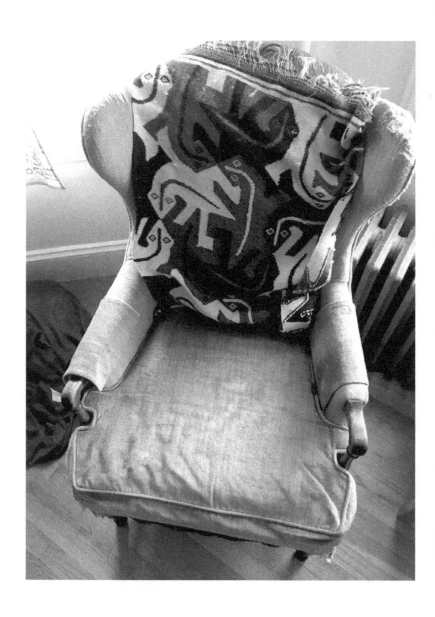

Cat Picassos

Bought this golden armchair throwaway at Boomerangs seven years ago. $20 bucks. I threw the faux Native American black n white rag over the back for contrast. Tom Appleman had my friend Deidre pose in it provocatively for the cover of his first record, *Big Flirt*.

Chair was beat up when I got it and has since been abused by Carlotta and Wasabi. Do I give a fuck? Not really. Happy to spend twenty bucks on a scratch-a-thon. I was never fond of the fuzzy, multi-leveled cat apartments where they're supposed to confine the sharpening of claws. My cats would never be fooled by those atrocities, they're butt ugly and cost a fortune.

This beauty has been completely adopted. I sometimes use it to read in, the afternoon sun pouring in over my shoulder. The cats stare at me as if I have no business sitting in their chair. It isn't the only victim. The couch in living room, the chocolate chest (antique), the 'coffin' in my room, all rugs and closed doors get the treatment. We had to add $50 a month to our lease in order for the landlord to allow pets. It was a non-starter. We would not live where we couldn't have our kitties. Pay up, Berlin. (Robby chips in.)

I bought no-scratch spray. Squirt it onto any surface and the wee cougars stick their noses up and demur. But the sauce wears off and they're back at it in hours, making art and opening wounds with cotton ball fluff protruding like an exposed armpit.

Closeted

I have a lot of over-the-years crap in there. Suits, ties, fancy shirts, hats; essentially stage drag for a big show, a special performance. I waste money on that stuff, but it provides a temporary transformation for the singer, for Berlin who, for a hot minute, is not a waiter. As a waiter, it's always the same deal. Black jeans, regulation T, black socks, black sneakers, apron and towel. Never changes. I never dress up. My closet gets poked into if gig essential, a sparkle shirt on an ancient LV[64]. Even so, The Nickel & Dime Band rarely makes a point of conjuring a look, a group persona. Maybe if we had, like The Police, dyed our hair in colored unison, or chosen a trademark costume we'd have had a better shot. But not really. Once you're up there, once your entrance is made, no one pays attention. Group Gaga we are not.

Some of these clothes are as old as Orchestra Luna, when dress up was mandatory theatricality. Some are gifts: shout outs to Randace Rauscher and George Dudley. Some are so glitter twin out-of-date I get ridiculed by the band when I wear them. What's worse is that they stink. I rarely tub wash, soak, squeeze and hang to dry. Dry cleaning is out of the question. Let 'em rot. If I spruce them up with a pro job, they'll smell like armpits in minutes. For the Luna years, the no girls hard rock Luna years, I wore black leather pants at every gig. They'd get so stiff with sweat that I could stand them up solid against a door until the next show. The gnarly leather scraped my legs when I pulled them on, but I felt sexy and put up with it, raised leg on a monitor like an old school rock stah.

The majorette coat, the flashy red and gold, has made several appear-

---

ances. I got it so that I could introduce The Upper Crust (rock royalty) in an appropriate get up. The court jester extending his fake Brit vowels at the JP Music Festival one year. The good thing about a coat like that? About wearing bright colors? It distracts from my face, from the eye bags, jowls and under chin hammock. Now that I think about it, I should dress up more often.

Longest lasting is the white linen Panama suit, Jacob Reeds. It's almost beyond repair. Pit stained, sleeve torn, a tape wormy thread loose, a missing button. The fit is lackadaisical. A belt has the pants hang low. Suspenders hike 'em high and lift the ball bulge for all to see. Wise to button the jacket and hope that the last men's room shake off didn't leave a spot. I bought two of them, one for Berndt and one for myself for the Marlene nights at the Lizard. Damn, we looked sharp. Photographed like Big Daddy Hot Tin Roof rock entrepreneurs in the cabaret spot light. Sharpshooter twins in radiant white.

As for the rest, beyond here and there weddings and funerals, they await moth infestation. They're wrinkled and ragged, but under woozy lights in a darkened club, no one can tell. I won't throw them out. I like knowing they exist, ready for their close up in the glitzy sun.

Cry Me A River

"Who's that girl? She's gorgeous."
— MD

"Actually? It's not a girl. It's River Phoenix. Photo by Gus Van Sant."
I am hardly alone in the culture as a fairy who loved River. From the get go. It wasn't how he looked (although that was high in the mix) it was the searing power of his eyes. They bore in, never held back an honest truth or the promise of some not-so-hipster romantic ideal. Clear-eyed, but susceptible to heart surge in the face of Big Love; all fiction in my fevered brain.

All I knew about him was based on his movies. *Stand By Me*, *My Own Private Idaho* and *Mosquito Coast* in particular. Part of me bought into the 'die young, stay pretty' pantheon. River did die young and he did stay pretty. If I was a high school bobby sox-ette I would have inked his name on the edge my biology book. I imagined taking long walks on the beach and arguing the Big Questions. Smoking a joint, laughing and skipping stones into the sea.

I'd heard that his sister's band, Aleka's Attic, was playing Passim's. Fuck! Gotta go! Gotta meet this dude! Gotta hand him my screenplay musical, *The Kingdom*. He would be The Perfect Actor to play the lead dude, right? (Convinced by the power of my fixation.) The problem: Aleka's Attic was playing in two days and the script was incomplete. No computer back then. Clacked away on a heavy IBM Selectric, like Kerouac unspooling on meth. Whiteout cum stains all over the pages. I finished it as best I could in one frenetic twenty-four hour eruption, raced to Copy Cop to print it up and grabbed a cab to Passim's.

The show was sold out. The door guy recognized me and let me in. The band was on stage, playing. I stood in back, just as they were winding up. They walked off stage, down the center aisle and as he passed by I stammered:

"Hey, River. So great to hear your band. It's cool your sister's with you up there. My sister was in my first band."

La, di, dah.

He was patient. Gracious. Stopped to hear what I had to say. Listened. Looked me in the eye.

"I want you to have this. A script of a musical I've written. A cassette of the songs. It's not Broadway. It's weird and dark. But if you have time, give it a read and a listen."

"Thank you," he said.

He took the script and cassette and walked. I was trembling. The only other time I meet a famous actor that I had goofy far away feelings for was Dai Bradley. I saw him play the lead in a Boston production of *Equus*. I ran into him at a table at a Landsdowne disco. No conversation. Gave him a drawing I'd done of a ceramic horse. Left. But the Phoenix encounter was over the top.

I raced home only to realize that I'd given him the wrong fucking tape! Instead of songs for *The Kingdom*, it was a recording of vocal exercises. *"Ha, ha, HA, ha, ha...ha, ha, HA, ha, ha."* I had so blown it, this after all the typing and frenzy. I found out who his agent was and called her in LA, waking her up in the early AM.

"Who is *this?!"* she yelled. I tried to explain that I'd given River the wrong cassette when she cut me off.

"You gave him a script, right?! I keep telling him, River! don't take any fucking scripts, but he just goes ahead and does it. Don't call again."

She hung up.

Might be wise, in future, to never wander far from the block I know.

Dead Wallet

I thought it would last a lifetime, this out-of-the-blue don't-fuck-with-me wallet, a present from gal pal, Sir David Minehan. Sadly, it suffered hard times, overuse and abuse. Credit cards fell out. The snaps didn't snap shut. The stitching popped and broke. I really loved it and didn't want a more basic receptacle so I bought a new one just like the old one. So did Dave. It takes getting used to. The old, discarded like a euthanized cat, is no longer with us. Friends made fun of it.

"Where did you get that purse?!*"*

Well, it kind of is, a purse. A man purse with a biker chain. You gotta grok the swinging metal against thigh and this new baby has an even longer chain, more swagger in my step. I feel like a 40's pimp in a lime green, double breasted suit with a neon yellow tie.

About Sir Dave du Lac.

Meister Rock-n-roll. His Highness. His Lowness. His Filthiness. We connect on so many levels. Principally music. Making records at Woolly Mammoth. Five of 'em: *I Hate Everything But You. Forced2Swallow, Cathedral* – Kenmore Woolly: 2-inch painstaking analogue. *When We Were Kids, Old Stag* – Waltham Woolly: ProTools up the ass, like everywhere else in the studio miasma.

"You're going to spend a lot *of money here,"*

I'd warn the newbie songwriter booking time with The David. He'd laugh it off, but truth is, Woolly ain't cheap. During The Shelley Winters Project we trial-and-errored for hours, making *Tusk* in our own private

Idaho. Try this. Try that. Bang on an upside down rubber trash barrel with an broomstick. Stomp around the studio in jack boots and turn up the mic. Have two people work the Hammond pulling levers and switch-spinning the Leslie. Incredible fun, creative and inspiring, but it never came to a money smart conclusion; a small fortune for a mere waiter. Between Robby's home gear and TJ's more reasonable Bitch Kitty there was no way I could revisit Mammoth, much as I'd love to. Much as I love spending time with the guy. We cemented our friendship there; all that remain are potty mouth texts.

His bedside manner, to which anyone who've worked with him can attest, is spot on. He can sense what it is you're after and encourage it out of you, push you to do your best beyond what you might have thought capable and the whole time, at least with me, cracking the foulest jokes, odious 'poke through'[65], vile YouTube clips and snarky remarks about local persona. And he has no objection to strapping on a Strat and adding windmill power chords to a song that needs them while your guitar player is nursing a hangover on the studio couch.

The Neighborhoods were the first band to win the 'BCN Rumble. I hardly knew him then. He was young, skinny handsome, snarfing up booze and drugs like a wigged out piranha, touring, climbing the music biz ladder, opening for Bowie at Foxboro and making friends all over the country. The one conversation I had with him back in the day was at The Rat. *Little Red Corvette* had just been released and he was ecstatic. It roared out of the house system in that club dungeon as he brayed along, eyes wide shut, impersonating His Purple-ness with a queenly vengeance.

He asked me to open for The Hoods at The Beachcomber (it took forever to convince him) as long as I promised to start my set with *How Can I Hate People I Don't Know?* which had, before I changed the lyrics, every possible, down-the-Trump-escalator anti-PC bad word you could think of. He lapped it up.

---

65   See 'Poke Through' *(The Paragraphs)*

We're both older. He spends less time on stage, although he did two tours with The Replacements. New shoes. New amps. New guitars. New haircut. New Minehan. Westerberg trusted him. He was the only guy in the new outfit who could sing harmony and not piss off The Big W.

WAR STORY
The Hoods were on the road. They caught a gig in a cavernous Chinese restaurant in the middle of corn fed Iowa. God knows why. Their agent just went for it. Take what you can get. They played to an empty house.

"You Neighborhoods not so hot. Nobody come."

"No so hot" joined the list of repeated phrases along with:

"That don't suck."

Which we printed on a t-shirt we had made for Woolly. It's what Dave's mentor, Phil Green, considered high praise. Green, another veteran of old school rock n roll, of *"run out and grab me a six pack of Ex-Lax"* shouted out to an intern in the middle of a session. The guy who mixed at such an overwhelming volume no one in any band could stand to be in the control room and Phil could slide the faders uninterrupted. These long-in-the-tooth days find both geniuses off the horse and booze, but the war stories still carry dirty water.

So yes, we text. Talk on the phone. Keep up the nasties. I give him our new records which he never listens to other than to pretend he has by saying:

"Nice guitar sounds."

Which I doubt he means.

> *"Does he still have that incredible ass?"*
> **— Billie Best**

He does.

"My ass is black and so is my groove," he counters.

Don't Sit On These

This pair, CVS lineage, has lasted months. They're perfect for computer, to read cooking directions, for a nauseating People Magazine lap at Fantasy Nails when my toes are in the tub and the mechanical fingers massage my lower back, to have and to hold at The Little Dipper so I can read the menu and not ask Mike. I resist taking them out of the house. I have a backup pair I take to work, but these dark-rimmed level 125-ers are top of the line. I wear them for hours working at my desk.

I didn't need glasses 'til I hit my 40's. My eyes were 20/20 sharpshooters until then. Maybe I wasn't using them as constantly as I do now. I do think glasses are handsome on people. I feel for the fat kid having dinner with his family who has to wear wire rims, for his feigned, seven-year-old, what-can-I-do-about-it nonchalance.

"Those glasses you're wearing are awesome," I rave, hoping I don't embarrass him. He reminds me of Piggy in *Lord Of The Flies* and looks vulnerable, but has wee balls of courage.

I visit my ophthalmologist once a year. His diagnosis, after ranting about politics, is that I have pre-glaucoma. He says it's an easy surgery, but my numbers remain flat-lined. The glaucoma is not getting worse. To this I attribute weed. The ganja keeps the Big G at bay. The pot doc who interviews me to see if I'm eligible for medical Mary Jane, promises miracle cures for just about anything, including glaucoma. He looks like Ho Chi Minh and drops his pencils on the floor. He wears high water pants, cinched up with a too-big-for-his-waist belt. He has black ankle socks and hairless chicken legs, but is an ok, on your side dude. Insomnia? Weed will help. Lower back pain? Weed will help. Good vision at a 3D movie? Weed will help. Hey, dude doc green lights my habit.

I pray that I never lose or crush these dark rim jobs, even though it's an eventuality. I hate atrophy, personal or otherwise, but there's not much I can do about it. I texted Mike one night about this dude who talking to me who had three heads. For real; the combo gummy and Miller Lite implosion.

"Don't deteriorate on me, Riggy."

– MD

Working on it.

Drill Press

I've never been effective in the promo homo department. Try this, try that. I burn money on a professional PR person who cynically promises crap results even as I succumb to the artist's hoped for Achilles heel:

"They could make you rich and famous."

I know it's bullshit, but I cross my fingers and imagine center ring at the circus.

My band, The Nickel & Dime Band seems an easy merch. 5 & 10 cent store miniatures. The obvious weed ref. Make no money authenticity. Ice cream sodas on us, etc.

I came up with this beauty. I collected (we all threw in) a pile of nickels and dimes. I borrowed a drill press from my friend, Bill Brown. It was heavy as a cannon and required goggles when operating to keep metallic shaving splinters out of bulging eyeballs. I obliquely asked attorney friends if drilling holes in money was a federal offense. With no clear answers, I went ahead.

The process was mad tedious. I hunched over a machine that looked like a giant wasp at which, while parked on a coffee table next to my bed, I drilled down. The coins got red hot, but the hole was clean and shiny. I picked up yards of toilet chain and hooked the two coins onto a neckless to sell at shows for short money.

Like CD's (which are so out of fashion that few people can even play the discs at home), few sold. We wound up giving 'em away. Everything is promo, right? Unless you're a giant touring act, locals make zip. So be it. The neckless swag wound up as presents to band members and studio engineers. The one above is the last of the Mohegans. The drill press, returned. I lost track of where the dimes and nickels went. I throw everything out.

You know what? I think the damn neckless is fucking brilliant, so shut the fuck up.

Ever Shoot Anybody?

I've thought about it, but I wouldn't have the guts. It'd have to be drilled into me and even then I suspect I'd rather take a bullet than shoot one. Could be, confronted with fight or flight, I'd grit my teeth and pull the trigger. You never know what you'll do until you're in the thick of defend or die, my passivism notwithstanding.

"I'd take a bullet *for you, baby, even if the gun is in your hand..."* –

a favorite noir lyric of mine that I have yet to successfully fit into a song as romantic masochism.

This gun[66], shoulder marched home by Dick the Dad one night, is a Civil War veteran. It's super heavy. To load and shoot requires precious coordinated seconds. You'd hope the enemy won't get the jump. You'd hope you'd have the strength to raise and hold it horizontally long enough to successfully aim and fire. It's terrific looking, leaning against the wall like a lieutenant on leave, drunk and puking in an ally around the corner from a brothel. The entire weapon can be taken apart, piece by piece, cleaned and polished. It's finely made, each brass section shines like gold if you take the time. It's wicked popular at our Christmas party. Guys and girls take selfies with the damn thing, aiming and jabbing the bayonet into the bedroom air.

It's an uneasy feeling to be light hearted about a firearm. War is unknown to me. I'm too old to enlist or be called up. During Nam, I got a deferment. A 4F. A Peace Corps shrink diagnosed me as hom-

---

66   See 'Guns' *(The Paragraphs)*

icidal *and* suicidal. Always thought both could be helpful on the battlefield, but I never went.

MY DRAFT PHYSICAL, 1969

After Moosup, I tried it one more time, teaching as a deferment. I shouldn't have, trouble afoot. This second shot was in Steamboat Springs, Colorado, at a co-ed boarding school. I taught English and photography and neither of them well. I became platonically involved with Kaleb, a kid from Santa Barbara. We drank bottles of Robitussin, got high a lot and were kind of secretly in love. The school, alongside the public school in town, put on a collaborative *Oklahoma!*. I landed the lead, Curley. In some ways, like all theater, our ensemble was a play within a play. It was also the drama bug that bit and ultimately encouraged me to apply and be accepted to the Yale Drama School, full scholarship; another tempestuous, ill-fated career move. At any rate, right after the curtain came down, I was given the boot, isolated in a motel the night before my physical for the draft. My sole faculty friend did me a solid and dropped Kaleb off to hang with me on my last night. We slept together, but our friendship was never physical. I should not have been a teacher in the first place, trying it for the wrong reasons. Wanting to stay out of the war no matter what it took.

BEFORE ALL THAT

Yuri was the first kid to get to school. He showed up a day early. I saw him sitting by himself in the dining hall. Straight black hair, morbid cigarette, blue-green arrow eyes that burned, razor-thin lips. He wore a too small military academy jacket with a stiff grey collar. He walked off alone, up into the hills and came back with a poem:

"Meglicorous ustings of contaminated foresight..."

He'd scratched it on the bottom of his boot with a nail.

We sat in the dining hall and talked rapidly, three cups of coffee prying it out of us. The place was deserted. We laughed a lot, jerking Yuri out of his brooding persona, his raggedy Beat ennui. He was from Chicago. We spent most every night, late into the night, sitting against the wall of his bunk, talking, keeping others up. Cigarette after cigarette. We'd hug goodbye. I'd stumble out under the dark, brilliant stars high in the Steamboat sky, hike to my log cabin, my Black Lab, Tucker, and my thank god electric blanket.

I drove the bus on a soccer trip in a heavy snowfall. It was freezing. As the assistant coach I was meant to stand on the sidelines and yell a lot. Yuri was the center forward, but a sensitive hypochondriac, not a jock. The snow got so deep they cut the game short. In the locker room his bony torso, pale arms, anxiety strong, hairy legs looked out of place. Never easy for never athletes to sort themselves out in a high school.

I looked him up in Chicago long after the Colorado fiasco. After my fall from grace, my dismissal. The headmaster had falsely accused me of 'being involved with' two boys and a girl. I'd sent Kaleb love letters after I returned to Philly which were opened before he got them and read aloud by the headmaster in the cafeteria in front of the entire school. Kid went berserk. Who wouldn't?

So when I saw Yuri I'm wondering what he thought of me after all the commotion. After he'd heard those letters read. How much had he figured out? He lived in a rambling house with a screaming mad mother and wild runaway brothers and sisters. I drove him home in Lilian's MG Midget, the one she and I took west and shortly after our visit to Leo in Pennsylvania.[67]

After a nervous silence:

"I don't know what to do," he says.

"About what?"

"Girls. It just doesn't work. I'm scared."

---

67   See 'Peter Barrett & Moosup, The Musical'

"Of what?'

'I'm a virgin, Rick."

"Jesus. I thought that all the time you spent with Angela...you were so hard-assed, so tough and poetic. That you guys..."

"No. We didn't. We never did."

Then he asked me to tell him, specifically, tell him or suggest something to do about this and I'm sure he meant to talk about being gay, but I passed. I didn't want any more blather to get back and hurt Kaleb. I opted out and left him stranded. I've done this before. Hurt secondary friends by favoring person number one ahead of the needs of another. I'm not proud of it.

Framed

My Sofi[68] looks so much like Wasabi. The locked on, golden-eyed I-love-you stare, the single outstretched paw, black fur that's actually dark brown. She was a lot smaller and a lot nicer in a girl's way. More affectionate, although not to take anything away from my juvenile delinquent boy.

I took the picture. Margie printed it. The frame came from the sidewalk. I see her every day, staring at me from the top of the bureau. There are times when I'm meditating that I feel a pressure, a presence near my leg; Sofi checking in, keeping me on track, letting me know there might be a hereafter. I ask if she might teach good manners to Carlotta and W, purring:

"I'm here you two. Close by. Keeping watch. You're lucky. Brother and sister in the same house. You have each other. Don't fuck that up. At least you never had to deal with Mao.[69] And don't you dare die on Rick. He won't be able to handle it. I know. He was with me when I went. See you on the flip side."

---

68   See 'Exit Ramp' *(The Paragraphs)*

69   See 'Friends, Enemies'

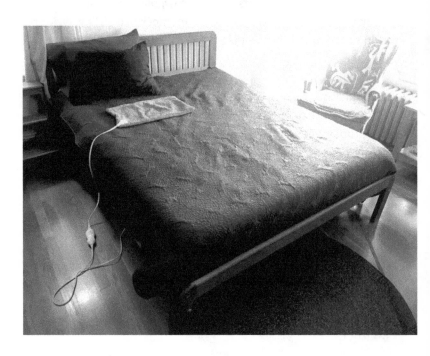

Futon

When I moved to Beacon Hill, I had no bed. My no longer boyfriend, Steven, kept ours. I always wanted a futon, the sheer Japanese hard-ass hardness of it.

"You might as well sleep on the floah."
– Kelly Mac

This when she sat at the foot of my bed to practice singing the chorus of *I Just Want To Go Down On You* with two other girls from Doyle's. (A song they actually performed with me at the Lizard Lounge, all three hot blonde back-up singers.) She's right. A futon is as hard as packed earth.

Mum and I drove to a store in Cambridge and she bought me bed and futon. They set up snug in my tiny new bedroom with the dark blue Auntie Marimekko wallpaper and many un-curtained, no venetian blinded windows.[70]

Over time the wood joints and screws are weakening. Some have fallen out. Too much behavior I suppose. The whole contraption could collapse, as hilarious as it would be mortifying. It has since been replaced with a Bob-O-Pedic. Fabulous, firm and a good bed fit for the money. Shamus[71] said that you have to spend at least $500 on a mattress if you want to take care of your back. That is *exactly* the amount I spent at Bob's. I had it delivered, lurched up the stairs at 370B by two impatient thugs who couldn't wait to get the fuck outa there.

---

70   See 'Angel vs Id'

71   See 'The Blue Ox'

"Could you also please roll up the futon and put it on the sidewalk for me?"

A real mood improver, but they flopped Bob onto the bedframe, hugged up the futon, over-the-shouldered it downstairs like a cadaver, dumped it and took off.

I sleep like a baby unless I have a guest. God knows how many visitors have slept, or tried to, on this thing. I do remember the first ever. Tobias, from Germany, after a trip to the beach. Blue-eyed and handsome; the perfect initiate. I'm lucky to log a snore on a shared futon or Bob-O, but there are issues.

1.   I have the old-man-has-to-pee-every-three-hours disorder. Up, down, up, down, in and out of bed all night long. One must gently peel away the covers and leave the bed on tip-toe without waking up one's friend.
2.   I wear a tooth guard. One does not want to be intimate with one with plastic-in-mouth, although I imagine a blowjob with that thing could feel oh so smooth, soft frictionless plastic gums riding the shaft, as creepy as that sounds.

I want to forewarn, but I don't. I don't want to freak him out with a situation that might have him fly the coop and leave me solo in a creaking bed. Then again, if he takes off I can get a decent night's sleep or entertain a hustler...

> *"You haven't had sex until you've paid for it."*
> **— Provincetown bartender**

Find him. Have him. Pay him. Offer cab fare and give him the heave. No pretense of like-to-get-to-know-ya BS, futon or otherwise.

Gentleman Songster?

Billie Best (OL2, Luna, Berlin Airlift manager) and Chet Cahill (bassist in many of my bands) had, as far as their friends were concerned, The Iconic Relationship. Love and art, a parallel parking of two oddball souls spliced seamlessly together. 'Fireplugs' was their email tag; they were both 5'2" short. At one point, well along, they split up. Or Billie did. Took a break. I'll never forget the call from Chet, the sound of his voice.

"Billie's leaving me," he said.

A blow to all of us who believed in what seemed indestructible. The details I won't go into. Not my place. Blood under the bridge. (Read Billie's book.)

What's wild is what happened next. Billie (with an eye pealed for Phlebitis, a blood clot crises that if untreated can be fatal. Nixon had it.) wound up in the hospital. If the clot wriggled up to her heart, a dead Best. The first person she called was Chet. Lo and behold, he came down with the first recorded case of Scarlet Fever at Mass General in decades. They wound up in the same room, side-by-side beds, together again. When they got discharged, they eloped. Ladder to window (no Marriage Industrial Complex for these bums). And they made a choice: no kids. Disappointing their parents, but opting for art, career and just-the-two-of-them over rug rats. They did wind up buying a real deal farm in the Berkshires with goats, cows, chickens and a big dog.

"If Chet dies, I'll have the dog," Billie laughs.

They were smart, cutting edged and rode their own rodeo of establishment and non-establishment horses, playing the ironic money game, making a sometimes decent living and spending it in cool ways. Ever the five year plan. They collaborated on projects (Chet's beautiful death design, the pinnacle) and worked solo (Chet: music production, farmer. Billie: author, farmer, green biz entrepreneur).

What I admired was how they set up house. The stuff they collected – rarified objects d'art and cool family heirloom clutter. My fav: a pale turquoise ceramic 'bass'?. A curvaceous Pisces with glowing, translucent white light marbles studded like chubby moles all over its body; a muted silvery glow when lit, for which, like Blanche Dubois, I opt. I always wanted the thing. The fish. Wanted them to give it to me. I never shut up about it, but, after Chet died, I lost out. It went to another friend.

On my birthday I got the above. Whiffenpoof Art Vinyl.

Singing groups were a big deal at Yale. I got in there in part because of the singing I'd logged in high school, a big loud baritone. Singing groups were a safe house for man-to-man romance, the homo closet ajar. You didn't talk about it, but you 'knew', platonic or otherwise. Rushing underclassmen (meeting up to persuade them to join your group) was like dating; long meaningful looks, deep confessional conversations[72], borderline flirtations. I was deep in the closet back then, hiding the truth of my persuasion even from myself. I refused advances even as I had crushes on many of my friends. Not atypical in the early 60's.

I loved the singing. The intricate arrangements. The boisterous acapella punch filling hall, dorm, dining hall, Morey's Temple Bar, but I felt the odd man out. Most of the guys in my group came from prep school. Compatriots, but not real friends. Not sure who my real friends were back then. One or two intense interactions, but un-fleshed out. Booze numbed but never liberated the truth even though Yale was all

72 See 'The Fierce Urgency Of New Love'

dudes in my day and, like English boarding schools, homosexuality permeated the ivy air.

Getting the Whiff record from Bil and Chet walked me back to those bygone years. The songs, the trips to Bermuda and Puerto Rico, recording live in a CBS big-room studio, the green cup at Morey's, the white tie tuxedos, the rehearsals – all come hurtling back when I stare at this vinyl tacked up on my wall. It has me remembering Chet. How he knew the artist I was, the song writer I wanted to be. How he cared about my being true to myself. I miss his critique hearing new work.

AN EXAMPLE
Chet re *Old Stag*.

When we performed it at Hi-N-Dry with Jane, a string quartet and backup singers from The Trans-Siberean Orchestra after Chet was gone, I started the night by reading his letter. I asked Billie if that would be ok. She said yes. More than anything I could write about him, this shows the dude he was.

"Rig,

Sorry it took so long for me to respond. The thing has laid around for a couple weeks waiting for me to carve out some time to listen. Wanted to sit down and give it its due and not blast it in the car while I was busy heading somewhere and not really paying attention. After prompting by Karla during a phone call (who loves it), I cozied up with the cd and gave it a twirl.

Love the cover, pix, & minimal liner notes. A rather professionally glossy, yet under-baked package for someone like yourself. If I didn't know you, the title 'Old Stag' would lead me to imagine you as an aging hetero rock star; propped up at the piano stool by Viagra and some well-earned substance abuse problem. Of course I can't keep my love for irreverence at bay any more easily now than I could during my purple spandex days, so I would've probably voted for a title like 'Old Stag Hag' or something... but that's just me.

I won't go into a song-by-song, note-by-note critique, cause that bull-shit always pissed me off back in the day. (On the other hand, I was also always pissed off by a general offhand comment like 'I didn't like it', which, in a split second, minimizes months and months of sweat & sacrifice slaving over a project... 'Half In The Bag' comes to mind...)

But yo, the strings hit the fucker out of the park. I'm not sure I can ver-balize it, but they really ramp up the intimacy of the songs. Karla also noted that your voice seems to 'fit' into the string quartet mix really well, like another instrument. Although I liked your last solo piano recording, the fleshing out of these songs by the strings give everything more depth & emotion, and, if I can be a musical snob for a moment, kind of legitimize your bare-bones composing style. The arrangements by Brendan were great. They gave you a lot of room, and would suddenly swoop in and take things to a different, unexpected level. (I'm also jealous that he got away with some pretty outside arrangements on a few songs, something I felt got squashed on our more pedestrian gotta-make-a-hit-record offerings.) Anyway, props to you for coming up with the quartet accompaniment idea.

Next impression is that the backup vocals really threw me off in a good way. They're this kind of goofy element that drops in occasionally, taking the more serious edge off the strings, and then disappear. They also add a little levity every time they poke their noses into a song.

Lastly, your voice, long the object of much discussion over the years. Well, I think your voice has found its voice, or rediscovered it anyway. I hear a lot of nuance that reminds me of the old, more tender OL songs. Great falsetto, as always. Of course, you can sound like a grizzled old drunk too, depending on the song's needs. But at this point, it's really kind of ageless. One moment I hear a befuddled, hormonally charged 17 year old, the next I hear some world-weary gasping geezer with one foot in the grave and the other, grate-fully, not far behind. Ya gots charachtah in them pipes, man.

I have one curmudgeonly jazz-musician grouse, about which I'm sure you'll never do anything: learn some new fucking piano chords fer chrissake. There, I've said it.

Fav raves (all links are videos from the live performance that night at Hi-N-Dry): *Always. Happy Lesbians. Elle. Michiko. Love On A Wire. Psycho. Your Light Is On.*

So, a tip of the glass to you, Mr. Kinscherf, for staying the course. For living an artistic life. For settling into your skin. For being an inspirational magnet to other creative nomads. For dropping out of Yale and getting booted out of Moosup. For not stopping. And for making a great fucking record. I hope you know how much you really rock.

X

Chet"

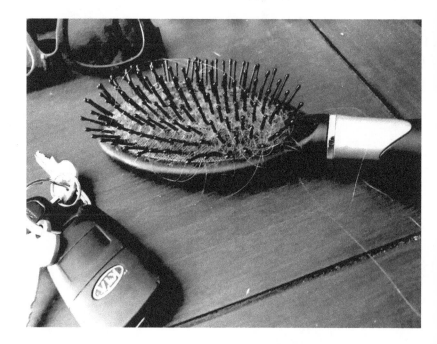

Gnarly

Is that word a Left Coast start-up? Surfer lingo? I never use it, but it applies to my disgusting hair brush and witchy strands.

Dad looked twenty, thirty years younger than Mom. No gray hair. No spot. New friends wondered if she was his Mother. Terrible for her to hear. Terrible for a kid to overhear. Thing is, I am similarly well preserved. But the hair? My god-awful cheap wig hair? A losing battle.

I'm in denial about it. I seem to have most of it, more mouse brown than grey. I continue to not use shampoo, just burning hot water raining down ineffectually, never squeaky clean. The good news: no fluffy puffy when blown dry. I brush it before, not after the shower, so there's less fallout. I toothbrush scoop the hair nest collecting in the tub drain and try to guess whose it is. (Probably mine.) Getting pretty for work, slicking my do back into a loathsome, legally required ponytail, I notice, top of head, a thin crevasse of bleachy whitening. I paper it over with artful strokes, but it's a failed cause. I do not want a fucking spot, but that's a serious eventuality. If I shaved my skull I'd unearth asymmetrical moles littering the landscape like ticks. No *Peaky Blinders* shave cut for this old bird.

For years I had a toothless hair brush. nine or ten bristle stalks in a red rubber field. Posted a snap of it on Facebook and got a lotta *"ew's"*, *"gross"*, *"do something about this!"* from the girls at work. Brandon Anderson, bartender of many bars, a raconteur with a laugh that should be copyrighted, bought me this CVS beauty. Handed it to me on the sidewalk.

"I was in there. Saw your post, so here."

Brandon did me a favor. Scalp happy, bristles fully represented, Berlin can thread the hairy needle. He also bought me a birthday 'grabber'. We old people need grabbers to pluck peanut butter jars off high shelves. I never use it. Too proud. The truth hurts.

> *"Why don't ya **not** tell me about it."*
> — **Harold,** *The Boys In The Band*

Good Idea/Never Happened

Jamaica Plain Spoken was a video/interview project that my friend Todd Drogy and I fired up after Dubya won again in '04.

"Let's drive cross country and interview people and make a documentary," he said.

"I can't stop everything and drive all over the place. I think we should narrow it down to just here in the JP hood."

So that's what we did. Over sixty interviews with people of all genders, beliefs, ages and ethnicities. Many were those I for one would never have encountered or spoken to had we not come up with the idea. I'm a snob of the handsome, less apt to strike up the band with the not so cute. We named our company 'Elbows In', an inside joke. (When a girly-boy runs, his elbows locate at the waist. Wrists, hands, forearms fly about the side like chicken wings.)

We bought Final Cut Pro with a student discount, booked interviews, filmed and started to edit. Thing was, Todd promised he'd never drop the ball, but in less than a year, he enrolled in a grad school program in Canada and flew the coop. I didn't complain because this was a godsend. For the time being there would be only one cook in the *JP Spoken* kitchen. It meant I could interview, shoot and edit on my own without niggling interference. My work was sketchy at best. I attempted fancy tags like a Channel 2 doc that were slap dash and amateur, but I was having a blast and the editing spurt set me free to make the more facile music videos for the band. Then Todd came home and we realized there was a mountain to climb. That without a significant video/tech upgrade no one would show it. No film festival. No TV. We hit the grant writing drawing boards, a death nell for the project because:

A.   We had to use that horrendously frilly grant language; verbose, run-on sentences explaining what we were pretending to accomplish, but essentially saying nothing. A friend of mine called grants: "welfare for ivory tower professors".

B.   We had to clarify that this was a community centric project worthy of real cash, but it wasn't, not in any legit sense. The only thing 'community' about it was that everyone lived in Jamaica Plain. In reality it was just a bunch of local characters mouthing off.

C.   Hardest of all, we would have to promise a storyline arc, a beginning, middle and end. We would need to select a restricted group of interviewees to build a narrative spine, leaving many fabulous interviews on the cutting room floor. Talking heads who had great stuff to say and who were, for years, part of the fraying JP fabric.

So we killed it. We killed the project, dead in the water. But just before we did, I came up with a cool intro scenario. We'd build and film a Punch & Judy stage, populate it with a handful of puppets that were JP representative and tell the story, history and present condition of the hood. It would be funny, informative and clarifying.

Where would we get the puppets? A college credit project at BU, right? What a genius idea! We scarfed up rags, t-shirts and baubles from The Garment District (a buck a bag) and turned them over to art kids at the college. We assigned general character parameters. A black lady. A priest. A drunken Irishman. A hipster. A musician. A grandma. A queer. A lesbian. A business owner, etc, meanwhile agonizing over the script. We never got it finalized, arguing incessantly about details, dialogue, structure. We did wind up with the puppets and they were outstanding, but had one problem. The neck hole where you poke your finger to operate the head was too small for a child, let alone an adult. If we drilled down to make a bigger aperture we would have shattered the papier mache widdle headsies.

"It's always something."
– Gilda Radnor

I gave the bulk of them away to Todd and to friends, save for the above and one other. Remnants of a good idea gone bad. JP Spoken, a worthy try. Many of the clips are up on my website/YouTube for all eternity with nasty comments about *2 Dads, One Family* from homophobes.

He Could Have Been
A Contender

This photo was taken by my friend, Heather MacCloud. The kid is wiped out. Sweaty. Heavy exhausted arms. But he'll jump back in the ring. Look at those eyes. Dude's game.

The shorts are too big. The shirt, loose. But the gloves, relaxed in his lap, are ready to punch the crap out of you. Kid has to be Irish. Patrick, Keagan, Ronan, Dermot, Connor. One of those. I'm pretty sure he'll flatten whoever they put him up against. No scratch on that face.

I ran into the man who trains these guys. His son was a busboy at Doyle's for a few short nights. I wanted to access a match, but it never happened. Might have been awkward. Berlin, zeroing in on the action. Like my reflection in the glass, Great Caesar's Gay Ghost, just off his left shoulder, the voyeur of the violent.

For me, fisticuffs have never been a turn on. It's just that I loved Brando in *On The Waterfront* (Kazan). One of the best movies ever made. Marlon was never more beautiful, even pretty. Eva Marie Saint on a fire escape, waiting for her man in a luminous, white silk slip, starkly vivid in black and with a searing Jazz soundtrack. These days b&w looks manipulated, post-production fake. Back then, it was just straight up film stock, silvery with exquisite chiaroscuro depth and detail. It looked more real than color.

I doubt this kid ever saw *Waterfront*, but he should and he takes me there in spite of himself. Maybe Eva's waiting for him in an Irish battleship, sexy with a cigarette on a JP porch.

Hey, Mr. Tambourine Man

I found this guy in the attic at our enormous half house on Washington Street two doors down from Doyle's. His girlfriend, in Flamenco drag, wound up elsewhere. They both had alien green skin and Asian eyes, nothing remotely Latino. Maybe the sculptor was blind. My green boy seems a bit fey, hip to one side, pointy right toe. His widow's peak, stylized. His chest, waxed. I imagine, under the influence of a psyche-delic, he might actually dance, his girlfriend magically reappearing. He's the perfect dude for my desk. We hang out every day. He knows more about me than he should.

The house where he was housed sat in the shade of the elevated Orange Line, which, at one point, groaned and tilted off balance and threat-ened to land in our living room. This happened just days before it was dismantled. Sad to say, because riding the elevated was one of the best views of the city ever, as if seated on a drone, floating above triple-deckers, factories and busy streets. Driving down Washington Street, under the El during a blizzard, was transformational. The street lights caught snow curtains slanting across the proscenium of the riveted steel beams. I miss the El, but I'm glad I never got my skull crushed by a lopsided train.

Accident witnessed; a sinkhole swallow. Outside our yard a Volkswa-gen wound belly up in the hole. The asphalt buckled and broke open gaping jaws that ate the German bug. Awesome to watch, not nice to be in the car.

Before we moved in I spent hours on the place, repainting, sanding and slathering urethane on the wide wooden floorboards, hammering together a wheelchair ramp so that the paras and quads I was working for at the halfway house could visit.

This was my boyfriend Steven and mine's third house in the hood. Too big for two. We needed roommates. Nancy Adams first. Nance was in our band, Rick Berlin: The Movie. Main recall was the sight of her ass on the ledge leaning out the dining room window.

"Nancy! What are you doing!?"

"I'm using my panty picker."

"Your what!?"

"My panty picker. My undies fell off the clothes line and I don't want to go outside so I made a panty picker." (A bent and stretched coat hanger with a panty picker improvised hook.)

After she moved out and we appropriated her room to record and rehearse. It was a coke den. Steve was dealing. I was using even as I complained about it. We'd hit bars on Lansdowne, bump up in the bathroom and coax a guest back to the house for a sometimes uncomfortable threesome, sometimes just for Steven and sometimes just for me. If the bar failed to provoke a tourist, there was always The Block. Fire up the Duster, zoom down to Arlington and see who might want to make a quick blowjob buck. I was once pulled over on a downtown mission. The cop made me walk a straight line. I was perfect. He wished me well and let me go. I took off, snorted a line on the passenger seat and scored a hustler.

Then Jane moved in. Jane Mangini, the most talented, gorgeous musician/best friend I've ever worked with. She always, always knew how best to interpret the piano parts to my songs. She was with us for several bands and then, after an inspired minute in an ad factory in the big city, originated The Trans-Siberean Orchestra with friends. Her phenomenal performance of *Jungleland* for a video she asked me to edit, thanking and honoring the frontline heroes of New York during the worst days of the pandemic – WE SHALL OVERCOME, AGAIN – is beyond words.

Funny, sarcastic and, way back then, busy in the boyfriend department. She moved into the closet under the stairs. It fit her bed and her dog, The Goose, a dumb Doberman who loved to swim in circles. Jane would take him for walks in Franklin Park. When he spotted a pond, he'd hit the water, kaboom! Thing was, he could never figure out how to make it back to shore. He swam round and round until Jane was forced to wade in and save him, returning home filthy with mud and reeds. Goose loved to shit in the car. Long trips were a scrape-it-up diarrhea hose nightmare. One Thanksgiving he locked his jaws onto our turkey and ran it out of the house. But we loved him, The Great Goose, how could we not?

When my Mom died, Jane took the bus up from New York to visit, drink and console. The door to the Lucky Star loo was busted and hung open. Vile fumes floated down the aisle for the entire hold-your-nose trip, but she made it. She showed up at Jacques and afterwards we walked a half block down the street to The Napoleon, a now defunct gay bar populated by elderly queens. They nicknamed it 'Jurassic Park', a tongue-in-cheek compliment. There stood the de rigueur piano bar with a black dildo candelabra, omnipresent Broadway covers, a semicircle of chime-in singers and a terrific lesbian on the keys. Jane and I sat in a corner, getting shit-faced, commiserating and laughing out loud. She was telling me about a co-worker's recent New York date.

"She went out with this guy from work. A cutie. They went from restaurant to bar, to another bar and then back to his place for a nightcap. The whole time he was carrying around this McDonald's bag. She had to ask, 'Why the fucking McDonald's bag!?' She said he looked really shy and embarrassed, but he opened it up and pulled out a strap-on. A fucking strap-on!"

And the kicker?, in Jane's reaction in her come-and-go Southern belle drawl (she grew up in Florida).

"Ah was intrigued and repulsed at the same tahme."

Then it happened, that rare moment when an entire room, cacophonous with conversation, stops talking all at once. An abrupt oasis of silence. And in that eye of The Napoleon storm I asked:

"How do you strap it on?"

You could hear a pin drop. My question bounced off the mirrored walls like a ping pong ball and then, you got it, uproarious, piercing whathtefuck?! shrieking gay laughter. I was outed as a strap-on neophyte and I'll never forget it. If you're going to embarrass yourself, this is the way to go. Classic Jane. Classic Berlin. Of these stories there are many to count.

PARTAAAY

After the work and redecorating was complete, we figured we should celebrate. Open the house up for friends far and wide. Unfortunately it rained. Bad idea to house-warm in the drench. Seven of my wheelchair buddies drove their chairs up the ramp, skid marks and wet rubber destroying my shiny happy floors. Did I care? Not really. I was out of my skull on weed, coke and LSD. From my on high distance I Magoo-watched as:

A.   A drunk stomped down the backstairs and blew a hole the third step up from the bottom, his legs dangling in the basement, torso above. No one helped. They stepped over him, as if he was a living statue.
B.   A projectile vomit-er fired a puke pipe so forcefully that people could duck under the arching spew. An Eero Saarinen's St Louis Gateway Arch of vomit.
C.   Some bastard took a dump and finger painted shit all over the bathroom tiles. Art for shit's sake.

Meanwhile, I was losing it. I spent a chunk of time alone up in the attic with Mr. Tambourine Man. I just wanted to be left to myself, to wait for the party and the drug intensity to die the fuck down. At some point, long after everyone left, I lay on the couch with a Golden Retriever who was, at the time, my best friend, my only friend, in the whole wide world. I held onto him for dear life. His empathetic you'll-be-okay brown eyes kept me from going upstairs and flinging myself like Turandot off the widow's watch.

Not long after, Steven and I broke up. Ours had been a rocky relationship. Open sometimes. Closed others. Massive jealousy and deceit. But that party, holy crap! To end all parties. It was written up in the Herald, back pages.

All that's left is Mr. Tambourine Man. Does he remember? I bet he does, but then again, he's inscrutable.

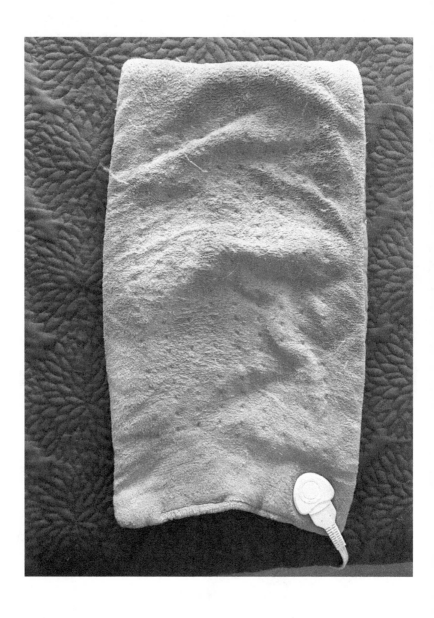

Hot Turquoise

I wear these out, these heating pads. They give up after a month. This one's lasted the longest.

I threw my back out lying on the couch, legs extended, heels on the coffee table. It felt like a knife in my side, requiring four weeks of physical therapy. Not fun, but helpful. The kid who worked on me was effective and good looking, which had to help as I lay silently under the pre-massage wet-hot towel. Ever since, I use heating pads. Twice a day during meditation. Lie down meditation, because I can't sit up and use the pad at the same time. My sister, Janie, says it's okay. You can do lie down meditation when you're sick. Why not when your back is messed up? Who knows if my meditations are spurious. No universal consciousness within range, but my back feels the bliss. It has helped. I haven't had a recurrence for months. I used to do yoga, stretches and pushups, but after the hernia invasion I felt a twitch-n-pull down there so I have yet to re-start those tedious isometrics. The turquoise has replaced true effort. At night I shove it under the covers, like those bed warmers they used in the olden days. Heat the sheets and apply one further ablution to my back. I leave it on longer than advised, but so what. No ill effects and it's a guilty pleasure to slide under the jacuzzi sheets. The cats appropriate it, their personal kitty chlorine swimming pool. They snug themselves on it precisely, no leg or paw out of the water, but I don't leave the heat on. No crispy kitties. Just one heat sedated old cunt drifting off to sleep.

I Like Heavy

My Mom, the same. When I was looking after her, after the big C diagnosis while I was in Philly, I'd help her climb into bed. It was Autumn cold. She had an electric blanket, but wanted more. The cocoon of warmth, lasagna layered under a blanket pile.

"I like it heavy," she said.

Watching her sleep on her side, one arm resting on her hip, wrist on shinbone, I realized that I did the exact same. Who knew? (Come to think of it, it's likely that anyone sleeping on their side would do the same damn thing.)

"I'm so sorry you have to deal with this," she said.

"No way, Mum. It's our turn."

She hated that her kids had to take time out to look after her. She never wanted to be a burden, but accepted the help. She had no choice and loved us being around. Janie and Lisa had gone home. I showed up after my trip to Europe. She didn't want me to find out she was ill and cut short my time overseas, so I heard about it only after I landed in Boston. Turned right around and flew to Philly.

While she was asleep in hospital, I'd go out and get hammered. Picked up a stranger. Brought him to her house. Got up early with a hangover and went back to see her, visitor out the door.

She moved to Portland to stay with her niece, Polly, with whom she was super close and who was a nurse at Portland Medical and whose husband was a hospital big shot. They found her a terrific oncologist. Mum would be in it for the long haul. I drove up every week, mid-Doyle's. We had an awesome time. Laughing. Doing the crossword. Taking walks while the chemo surged in her veins. Bought her a wig.[73] Drove her to appointments. We'd grocery shop and fight over who would pay. It was the way we'd been when I was a kid when we did so much together. Easy close, Mum and me.

> *"I'm only going to say this once. Spend as much time as you can with your Mother. If you don't, you'll regret it for the rest of your life."*
> **— Jane Friedman**

She died at Lisa's house on Long Island. Both sisters were there. I'd rushed home to mix a record thinking she had more time. I called from a gas station on the Connecticut highway. She sounded upbeat, but she left this world shortly after we spoke. I think of her every time I drive past that off ramp. I can see the now useless payphone from the highway.

Nearing the end, she experienced that phenomenon we've read about, when life's calendar flashcards before your eyes.

"I'm with John. John Dudley. We're sneaking a smoke on his back porch, a yellow light bulb overhead."

Like Falstaff, she saw flowers on her quilt. Picked at them.

"So beautiful," she said.

She was Yankee self-willed, but it took her most of her life to give up the cigs. It infuriated her. She quit a mere five years before she got lung cancer. She'd roll down her window at stop lights when she saw kids smoking on the corner. She'd yell at them to give it up. The young rarely listen to the old.

---

73 See 'Cute' *(The Paragraphs)*

Back to heavy.

I got the quilt on sale at Lord & Taylor's. I needed something. All mine were light weight. I'm not a fan of goose down puffery, warm as they are. Like Mum, I wanted heavy. I wanted it to look old fashioned, a 'winter throw' in a log cabin at the turn of the century. This comes close. It had a tear I repaired. It sprouted another. I'll leave it as is. It does heavy regardless, no patch work necessary. Like an asshole, in summer, I crank the AC and twirl the quilt onto my bed. I don't think I can sleep without it.

Imaginary Cities

My friend, Paul LeTarte, speaks five languages, likes to seat his cell-phone (lit) under his pint of beer and admire the illumination. He has a degree in foreign affairs and city planning, is a considerate person and of late has a lot of hair. If he lets it loose, it hides his face. He also likes to somersault into a snow bank in his underwear as his brother films.

A few summers ago he asked me to go swimming (Turtle Pond, Roslindale) on a hot summer afternoon. I resisted. Pre-Melanoma, burning sun anxiety, reveal of hideous crêpey alabaster legs, ill-fitted in the bathing suit department and decrepitude of body in front of handsome boys were imaginings fast at work in my gonzo skull. Still, I like the smell of a lake under nostrils, like rain, the soft music of children laughing in the splash, the inverted bowl of blue sky, the anthropomorphic clouds. I had the time, so fuck it. I borrowed my roommate's bathing suit – black, cool, hip-hop style so I don't look weird in silly shorts. I slathered on the anticancer sauce and we drove out of the hood, windows breezing down, blues on the radio. We parked roadside, kicked off our shoes, hid phones, hippity hopped over gravel and grass like living dead marionettes and traipsed a sandy path to the dock where kids, young adults and happy dogs were goofy in the sun.

In seconds Paul's in the water and swimming at a smooth crawl across the pond to the 'party dock'—weed, booze, boom boxes blaring. I dove in, water curling around my body, filling my ears until, uh oh, not salt water! I forgot. I always forget. Fresh water is nowhere near as buoyant. My seventy-one year old sack of bones was heavy and awkward. Flailing, stabbing and squinting underwater as ten-year-old kids and an elderly woman seemed completely afloat and at ease. I did not swim far. I tried not to think about the snapping turtles the pond is named after, or what part of me they might snip and snap. I did yank up the shorts that fled past my waist and climbed onto the dock, no easy lift. No legit ladder, just planks nailed together at an uneven slant. The wood, slimed with algae, was laughing at me, at how foolish I looked slipping, sliding and jerking about like a total spaz.

I flopped onto the dock, exhausted and embarrassed, as small children leaped in and out of the brown water like penguins. I was awful at any of this, but loved it anyway, lying back on a tiny towel, trying to avoid late afternoon death rays when Paul returned, climbed up and stood dripping, smoothed out and breathing heavy from his swim, from the swim that erased his axe-in-head hangover. I tried not to look 'there', but of course I did, stealing a mental GoPro. He chatted it up with a burly ex-punk rock Dad who was there with his son. Dad dude offered me his truck-wheel sized inner tube. I declined, but when Paul arched back into the drink for swim-across #2, I took Dad up on the Dad tube, hurling it like a dyke with a discus and galumphed back into the water, limb heavy and floundering.

The tube, which seemed manageable for others, was next to impossible to navigate. I lurched my elbows up on either squeaky side, head in hole, but couldn't lift my legs into that oh-so-relaxed float-about-the-pond position, ass underwater, chest to sky. I squirmed and shifted and struggled like a maniac until I forced my knees up under my chin and was able to yoga through the rubber ring. Woo hoo! Proud and panting, a cheerful Jeremy Irons in a tube, paddle, paddle, spin and splash. I noticed that I was drifting towards the lily pads where the snappers lurked. Enough already, as I frantically inched away from the turtle bite real estate. I worried about a dog-paddling Irish Setter's stabbing toenails digging into my side as I hurled the shiny black rubber onto the dock and clambered out, wiped out. I feigned calm, but was grateful to be out of the water and to lie the fuck down. A swimmer I am not. Went out for it as a sport in high school and puked in the shower after five laps. I wasn't fond of here-it-is-have-a-look-ya-can't-miss-it speedos. At any rate, I doubt I'll be going back. I will stay home with a mint julip, sexy sun glasses and a candy cane parasol.

Paul's brother grows intense weed. Two hits and you can't move. Paul seized an opportunity. He places a 4'x8' swath of butcherblock paper on the floor, smokes a fatty and then, with ink and pencil and on hands and knees, begins to draw. The THC focuses his pen. He's at it for hours at a stretch, creating a bird's eye view of a fictional middle eastern city. Narrow streets, ribbon rivers, small open spaces, tiny houses. The brain eraser oblivion of making art.

I want art work from my friends. I want their stuff on my walls. I don't have the bread to pay for it, so I charm it out of them, one guilt tripping manipulative drop at a time. I have a collection of at least eight to ten of these. Some from the accomplished. Some from the less so. For me it's personal. Having art made by friends keeps them with me as I might not see them ongoingly. Preferable to a photo of a face which never seems to fully restore their being into a forgetful heart.

Every time I ran into Paul, I'd ask for a 'city'. It took a while. He's usually high and a mañana procrastinate, but one night, at the Behan, he brought it. A section the size of a high school lunch tray. No room for the big honcho in my house. I adore it, especially the frenzied scratchy ballpoint blue lines indicating water in the lower right.

NON SEQUITUR
He told me that his roommate, Peruvian, masturbates at least seven times a day. That's gotta chafe. Why does he tell me this?

In The Dunes

Orchestra Luna was my innocent first foray into forming a band. There we are on the dunes just outside Provincetown. Two gay guys in berets, two girl singers in retro dresses, three jazz musicians and a cloudless sky. We had no idea what we were in for. I no longer have the LP. Others might. Some company in the UK decided to press a re-mastered CD. Glad they did. I have just this one. That's it. The cover shrunk into a 5x5, under hard plastic. Tom Werman's liner notes on the back, saying terrific things.

Mike saw the disc one night and read Werman's words aloud, astonishing me with what had been written, capturing the essence, the magic of that impossible band.

"This album was recorded less than a year after Orchestra Luna's first live performance in a small Boston folk club. In that year, they have developed from a collection of very talented individuals into a powerful, sensitive and unique musical unit. Having no obvious comparisons, they are at once progressive and nostalgic, exploring the limits of theatrical and musical form and traveling the whole range of emotion from the depths of desperation to the pinnacle of celebration. To experience Luna live is to take the first bite of a strange but delicious fruit; after your first taste, you may not know precisely from whence the fruit came, but it's too late. You've already developed a strong appetite for more. Familiarity soon breeds dependence and you too may find that an evening of Luna's music can become a regular need. This album has the same effect; you'll want to turn the record over and do it again, to try to absorb just a bit more of the wealth of sound that swept by you on first listening. I've seen it happen to all different sorts of people; they encounter and inevitably embrace Orchestra Luna. In these times of all too much musical predictability,

Luna gifts us with a brand new approach to live and recorded music and evokes a brand new reaction from its audiences. Luna wrings more from its fans than enthusiasm... it engenders love and devotion. Having watched the fruit ripen over the last year, it's evident to me that Richard Kinscherf is an astounding and unique composer and pianist, whose vocal style sets a standard for a future wave of entertainers; that Scott Chambers plays the bass with definitive taste and authority; that Don Mulvaney is one of the most inventive percussionists in pop music; that Randy Roos is absolutely unparalleled on the guitar; that Liz Gallagher and Lisa Kinscherf could be the most endearing and appealing female vocalists of the decade; and that Peter Barrett is simply a verbal genius. But those are the feelings of one who has partaken of this fruit many times over. Help yourself. Orchestra Luna is a musical feast-a provocative gesture in a medium which thirsts for new directions."

– Tom Werman

I got all twisted up hearing it. He had been the guy who humiliated Lisa at a party after a Hippodrome performance, ridiculing her voice by grotesquely imitating her singing *Little Sam*, making fun of Liz's armpit hair, my eye make-up (which, I admit, was cartoon whore horrendous) and wanting changes to all the things that made us original. He was bombed. Hearing his words in Mike's voice, I forgave him, but it cut, him doing that, hurting my sister.

ABOUT OL

I started writing songs in New Haven on a discarded church piano, in a house jammed with artists, musicians, poets, architects and a guy who ate Christmas Tree balls and played the clarinet. *Little Sam* was among the first.

Lisa had moved to Cambridge. She thought I'd like it. I hitchhiked, sparse gear on my back and wound up first in Central Square and later, Somerville. Got a job in Quincy at a group home for delinquent teens. The salary saved bought me an upright and I hoisted it into my third floor apartment. I put tacks in the hammers and continued writing weird songs. I had no ambition. I just liked doing it. Sublimating experience, observations, romance and friendship into a safe house collective. I had to practice them every day or they'd be lost, no recording device to refer them back to me.

One summer afternoon I heard a shout outside my window. Harry Bee (in a management partnership with Bruce Patch) asked if I'd ever thought about starting a band. Why not give it a try?

We began with Lisa and Liz Gallagher, a friend I'd met at an actor's workshop in New Haven. We learned twenty songs, piano and back-up vocals only and a couple of solos for the girls. Once locked down, I put a notice up at Berklee for a bassist. Scott Chambers joined up. We added bass and voice to the twenty.

Lisa waitressed at Club Zircon, a jazz bar two doors down. Randy Roos (guitar) was a regular performer with his band Softwood. She asked him to listen what we were working on. He went for it. Lucky us. Randy is a phenomenal, one-of-a-kind musician. Short, a cloud of curly hair and a composed persona. His fingers fly over the fret board and his jazz sensibility moved our repertoire into a new realm. All of this was unplanned. It uncoiled out of my head, one domino following another, each surreptitiously leading to the next. Got the girls. Need bass. Got bass. Need guitar. Got guitar.

We moved to a house in Allston, auditioned drummers and chose Don Mulvaney (who played piano and sang with a voice like Stevie Wonder). The material expanded. Arrangements became more intricate. Enlarging on the idea, I asked my poet friend from New Haven, Peter Barrett[74], if he'd join up as a singer/performer/spoken word artist. Peter brought an entirely new tone and presence. Got poet. He named us: Orchestra Luna. The girls: The Lunettes. Got name.

My sister, unsure of herself on stage, wanted guidance. I asked Barry Keating (whom I'd met in Grenada, West Indies, on a wild ride, failed

---

74   See 'Peter Barrett & Moosup, The Musical'

movie[75]) to choreograph. His New York compatriot, Basha Johnson, designed costumes for the Lunettes. The whole picture was becoming coordinated and ornate with props, spoken words and structure. We rehearsed at least twice a week for hours. Got choreography. Got costumes.

Harry and Bruce booked us a residency at Jeramiah's on Harvard Ave (a short walk from where we lived). The place was packed from the get go. Our oddball band found a quick and rabid following. We wound up on the cover of *The Phoenix*. Opened for The Cars at BU. Lenny Petze (Epic) came to Jeremiah's and signed us up. Got gig. Got record deal.

Learning the songs, developing the act and signing the deal, a six month whirlwind, made winning in the music industry seem stupid easy. (We were so naïve.) Epic hired producer/composer Rupert Holmes and we began to record our first (and only) album. Holmes added a full, real Orchestra. After it was completed, Ron Alexenberg (who'd take over at Epic) came to see us, heard our cover of *You Gotta Have Heart* (Damn Yankees) and played on WBCN on opening day for years, plus our signature song: *Doris Dreams* and wanted them both on the record. We went back in the studio and folded them in. Got record.

Jane Friedman had us to play Frank Zappa's 10th Anniversary party. Jane was Frank's publicist and worked with LaBelle and managed Patti Smith. Both played the anniversary. LaBelle sang an acapella version of *Please Don't Eat That Yellow Snow* and Patti played as a duo with Lenny Kaye. I told her to hurry up and get off the stage because we needed to sound check (having no clue about the inspiration she would become for me down the rock n roll road). We played just the one song: *Doris Dreams*. When it was over, Zappa rushed the stage, picked Randy up off the ground and hugged him. Susan Blond (Epic's publicist) booked us a residency at The Little Hippodrome where we met The Famous and began dropping too many names to count.

---

75   See 'Busted In Grenada (Above and Below): The Janeen' *(The Paragraphs)*

The dream was over as soon as it began. Epic signed Boston. Springsteen's *Born To Run* came out on Columbia. We got left in the dust. Who were these weirdo Orchestra Luna-tics? How did they fit into the CBS hit record roster? Steve Popovich[76], who took over at Epic, took one look at OL, didn't care for us and we got dumped. (Years later, Pop tried to sign Luna, a no frills version. to Cleveland International. Big fuck up. Long story.)

So there ya have it. My first toe in the slime water that is the music business. Addicted ever since, though not to the biz, but to having bands. One of the great gifts in my life.

---

76   See 'A Tisket, A Tasket'

John

You could safely say that JL (more than any other Beatle) changed my life. Not only his songs, but his interviews, his earth shaking romance with Yoko, his horrific murder, his Liverpool, thumb-your-nose-at-pretense origins, his consistent doubling of vocal tracks (he hated his voice), his calling out of Paul, his love for Paul, his jokester middle finger to the press, *Imagine*, etc.

We'd moved the Orchestra Luna house from Allston to Newton High-lands. A giant musician/art zoo next door to the Episcopalian Chaplin's house. Peter, Karla, Liz, Lisa, Mike, Steven, Billie & Chet. A houseful. Orchestra Luna II. We set up rehearsals in the basement, got odd jobs in the neighborhood, shoplifted duct tape, steaks and Christmas pres-ents. At the same time, Steven's and my relationship was coming apart, the early beginnings of an open relationship experiment. One that, in most cases, ultimately fails. Break up or stomach the pain of sexual jealousy, perhaps the worst of its kind[77].

I got my own place across the street, an attic apartment with slanted ceilings and long views. I painted the walls butter yellow and moved in. Put a writing piano in a corner. A respite from the Sturm Und Drang we were tangled up in. I'd threatened suicide. Had there been a gun... Walked outa the house stark naked and lay face down in the grass hoping for rescue, a pathetic drama exploitation. But yes, smart to move out of the Luna house. Out of sight, out of apprehension, real or imagined.

After The Highlands, Steven and I moved to Jamaica Plain. Billie and

---

77   See 'On Your Back'

Chet as well. Karla joined Meatloaf. Mike Scopino moved to New York and ran a famous music club. Peter quit and moved to San Francisco to start a band with his brothers: 'No Sisters'. A tearful farewell to one of the best people in my life. The end of an art era. Bands come together like an elopement, filled with honeymoon promise, an instant marriage of three to eight people who barely know each other. The music is their bond. Their relationship to each other is a work in progress with many false beginnings and abruptly ended shelf lives. All I have left of that phase is this photo of John. The frame came from that second Highlands house. It's middle America motel. Where I scooped up the Lennon portrait I have no idea, but John and his frame have been in every house I've lived in since, staring down at me as if to warn:

"Don't stray from the truth, Berlin. Write real. Do not concern yourself with success or shallow adversaries. Keep it up with humor and a doe-eyed, disturbing romantic heart."

Doing my best, JL. Doing the best I can.

THE NOSE
Among many quack concepts is my assertion that not all, but more than a few great musicians (men and women) have the same nose as John, frontal view. The soft downward pointing tip flanked by parenthetical nostrils. I noticed this for the first time watching my friend, Tom Janovitz, perform at Toad. I wrote lyrics for what became *John Lennon's Nose* (Old Stag) on a napkin.

I do not have this nose.

A DIFFERENT JON
(I fear we used him during Orchestra Luna. I'm pretty sure he feared the same thing.)

He grew up on his Daddy's farm. His mother was a substantial, in charge woman. She kept tabs on the money. Jon had to ask her for his allowance, otherwise she'd set it aside in a drawer in her upstairs bureau. She stuffed it in a nylon stocking and shoved it in amongst her underwear. Jon never wanted to go into that drawer.

He was responsible for small chores around the farm. He had to stack firewood in a tidy pile next to the living room hearth. He had to walk out to the end of the driveway and pick up the Sunday Globe. He had to burn the trash and take out the garbage. He had to mow the lawn with the Gravely tractor and occasionally trim ivy back from the upstairs windows.

He was a quiet kid, shy. He smiled all the time, but if you looked closely you could see that the space between his eyebrows puckered and his eyes spoke of an anxious heart. He was good-looking, a bit on the feminine side. From an early age he decided to let his blonde hair grow long. It might have caused a family crises had he not been so obstinate about it. He was well behaved in the other areas of his life, so they let him get away with it. The hair. He would comb it carefully in the morning and lift it back from his shoulders before leaning over his cereal bowl at breakfast.

He loved his father. The man was tall and well-muscled. He had a strong back from having worked the farm from the time he was a little boy. He had a good head for business and managed to buy up large tracts of neighboring land. He had an exquisite taste in classical music and would dress up and drive into Boston to hear the Symphony. Jon would tag along, but there was little air in the car for him to speak up. Conversation was kept to a minimum. His father's deep blue eyes did the talking. They were stern and kindly at the same time. If you did something he disapproved of, you would know immediately and shame would spread over your body like a fever.

On rare evenings he would visit Jon's room, sit on the wicker chair next to his bed and talk. Not a two-way, heart-to-heart, father-and-son, more a monologue, spoken softly by the older man to himself, enlisting the silent affirmation of his son's wide eyes and held breath. He would talk about the difficulty of living 'rightly'. That it was the tragedy of the world that most people had no sense of the refinements of life, especially the arts. They chose to purchase the flimsy byproduct: a smarmy greeting card, a cheap Van Gogh reproduction, a gaslighted biography; impotent cousins to the truly meaningful. The 'shallow ones' had cowardly values and a voracious acquisitiveness. Jon never fully comprehended the ramblings, but at the end, in the silence, when his father turned away and gazed out the window at the evening sky, he felt a great rush of emotion.

When he was twelve, his Dad died. He had been out in the barn assisting the delivery of a colt. In the midst of the birth, as he was struggling to pull the babe out of his mother's womb, he suffered a stroke. He seized up and died. Jon had been holding a lantern over the mare's backside and saw his father fall. He shrank from the sight of it and ran home to his mother.

Large tracts of the farm were sold and his Mom started a music agency nearer to town. Her indomitable size and spirit carried her quite far. Her agency became reputable and successful. Jon lived at home with her, but in the absence of his Dad, found her domineering personality difficult to bear. He became quieter and waited stoically for his twenty-first birthday and his inheritance. He was determined to realize in himself, and in the spending of his money, that yearned-for Eden perfection of sweetness and fairness, of what his father had so wistfully imagined in those unguarded moments beside his bed. He fell easily into the dream of the flower children of the sixties and although he abstained from the drugs and loose sexuality, he believed in the widespread kindness, love and open heart of that generation. When he became a young millionaire at twenty-one, he retained his long hair and diminutive ways.

He tried to start a community with his closest friend, Lance, and bought a farm on a hilltop in New Hampshire with chickens, cows, cats and dogs. He acquired an incredible amount of musical equipment, all that he would ever need to start a band. He tried to find other people with whom he could trust to join his fantasy, but as the hippie sixties moved frantically into the dirty seventies, things got a lot harder for him. He lacked the tough edge of mastery and command that his father had. People ran over him and abused his generosity. The farm was a shambles. The vegetables rotted in the garden. There were cats all over the place. The shiny new gear sat unused in an upstairs room in the barn. Lance fiddled around with seven guitars and as many pedals, foot-switches and effects while Jon tapped on his drum kit when he felt inspired.

Sadly, the music that he had hoped would come together never materialized. Bass players and singers came and went, but at the end of a year it was still just Jon and Lance. They spent a lot of money and had nothing to show for it. In the meantime he discovered, through his mother's agency, a struggling band and he fell in love with their music. It was a carnival band with two girls, a poet and a bizarre singer/composer. The event of their performance filled him with feeling. To him this band cut an undiluted magical path across the hazards and misfires of all other musical aggregations. He saw them live as often as possible and, after several months, through an introduction from his mother, he met their leader, Rick. He idolized Rick as someone who seemed to have everything needed in order to be fulfilled in life. Everything except money. He followed their haphazard career and eventually helped them survive multiple financial and equipment disasters. The band continued to fire him up and he felt that his money, even though it wasn't earning a single dime, was well spent. He still lived on his hilltop farm and left only to buy supplies or to tack up flyers inviting potential members of his unrealized band to come to New Hampshire Heaven and strike out on a sincere path in the oddball wake of people like Rick and his Moon Band.

He slept alone and rarely masturbated. He was not a particularly sexual person. Nor particularly spiritual. In the back of his head was his vaguely formed whim and whenever he became close to a person, a project or an object that clarified his vision, he would shine. The smile on his face, intended to project his Positive Philosophy, would become more genuine and he would have happy thoughts. If the vibration was negative, the smile would remain, but the City of Light would cloud over and he would have secret misgivings of a gloomier nature. He would become more like his mother and friends or associates would be unexpectedly cut off from the spigot, from the wallet.

Down the road he worked it out with the Moon Band. He would roadie, tune guitars, set up gear, most of which was his anyway, and be more directly involved, both he and Lance. It could have been an ideal situation, except by now the Moon Band had lost the girls and, having struggled valiantly for years, decided to iron out its sound and shoot for a more commercial approach. It was hard to explain. How does an art form or an artist change over the years and become something unlike what it had originally set out to be? How can one justify the shift? To an original fan, to someone like Jon, it was a travesty. A betrayal. He hated the new band. It had lost its magic. Rick had been tragically led astray by the force of circumstance. His alliance with the new guitar player dumped a lot of offensive power chords on his delicate, jazz influenced material. Instead of winning the hearts of sensitive souls, he sold out. Rick had become just another meaty red fist pumping the air.

Jon was sad, angry and disappointed. He wasn't sure what to do. Rick explained it all to him in a hundred different ways, but he couldn't understand it. He had wanted to support an underdog, and now, with a potential success on his hands, he didn't feel right about investing. He wanted to assist a limping failure so that it would continue to gladden the hearts of the lonely. He wanted to retract his support and go back to his farm and start all over again. The innocence veil he had painstakingly protected and maintained over the years had been ripped away from his eyes and he did not like what he saw. He didn't like to watch Rick posturing around the stage like some cliche rock n roll rooster. He didn't want to have to block his ears because the sound was deafening. He didn't want to watch his equipment get lugged in and out of murky clubs just to have bullshit cock rock music blasted through it. He didn't want to deface the dream his father had initiated by perpetuating a project he could no longer believe in. Worst of all he hated to lose the one thing that he cared about in the first place: unadulterated musical magic. All he wanted to do was go home and sit under a tree and stare out. To vanish.

He lost touch with Rick and with the Moon Band. No one knows where he wound up. We can only hope that his grain-of-sand pain became a pearl.

Maman

Mère. Mother. Hard to catch it in the photo, but this French boy has that word tattooed on his forearm. I never asked David Armstrong, the photographer, what it meant. On a face like his, with forehead frown and anxious stare it was an unusual choice for a tatt. Or not. It deepens my fabricated sense of who he might be, besides gorgeous.

Backing up.

During the formation of Orchestra Luna[78], I was out and about. A lot. Made close friends with Pamela Norton. She seemed to know everybody interesting. Everybody in art, everybody gay. I tagged along with her to apartments and parties and, to use her expression, was *'gathered up'* by them or they by me. Pamela said that about three years ago she was with this guy and all of a sudden she became known as Pamelaandthisguy[79] and she wasn't Pamela anymore. She wants to wake up in the morning and be loving somebody, but she wants to be Pamela. Pretty sure this had a lot to do with why we were friends.

One afternoon, on a floral couch in a Central Square living room, she and I were drinking shit wine from the bottle when through the door this beautiful guy in a house dress made his spectacular entrance. A David-Bowie-Hunky-Dory album cover mock-up – lips, body, hair, dress, joyfully laughing, full of life. He knocked me out. This was, turns out, David Armstrong, the guy who, years down the road, took the portrait, Maman. The portrait of his French boyfriend.

---

78   See 'In The Dunes'

79   See 'Miss Pamela Running It On Like It Is' *(The Paragraphs)*

At another party in another found object living room, this time on Beacon Hill and again with Pamela, there he was, Monsieur Armstrong with his best friend Nan Goldin. Nan was a short, curly red head, who took everything in with a subdued observation, like a young Margaret Atwood. They were just kids then and had been close from the age of fourteen, now in their early twenties. Carefree and at the beginning of what would become a long, full life of photography, friendship and drugs. A life that took them to New York, LA, Berlin, Amsterdam, Paris. How they managed so expansive an adventure was beyond me. I was the guy writing songs on heavy upright pianos, forming a band in spite of himself and anchoring my world here in Boston for the foreseeable future. I had been the romantic nomad, following a firecracker heart all over the country. That stopped as soon as I had a band; been here ever since.

Years later, at a chaotic loft party downtown (why have I not been to any of these recently?), I ran into David. He had yet another boyfriend, not Maman, but super cute and on-his-lap affectionate. This, as I was can't-help-it narrowing my choices to straight guys and wondering if I could ever be in love with a queer. But here he was, a proper, well-adjusted and in yet another relationship, homosexual. On the other side of the tracks, an untethered Kinscherf was, would he ever be?, not quite on the same team.

"Ricky! How are you?"

It felt cool to be recognized by someone who had blown me away all those years ago and who had, it seemed, made it, along with Nan, in art land. I asked for a photo. Like I said, I do that, ask friends to give me work I could never afford. I buzz through galleries and museums as if riding a dirt bike, quick scanning paintings and sculpture with no more patience than I have shopping for cereal in a super market. I want work in house.

"Here," he said. *"Have this."*

Which was Maman. Which still lives in the silver frame it came with.

Much later (these lapses) I went to a Whitney Biennial in New York. I went because I'd read that both he and Nan had a twin show. Nan's work had become super famous. Brutal, biographically honest, rich colors, off-hand camera. David's, black and white. A perfect pairing. I skimmed along predictably and on my way out I heard a voice behind me:

"Ricky! You're here! Did you like the show?"

I fumbled about. Then I told him how much I loved Maman. How lucky I felt to have it in my house.

"My dear, there's two of that boy. Two portraits."

"What?"

"Underneath Maman, in the same frame, is a second. I thought you knew."

When I got home, sure enough there was the other, hidden like a scarlet letter beneath the first. I had a Boomerang Baby Jesus sepia print of the creche, the *Adoration of the Magi* which Rene Ricard re-named *The Adoration of the Shepherds* (naked ass on one youth in the manger). I replaced it with Armstrong portrait #2. I prefer Maman because he was first, or because he seems less posed. Both are compellingly beautiful. They might be worth a shitload of cash, but like the obstinate lover who holds tight in his heart to the one long gone, I will never part with either.

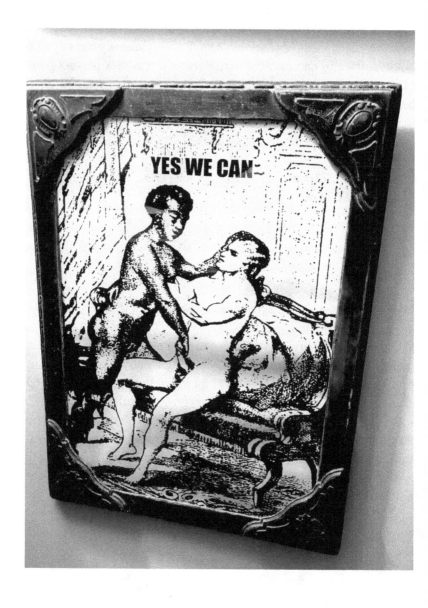

Master/Slave? Slave/Master?

This, to me, is not so much about the graphic or what it implies (fill in the blanks), but about the frame. It was never supposed to *be* a frame. When I was on the phone with my sister, Lisa, it all came back. This was the wood that held the blotter that lay imbalanced on my Mom's desk in the living room in Wayne. It was not intended for boner pictures. The desk, an intricate in-laid chestnut/walnut hunk with drawers that got stuck and where she sat in high curved neck concentration to pay the bills Dad would not. The green blotter was stained like a Rorschach. Mom would be appalled if she saw what now shouts from that rectangle. Hard patriot cock-n-balls, a ready vagina and man control in her hands, which, in some far-fetched way, my mother might have approved of. I love the damn thing. Next to my desk and hidden a bit in the shade to be discovered by some unsuspecting, curious visitor. Will he ask me about it?

TENDER TOUCH

I used to love it when Linda Hogaboom (real name) got down on the ground with me at recess and drew diagrams in the dirt with a stick. Each line was experienced inside me as if being drawn 'down there', or as if traced on my back, carefully and suggestively, as I was lying face down in the sun. At camp, during Capture the Flag, the captain would have to draw the plan of attack with a branch. We would crouch down beside him and listen. My skin shivered as he did it. It was, I suppose, my first sexual experience, drawing.

The fabulous black lady of YES WE CAN knows all about that.

Me, Dick & A Cactus

Tuscon. Lived there four years. Attended the Arizona Sunshine School. Weathered a sandstorm on a cot during naptime. Whiskey on Santa's breath at Christmas, but I still believed in Jolly Ol'. There was the story about a monkey who Tarzan-ed through the house and machinegun shat the walls. There were home movies of L'l Ricky pushed around in a broiling back yard in a baby buggy by identical twin, red-headed sisters, laughing like a duck. I lost the reel evidence in a garage sale.

I've had this photo for as long as I can remember. The glass splintered and was thrown away, but I'm fond of the paper bulge distortion catching light and moved by the seeming happiness and good will the two of us purport. I'm not sure it's real. Dad used to say that he 'felt wooden' around me as a boy. Throwing the ball back n forth was never something I was remotely good at or that he was able to improve. But here we are, in the dry southwestern heat, his hand on my tiny shoulder, a charming cock-eyed smile on his face. We seem ok with each other. I had no idea he was already unfaithful to my Mom. If she knew, she never let on and we were none the wiser.

After the shot, did we lie back on those canvas cots and squint against the red sun? Did Dick let one ride and make me laugh, inspiring a life-long love of gas? Did I realize that 'Dick' was in no way ever going to be my tag? Did he suspect, could I have possibly known, that I'd wind up a homo? Did he know I'd love as frantically, as a romantic incurable? That I would become an artist when he did not, fearing the penniless? That he would die[80], vomiting into his lungs at Tufts Medical on *Christmas Eve*?

---

80   See 'Christmas Ash' *(The Paragraphs)*

We moved to AZ so Pop could start a business which, shortly after he quit, became Armstrong Tile!? Motherfucker! We could have been loaded! Where he and Ma played golf with Barry Goldwater, who famously said:

"I don't care if they are straight, as long as they shoot straight" about gays in the military. Who argued at a golf club that didn't admit Jews*: "I'm only half Jewish. Can I play nine holes?"*

Like me, Dad was a name dropper. Barry Goldwater, Bette Davis. Groucho Marx. Princess Grace. Thing is, he was wicked funny. And quick. And charming. And handsome. Insanely popular with the ladies. I doubt he ever turned one down. He loved women as women, not objects. He really did. He made them laugh. Got who they were. Which is why they fell for him. Handsome is one thing, connection the more powerful seduction. Of course once the booze took over, it scattered the 'broads' as he called them. As soon as they maneuvered to shut him down, he'd throw them to the curb and move on. There was no way in Hell he would stop drinking. In the end, I still believe, his death was a suicide. He wasn't a happy guy. The only song that sang in his heart, as romantic as he was, was liquor. So he drank himself to death on purpose.

I love him. I do from my advanced seventy-five year old distance. I loved how my high school friends wanted to get fucked up with him. His naughty laugh, his phony pipe-in-mouth, his teary readings out loud of love letters from college girls, the ice tinkling vodka glass at an angle on the lawn as he teed off a golf shot, blackballed from all the uppity clubs on the Main Line, making loud un-censored comments about the membership. (Is this where the iconoclast in me came from?)

He won Miss Kansas in a raffle at a Philadelphia bar and brought her home. Her teeth clacked when she smiled.

"Hello. Ricky, is it?" Clack!

Steel trap teeth shut with a brutal incisor shattering smack! The sound of it sent me scrambling upstairs. Did she flash 'em for Pop?

He told Janie three things before he died.

1.   Never think you know all the answers, because you don't.
2.   Never be afraid to love somebody.
3.   Don't be too free with your 'chocolates'.

I Wish I Could Talk With My Dad

FOUND OUT

Tom and I took a long walk out to the rocks in the middle of the farm property on Chilmark, Martha's Vineyard. We'd dropped acid. Everything seemed important. Everything was bullshit. Rick once again going for the farcical acid seduction, the phony build-up to hoped-for sex. We came back from the rocks and went up to my room, moonlight and a kerosene lamp. (The house had no electricity.) He took off his clothes and lay face down on my bed, his body smooth and bathtub white. I 'accidentally' nudged the place between his asshole and his ball sack and he was super hard. I reached under, a giant erection. Biggest I'd ever felt. I rolled him onto his back and was kissing him all over and although he wouldn't let me kiss him on the mouth, he obviously liked what I was doing. Then Dad stumbled in.

"What's going on!?"

I'd forgotten. He'd been with us on and off all day. He'd been at the pond earlier and was staying the night.

"Get outa here, Dad. This is none of your business."

A flourish of sheets and Tom, unsure about the whole thing to begin with, was now hiding safely behind his defenses. We talked about it. He said he wasn't into it. He had to imagine that I was a girl. (No problem.) Eventually we fell asleep. When I woke up later his arms were around me.

Including here the first chapter of the first part (about my Dad) of my unfinished novel: *Armchair General – A Fictional Biography of Dick & Jane.*

Get Out Of Bed *(1928)*

Rit liked to stay in bed in the morning. To sleep in. In his favorite room in his favorite house of all the houses of all of his whole entire life of twelve years. The house on Myrtle, the yellow clapboard two-story with the uncut grass. He had his own room at the top of the back-stairs, off the kitchen and he'd lie awake, eyes half open, peering at the world through a gauze of lashes, dreamlike, listening to breakfast, to his brother's bare feet scudding across the orange and grey, marbled linoleum, to Teddy, his Mama, her laughter belting up towards him in hacking sheets.

"Cut it out, Karl!" (Cough.) *"Damn you!"*

His ten year old brother had untied her apron, the threadbare one with the blue and white Lilies Of The Valley and the torn pocket. Jiggled it loose, nicked it with his knuckles and, as it slid to the floor, spun backwards; a naughty retreat. He thrust his carrot topped head, chin forward, into the icebox, meaty hands around a thick blue glass milk bottle, the guilty flap of his long johns peeled, a chubby pink ass-crack grinning vertically through the gap.

Rit rolled onto his side, pulling the covers over his head. He could picture the whole scene. The repetitive motifs of the Kinscherf family engraved on his spirit like a secret code.

I am this family, he thought. Mama is me. Her smell, like clean laundry, her thick, waist long hair, her big green eyes, my face against her chest. My brother Karl. I am Karl. I know him like I know my own foot. Nothing he thinks falls far from my head. Even laughs like me. Something dirty about it. Dad – black brown eyes, grey, thinning hair,

widow's cowlick, same again, same as me. And he has my name. I am
Papa. Before I get outa this bed, before I make one sound, before I see
my ugly mug in the mirror, I am these four people. I own 'em like the
Brooklyn Dodgers.

"C'mon, Ma. It ain't fair. Rit said trash-out's his turn this week."

He knew Karl knew he was listening, but he wouldn't take the bait.
Wouldn't shout back and have to drag those damn cans outside in the
knife cold air. Nice to hear his name said, however. He liked that. Being
known in that taken for granted way, a piss warm secure sensation
creeping up the inside of his pajamas, sound as a silver dollar. They
are me and they are saying my name, he smiled.

They called him Rit. His name was Richard, like his Dad, but they
nicknamed him Rit. Something about how he couldn't pronounce
Dick as a child.

He hated getting up, facing the music and leaving the womb of bed. He
hated flipping the covers off, being jerked awake by the cold, scuttling
into the unheated bathroom. When they'd yell up for him to get the
hell out of bed, get dressed and get ready for school, he'd delay by not
answering. By playing silent checkers with himself trying to predict
how things were going to be. His corduroys, where were they? (On the
floor, kicked under the bed.) In what position? (Rag doll, face down,
dead.) What's to eat? (Bacon. French toast. Shove half of it into my
mouth with fingers. Teddy'll yell. Then laugh. Shake her head. Wipe
her soapy hands on his shirt. Ma!) What kind of day would he have?
(Blue? Yellow? Yeah. A yellow day.) There's no yellow day, sneered
Karl. You're nuts. Anyhow he usually got it wrong about the weather.
Couldn't visualize it unless it was extreme, like snow, something he
could overhear his Mama commenting on.

"Karl, look at it come down." (Cough.) *"Holy Jesus."*

His Mom was Teddy ever since she was a kid. She idolized Theodore

Roosevelt. Dick called her Ann. When he met her that's how she introduced herself – Ann Maynard Bartoldi. Met her on a stinking hot beach in Cape May. Wasn't interested that his wife was a former Rough Rider. He hated Teddy Roosevelt anyhow. And later, FDR. Hated any Roosevelt.

"Karl. Run up and kick that good-for-nothing brother of yours outa the sack."

"Ma! Somethin' died up there. I know it. Somethin' rotten and bad, and Rit's jus' layin' in it, waitin' for me t' come up an' suffer. No, Ma'am, I won't go."

The spatula hit the floor. Teddy laughed and then she coughed. She coughed and laughed. And then she farted. The laughing forced out the fart and the fart made her laugh. The circle of flatulence. Rit shook his head.

My Mom's a goddamned farter. She'd read somewhere that letting out wind was good for you.

"Ri-it", she called up, dividing his name into two syllables, sliding down to the second. *"You up yet?"*

He rolled onto his belly. Slid his arm into his flannels and cupped his fingers under his genitals. He'd wait for the second call. Ann would take a few steps up the stairs and tap on the wainscoting.

"You alive or are you dead? Karl thinks you're dead."

"Mm, mm."

"Get up and get down here, you hear me? I'm serious."

"Yes Ma'am. I sincerely do."

He couldn't help the sincerely, his latest overused word. Teddy went back to the stove, lighting up. Pack of Camels a day, he figured. A shattering cough. The cigs looked right on her face. Sharp and defining. Always within reach. A snapshot of her with Dick, when they first met and fell in love, barely twenty, arm-in-arm on that boiling beach in Cape May. Dick in a full body, skintight bathing suit, his sex sticking out like a stone. Ann, the carefree flapper in a big straw hat. Cig stuck on her lips then, just like now. Crisp and smart. Like a Saturday Evening Post ad.

"In love and smoking you own the world," he sighed. *"Sincerely."*

He rolled over for the last time. The sun hit him square, making his eyelids red. He could see microscopic tadpoles swimming in blood. Time was up; his conversation with himself over.

Dick was in the john clipping his moustache with cuticle scissors. Slow, deliberate and imprecise. It always came out crooked, like a picture frame which never hung straight. Rit wanted to adjust it, to clip it right, but he never said a word. One of a million things that raced through his head.

"Got a job, Pop."

"And what is that?"

"Paperboy. Delivering on my bike, just like you."

"Gazette?"

"Sincerely."

"Good for you."

Clipping moustaches was too formidable a concentration to interrupt. News like a paper route rarely made a dent in the old man. Worried more about politics. Or Ann's cough. Or about Yankee Jewelers, where he worked until his eyeballs fell out of his head. It wasn't that he didn't care about the paper route. His muted reaction seemed artful to Rit.

He didn't appreciate this fully until later when he got further along and realized how much pretense passed for authenticity. How people performed responses to things out of calculation and habit. He would learn and love to spot a phony, one of his future trademarks.

Today was Tuesday, February 5th, 1928. Winter nearly over, spring about to hit and it felt like the rest of the school year would float away like a helium balloon. More time outside. A dog's life. A baseball summer.

It was easy then. Plain old life. At least that's how he remembered it. Disarmingly easy. Easy to look into his Mama's eyes. Easy to not doubt himself. Easy to have thoughts of his own that didn't threaten anybody. Easy to believe in the self-evident: a father and his boy silent before the sink in their underwear, a son who can laugh at his Mama's irritated mood, a brother – his unselfconscious best friend. The whole portrait, his life and the people in it, made exquisite sense. He had a room to himself, a job, he knew the trees, the back way to school and how to charm the sweater off his teacher, heart unbroken.

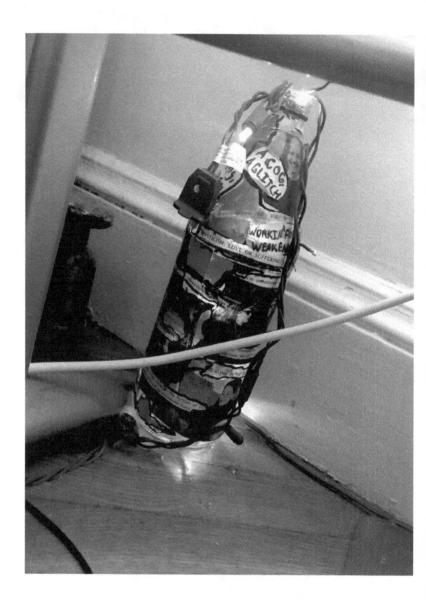

Message On A Bottle

Tommy Dean. Great name, right? Sounds like an author. No need to change that shit. Met him at the Behan. Another one. Alone, but not lonely. A fast talker. A punk rocker. A depressive who keeps the blues at bay by working his ass off – teens in trouble, art, words, music. A sexual Casanova. This one here, that one there. Arms in tight T-shirts, tight jeans. A come-hither bulge. He was always up to talk. Leaping from lily pad to rock to water like an inquisitive frog. Each conversational thread teasing out a new ribbon. A decent respect for talk that matters and doesn't, all at once. He's in San Francisco these days. Doing what? More poetry. Many ladies in the stable, but never a misogynist. He just plain loves women and loves fucking. He makes them want to know him, to be known and to be wanted.

He gave me the bottle before he left town. Brought it to the Behan with its Elmer's-pasted words and images. He just gave it to me out of the blue. I filled it with white Christmas lights, my predictable addition. It sits under my glass desk and illuminates, much like its author, my room at night.

Here's to you, Tommy Dean. Keep fighting the good fight. Keep being true to yourself. I know you will. I look forward to reading your some-day-novel, bursting with sex, like an erection salute.

Mic Unfriendly

There was a young hippie in Seattle (late 1960s) who wandered downstairs where I was playing piano. I'd smoked a lot of dope, found the piano and played, eyes shut and lost in the sound. I didn't hear him come in. I was strung out and improvising. Gradually I began to notice, unobtrusively, guitar harmonies caress, swim, touch the music I was playing. To hold hands with it as if by symbiotic magic. This had never happened. I had never played with an honest-to-god musician. I was in awe of them. I had not even written a song, figuring I was just some crackpot key-banger lost in a delusion that was triggered by whatever drug I could get my hands on. But this was different. This was new. When I stopped, I looked over and there was a young man, a trace of beard, no shirt on, overalls. He was looking right into my eyes, and he was crying. I could see the streetlights from outside reflected in his tears.

"I can't believe it, man,'" he said. "That's the music I hear in my head. Nobody's ever played it before."

There is an inexpressible waking dream in just sound. With no add-on song structure, lyric or goal line to aim for or score a musical touchdown. That simple innocence is the field I plowed for years. No song remotely within range. I'm not sure that this Seattle dude was truly locked in to what the fuck I was trying to say that afternoon. Those were his ears, not mine. But I believe he's right about the extraterrestrial connection that boings around in that rare air. Not unlike the Na'vi in *Avatar*, whose hair braided into the manes of those flying banshee creatures and won their trust. One is taken over by it, the simplicity of just sound, just music, which in no way relates to the ambition that can, out of necessity, addict the artist to his industry.

Ambition is more intoxicating than fame, desire makes all things flour-ish, possession withers them; it is better to dream one's life than to live it.
— Marcel Proust

That kid was on his own planet. As was I. It was only later when that bitch, the ladder climb to success, began to haunt. When I shifted gears and chose to write hit songs (whether they were or not), thus beginning my paranoid affair with the microphone. A love-hate relationship. Partly because, like anyone who hears their voice for the first time, I hated the sound of mine. You don't hear what your friends hear. Your ears misconstrue. Do they lie? They do not.

During my first crack at recording, a reel-to-reel on a table next to a piano in Lenox, MA, I was appalled. Who *is* that? I wondered.

It got worse. Working on the OL record, listening back in the control room, I thought I should try to sound, you know, more rock 'n' roll? Get the fuck away from that big gay Yale Singing Group Broadway tenor. Fat chance. With Berlin Airlift, same deal. We tried mic after mic. Neumann's (the Hitler mic), SM-57, SM-58. None seemed to sufficiently darken or rock-legitimize my sound. I had the voice I had. Deal with it, girlfriend. This was problematic, because my boyfriend, Steven Paul Perry (he insisted on "Paul," not wanting to be confused with Journey) had classic Bad Company pipes. No one ever thought *he* sounded weird. Whatever. Write for *your* voice, Berlin. Learn to like it. Sing *your* songs with *your* voice. Screw the doubting and the doubters.

New recordings with the Nickel & Dime Band sound OK. TJ's[81] been able to post-produce my vocals into something I approve of or have become used to. I sound like me after nearly fifty years in the game.

Working up demos at home, I use this baby. Robby thought it would add warmth to my crappy GarageBand hurry-up takes. The grey foam,

---

81   See "A Forever Cat"

scruffy with cat hair, might help, a follicle transformation of what my vocal therapist, Mark Baxter, calls "the vocal folds." (Picture a vagina.)

Thing is, given my kindergarten recording technique, my voice still sounds odd to me. My sketches – piano, LVs[82] and over-the-top backgrounds – remain sandbox stabs at new songs, which the band ultimately transforms into sonic righteousness and beauty.

Face it, Berlin, no vocal cord surgical transplant "fold" is available on an ice pack speeding in an ambulance to turn you into the Boss.

---

82   Lead vocals

My Benefactor(S)

... have been many. Friends and family who, thank god, believe in my made-up world and speak with their wallets. Dick & Jane Kinscherf, John Frothingham, Peter Walsh, Gary Cherone, TRIIIBE, Jane Mangini, Carol Bednarz, Eddy deSyon, Ellen Wineberg, Andrea Juan, Jane & Chris Clark, David Jasper, Clint White, the phenomenal GoFundMe[83] money contributed by so many friends during my out-of-commission-and-on-the-couch hernia-surgery hiatus, and every member of every band I've ever had who never made one thin dime for all the inspired work, music and time they put in. Without these flying-buttress arms and with no art-pro-quo income in sight, I would never have had solid, hard-copy evidence of the work I've done. The Medici cavalry showed up. I have been Master Pip, they my *Great Expectations*.

Among these, after my family, David Jasper is the longest standing. During the Luna Band era, he was a constant presence. His limo would glide into the parking lot of the Channel or a North Shore venue. Piles of powder would be cut and snorted on a dressing room table. Hash would be pin-poked and huffed. Solid cash would save the day when we most needed it. Over time, he ran into trouble with drugs. He'd call from a motel room in the wee hours, imagining that the exercise lady on the tube was scolding him. He was convinced the Feds were on his case and wrote a book about it, *Me, Myself & the FBI*. (I contributed.) He mailed succinct and challenging op-eds to small town newspapers all over the country. (All were printed.)

Paranoia notwithstanding – and god knows we all felt it from that dirty drug – David was still Santa Claus. Or Hemingway. He resembles

---

83   See "The Blue Ox"

both. His jolly beard, smile, and positivity shined down on the band and on me whenever he showed up. His mainframe predilection was the planes, the jet planes that spoke to him from the sky, predicted his future, and promised the moon. I never doubted his belief. I have my own plethora of questionable, unproven creeds, conjured up out of the ether. Why would the planes not speak to David, no matter how incredible or bizarre? Creative imagination generates a reality as real as any *de facto* material evidence. If Beethoven composed the 9th Symphony while he was deaf, hearing that towering music in his head in advance of pen to paper, why could not David read the signs sent by the planes, trust them and write his own symphony? Same difference.

One night, at an out-of-town rock club, he asked me to follow him. He wanted to show me something.

"Walk ten steps this way. Stop. Make a ninety-degree left turn, walk ten paces, and look up."

There they were, the jets, high in the starry sky, their sleek exhaust trails, hieroglyphs that spoke in code. Dave was beaming proud.

A few months ago I got an envelope left for me at Doyle's. Inside was a check for $500 and a note from David. He had been thinking about me, my age, and the possible end of employment for an old fuck. He wanted me to know that he'd look after me when and if he could. And he has. I am not the sole recipient of his unconditional generosity. There are many others in the Jasper orbit who receive and rely on his help. I try not to.

I could not do what I do without the thoughtful aid-and-abet from friends and family. I try to not feel guilty about it. To be genuinely appreciative and not ass-lick. Like I said, it's harder to receive than it is to give.

None of us ever feel fully deserving of the money gravy, unless it's a Presidential narcissist tweeting and evacuating on a gold toilet.

My Friend, The Chair

Had this baby for as long as I can remember. To sit on, hang towels from or stand on to hammer a picture hook into a wall. It's a classic. Sturdy, plain and design-simple. Shaker? Who knows? Never been up on that. It's darker now. Dru Toews used it as a platform to put a paint can on while he was fixing up his room at 370B. He ruined the surface. (Song for Dru: "Party Dress.") I didn't yell at him, but I did insist that he sand it down and restain. Which he did, perfectly. Of all my here 'n' there, found-object furniture, it's my favorite. Like a friend who lives to be used. To be useful. I feel good just looking at it. Like a dog, long in the tooth, who refuses to die, and wags his tail in spite of the arthritic legs that keep him from standing up. My chair is a dog.

Old Toes

I'm on my feet at work most of the night. My gnarled big toe and the one next to it overlap. I can uncross them with a twist if I take my shoe off, but they pay no attention, returning to toes-as-X seconds later. My boss lady, Mickey O'Connell Sholes, told me to buy separators. Toe separators. The kind they use in nail salons when they paint you up. No beyond-the-nail-itself splatter. CVS has them. Every night I work, I slide the rubber lozenges between the old claws. Toes will now be friends. They will not compete for space in my socks. They will be cheerful and not chafe. The separators do get revoltingly filthy. Or flicked under furniture by curious critters. Or don't make it out of my socks and melt in the dryer. Or wind up under the covers when I forget to fish them out when I make the bed.

Best thing of all? Every time I get pretty to go to work, server on foot, I think of my hilarious, dear, smarty-pants friend, Mickey. With Doyle's gone forever, we don't see much of each other. Used to be at least four, five nights a week. After the Doyle's diaspora, new jobs, C-19, new directions. It's as if we live on the opposite ends of the earth. Fucking sucks. But having to put those weird miniature rubber hourglasses between my nasties brings her back every single day I work.

True toes. True friend.

Once She Was Blonde

This portrait, the little girl with the toy rabbit who became our mom, Jane Porteous (1921), is timeless. The quiet way her eyes draw you in, sitting in an art studio garden, is Peter Pan Wendy magic, as if, at this early age, she knew that one day she would fly.

She had the original duplicated and framed before she died so that each of the three of us could have a copy. I can't tell if it's a water-color, a pencil sketch or both. She made the original frame part of the print. The frame is framed and endearing to notice. When it was painted she was, like my sister Lisa, blonde. As a child, during an ice hockey game, she was hit by the puck, which cracked her skull open. They shaved her bald and drilled a hole in her head (which, years later, she would ask us to feel with a fingertip). When her hair grew back it was brown, like my sister Janie's. Like me.

I wonder: Who *is* this girl, this child? What fascinated her? Hurt her? Made her laugh?

I'll never know. That small kid is as impressionistic a Monet blur as my boyhood. I inaccurately recall what happened to me back at the Arizona Sunshine School when a sandstorm smashed the windows during a nap. Or when a rabid dog on the other side of a chain link fence was buckshot-killed in front of me. Or why the three of us trying to sell tin foil-wrapped turds to neighbors in Oakland thought it was a terrific get-rich-quick scheme. All seem vividly real, but when I bring memories like that up to my sisters, they invariably dispute the details. Maybe the past is fiction after all.

So who *is* my mother?

I never could figure her out. Or my reaction to her. Or my reaction to other people's reaction to her. Not fully. Can any of us? On the surface she appears to be easy to categorize: an upper-middle-class divorced woman of sixty with grandchildren on her mind and a paradoxical queer for a son, who might as well bear children himself because he has the Perfect Apartment for it, not to mention a sort of wife/husband/lover. What a brood we became.

Details:

She liked the color green. She was an OK cook. Jewelry had to be gold, not silver. Bought American for patriotic reasons. Was frugal and generous. Ski-jumped and piloted planes in her youth. A lifelong Republican who played backgammon on the beach with the Kennedys in Hyannisport. Called the beauty parlor the "hair house." Played tennis and golf, both well. Liked to have her toenails painted. Baked herself a deep tan every summer until – who knew? – pre-melanoma dented her skin with surgical lift-offs. Never finished college (Smith) because she had to look after her mom when her sister, Franny, died in childbirth. Liked getting to know our friends one-on-one without us around. Got a bang out of working at the Villanova Cheese Shop with fellow divorcees. Loved the Philadelphia Eagles. Refused to call in sick for husband Dick when he was home with a hangover. Was head of her high school entertainment committee and the editor of the yearbook. Liked to garden, preferred bare feet. Elected best party girl in her class at Smith. An undeclared sculptor whose green clay statue of a naked woman wound up in the garage. Scored a receptionist job in a quack dentist's office when she needed to make ends meet. All about being fair with what she gave to each of her kids. Unforgiving of the overweight. ("Why do they wear those awful short shorts and mini-skirts?!") Worked into her mid-seventies. Partly for fun, partly to safeguard her nest egg and have something to leave us kids. Appreciated peace and quiet after Dad moved out, although the under-the-breath slings and arrows of that judgmental town could sting. Volunteered at the Women's Exchange; believed in the mission. Each of her kids expanded her horizons in spite of herself. Learned Transcendental Meditation even though it was never her thing. (It brought her cholesterol down.) Deeply connected to her niece, Polly. Maine may have been her truest home base. Routine was important. Looking on the selfless side was critical and an example for us – the antidote to Dad's *me, me, me* egotistical carryings-on. It was painful for her when I left for college. Ripped her heart out when the car pulled away. (I never knew this until Janie told me about it years after Mum died.)

And soon, the dream of her life: She's going to Africa, on a safari with a manic-depressive Aunt Bump and her brother-in-law (my Uncle Andy), the husband of her sister, who is paying for both the trip and the camera with the telephoto lens, because he is in love with her. He is in love with his wife's sister, and in the meantime his wife (my Aunt Polly) is grinding to a slow and agonizing halt as she succumbs to rheumatoid arthritis. And while Ma was here, visiting for the weekend, she didn't want to discuss any of this. Nor did I bring up any of the details of my relationship with my boyfriend. She bolted down two vodka tonics at Ken's Pub before we saw *Escape from Alcatraz*, got a bit flushed in the face, and really seemed to warm up to the both of us. Mostly, though, she talked about animals.

"I don't know why," she said, "but I've really gotten to love giraffes."

She told us about Andre, the harbor seal, who is brought to the New England Aquarium each winter. He entertains the kids; later on, in the summer, they dump him overboard, off the coast of Marlborough, and he swims north, all the way to his original home and trainer in Camden. "Sometimes in three days!" (I'd read that people who overly love animals are less fond of humans.)

I noticed later (did I imagine this?) that she took a long, somewhat curious (erotic?) glance at Steven's crotch while we were making dinner. But she didn't kiss him goodnight, and she didn't take a very long shower. I'd read in a magazine at a nail salon that the longer the shower, the greater the evidence of personal sensuality. The detective son grasping at straws, at clues of irrelevance.

Meanwhile, she never confessed to being confused or hurt by the Maine Triangle (Uncle Andy, Aunt Polly, herself), or upset by the goings-on with her children or their spouses, or put off by the outrageous Christopher Street gays at Jimmy Bucalo's farewell party. My mom – the Great Mystery. All and none of the above. It is fair to say we were really good friends. We laughed a lot. We did projects together when I was a kid. She helped all three of us with homework, especially math. She'd stay up late worrying about an algebra problem that confounded. She was tremendous fun. Always. Her dysfunctional marriage upended a lot of that, but after Dad died, she was, for the most part, the good-time Mom we loved to be around. That, and our moral compass – which I both respected and resented. Someone's got to be that for us, right? That she loved us unequivocally is undeniable. That she expected us to be fair, honest and good to each other and to our friends was non-negotiable.

Including here the first chapter from the second part (about my mom) of my unfinished novel: *Armchair General – A Fictional Biography of Dick & Jane* (click on "Jane").

Sammy, the Seal (1926)

Horatio Porteous *was* Porteous Brick & Mortar, the bricking factory that baked the bricks that lined the sidewalks of Portland. PB&M made Horatio a rich man. The color of Portland was Porteous red. Blood-dark and coursing through the alleys, commercial districts, houses and apartments of the city.

He didn't stop there. Though bricks were never out of fashion and bricklayers never in short supply, in 1904 Horatio, with his best friends Frank Mitchell and Andrew Braun, opened Porteous, Mitchell & Braun – the town's first, and for nearly a century largest, department store north of Boston. PM&B made piles of money. These three men and their families essentially, if indirectly, ran the city of Portland for decades.

Horatio had an only son, Johnny, a well-mannered boy, popular, unspoiled and bright. Unlike many children of the well-to-do, he was less interested in expanding his fortune than in serving the community. He went to Harvard Medical, became a GP, and returned home. Well-liked and sought after, he earned his reputation as a decent man and a trustworthy diagnostician. His were among those years of house-call docs; men familiar with their patient's lives, histories and families. Dr. Johnny was welcome in their homes, delivered their babies, mended broken arms, stood watch over breaking fevers. He was funny, he listened, and he loved his work.

"Dr. Johnny doesn't interrupt when you have something to say."

"He never acts like he thinks he's smarter than you."

"His eyes say more than words."

"I just feel better when he looks at me with that quizzical, warm-hearted smile of his."

Johnny's friends were the sons and daughters of his father's friends, a socially incestuous crowd that belonged to the same clubs, gave to the same charities and were guests at the same parties. They stood at the pinnacle of a Portland society which, though not as deep or as well-heeled as the bluebloods of Boston or New York, was no less inverted. A handful of wealthy families controlled the greater part of the city's real estate and business. They sent their kids away to school but preferred to live in Portland, contemptuous of the elite to the south. They indulged in rare but elaborate dancing parties in the fall and winter. (One Christmas, Johnny hired the Boston Symphony for a concert of waltzes, in honor of the birth of his first daughter, Frances.)

Winters were harsh and isolating, but the summer made up for it. Families retreated to Prouts Neck, a stubby peninsula twenty miles southeast of the city. A thumb of rocks, pine trees and sand, Prouts was the gated preserve of the privileged. Over the years it attracted rich families from as far away as Washington, San Francisco, New York, Philadelphia and Boston, but it retained its Portland identity. An eighteen-hole golf course was carved out above the clam flats, smelling of the sea. Clay tennis courts dotted with the handsome-in-white were filled with muted volleys and gentlemanly sportsmanship. A shingled clubhouse served sarsaparilla and lemonade to children who signed for them. A diminutive yacht club clung to a spit of rocks across the bay. Ivy League undergrads taught sailing, ran boat races and anchored yachts. At the Sunday "sing," families were conducted in rounds and chanteys by a mincing Princeton baton.

Unlike Newport or the Hamptons, Prouts was the converse of opulence. Summer houses were substantial, but not flamboyant. The unwritten rule: good taste is unostentatious. Summer "folk" graduated Yale, Harvard or a lesser Ivy brother, but the degree was a matter of course, not something to have one's nose rubbed in. "Cottages" sprang up in the 1920s, fitting snugly in the coves and groves of pine trees, rarely intruding on the landscape.

The Pride of Prouts was the reclusive painter of rocks and sea, Winslow Homer. He moved there in 1887, setting up shop on the outermost point. Though he died before Prouts became a haven for the well-to-do (in 1910), his imprimatur of vision, eccentricity and art lent bizarre credence to the cocktailed. They fancied themselves a cut above their bank accounts or their Groton educations. A delusion of creativity and eccentricity softened and forgave (however circuitously) their ownership of anything own-able on the Neck. If a Real Artist had thought of Prouts as home, perhaps some part of him was a part of them. Hell, they enjoyed the rocky surf, the fog, the pinewoods – a voyeur's empathy. If Homer painted a world made world-famous, they would keep the place unmolested.

Winslow would have been uncomfortable at the cocktail parties that were *de rigueur* over the summer months. His world boiled over with the dark greens and blues of an unforgiving sea. Prouts vacationers kept to warm fireplaces and manicured lawns. They knew not the impartial ferocity of nature. Their summer sea was a shimmering surface upon which to chart afternoon picnic excursions or race children's

Runabouts. Cooking fish chowder, acting up a storm in the Country Club's talent show or sharpening their wits in the back rooms of their parent's parties would not unlock for them Homer's depressive, solitary vision. Nevertheless, he bestowed upon them a disadvantage. Doubt wormed into their psyche. Many drank heavily, or could be found on the rocks at sunrise, head bowed, questioning a marriage, a banker's career, a sexual confusion. At the same time they fostered a snotty pride in being true Yankees, untainted by social registers or ladders climbed. They stuck it out and they stuck together. Their kids went to the same prep schools as their New York and Boston pals, but honored hometown simplicity and loyalty.

"We shall remain independent of those southern sensibilities," Dr. Johnny was fond of saying.

(Any place south of Portland was "southern.")

It came as no surprise to anyone that Wilma Mitchell and Johnny Porteous would marry. They courted for a year and tied the knot on June 2, 1912. A Protestant ceremony took place on a Prouts Neck lawn. A salty breeze curled hair and forced the pastor to raise his voice. When, after a night of champagne, cake and waltzes, Wilma felt Johnny stiffen against her under the covers, she let out a small cry and dutifully allowed his advantage. She was not disappointed when he ejaculated prematurely and fell asleep, limp and snoring like a bear. After an "eternity," Wilma wriggled out from under and crept downstairs to scratch out thank-you notes to the two hundred and fifty who had attended.

On an Egyptian honeymoon, Wilma rode camels and photographed Johnny standing smartly in front of the Sphinx. They spent four months abroad, and when they returned she was pregnant with Franny. Polly followed, and then Janie. As the years passed, they retired the evening ritual and rarely kissed in front of the children, but their mutual regard and affection was conspicuous. Wilma was proud of Johnny's reputation as a trusted doctor. She knew he was a good man who bore her pesky criticisms with humor. When he added an irritating red beard and mustache she nicknamed him B.S. – "Benevolent Satyr."

And Johnny adored Wilma. He looked up and smiled when she entered the room. She amused him with her no-nonsense approach to household and children. She made him laugh, though unintentionally. She was so certain about everything that when caught wrong, he delighted in her refusal to admit it. This made her a target. She secretly liked that she could "get at him" with the obstinacy of her character.

They bought St. Cloud, a three-story limestone, which stood tall and grand on Fountain Street. Floor-to-ceiling windows filled the rooms with sun. A granite walkup led to a red painted door with a brass knocker – a fat man's belly that resonated in the kitchen and brought a maid's face to the window. The entrance hall was two stories high. A rust-colored carpeted staircase rose to the landing like a queen's train. The upstairs rooms were deep and dark and off-limits to visitors. A pitched slate roof lidded the house, covering the attic protuberances like a cowl.

"This house looks like a person," she said. "Like an actual person."

"What is an actual person, my dear?"

"It's obvious. Actual, not real."

"I thought actual meant real."

"No. It doesn't. It means what it says – actual."

"Actually I think you're way off on this, Wilma."

"Look it up."

He did. She was wrong. She snorted about it. She still thought she was right.

"Actual is actual, no bones about it. Dictionary's wrong."

His shoulders began to move.

"Don't you dare laugh."

"I'm not laughing."

"You are. You're laughing at me."

"I never laugh at you, my dear."

"You only laugh at me... Doctor."

He hid behind his paper. She left the room. He exploded with his "B.S. bark," as she called it. She slammed a door. He shook his head.

Wilma gave beautiful parties. Not many, never too late, just-right parties, the first Saturday of the month. Six couples for dinner. She enjoyed creating the menu and arranging flowers. Every Christmas Eve they staged a spectacular. A fifteen-foot Scotch pine, chopped down and dragged home by Dr. Johnny, would be raised and dressed by family and friends. The final heart-beating *coup de grace* found their youngest, Janie, lifted by Daddy, jamming home the uppermost tin star. Everyone cheered. It was among her favorite things in life, and she waited for it anxiously. Theirs was a secure and happy home. No question about it.

In her freshman year at Emma Willard, Janie wrote in a paper:

FATHER
...A strong one, not given to extremes of temper, whose reserve fits him handsomely and entertains a reservoir of shy goodwill and love.

She labored over this sentence. She wanted to explain, if only to herself, someone whom she'd taken for granted. Someone who, in his absence, seemed all the more wonderful. But that was later. Tonight Janie (nine years old) reached up and locked her fingers behind Daddy's neck. She felt stubble where the shaved place in back was delineated in one clean stroke, his hair combed back with opened fingers. She shut her eyes and waited for him to begin a new episode of *Sammy, the Seal*. His voice, warm and deep, would stand on end the hairs on her arm. With eyes closed, nothing else existed. He'd left off where Sammy had caught his flippers in the ropes of a lobster trap and was waiting for Alissa, his best-friend-in-all-the-world, to row out and rescue him. Janie was worried Alissa might not make it. That Sammy would be hurt. But she knew that always, always Sammy would survive one narrow escape after another. This was her favorite part of the day. The fire roared. Polly and Franny pretended to do homework upstairs, and Mummy was instructing the maids about a dinner party.

"You have the most marvelous voice, Daddy," she told him.

Minutes later she fell asleep, her mouth open. Her hair fell across his arm. He picked her up and carried her to bed.

"You spoil that one, Johnny."

Wilma entered the living room as he came downstairs.

"You never give as much of a fuss about the others."

"She's our baby. Our youngest. But I care for them all, Wil, as you of course realize."

"And you love talking her to sleep."

"Won't deny it."

"I miss our bridge games."

"We shall become sick to death of cards in our old age."

"I suppose. Sherry?"

"No, thank you."

He took a pipe out of his vest pocket and tapped it against his open hand. He looked at her. She was tiny next to him. Tiny, but determined – set jaw, hands emerging like tongs from the sleeves of her dress. He noticed that her shoulders shook as she stirred herself another gin and tonic.

"Gin's a summer drink, Wilma."

"As you've told me any number of times. You're a doctor. You know what's best. But I like gin. Gin is not a summer drink as far as I'm concerned. It is *my* drink."

He smiled and cupped his hand over his pipe to light it.

"You're quite a girl."

"I am not a girl. I'm thirty-two years old. You are thirty-five. We're in our middle years. Gin and tonic. What does it matter?"

"Not much, I suppose."

"That's right."

Janie listened from her room off the second-floor landing. The flickering shadows of the railing danced on her bedroom wall. Her door was ajar – a requirement. She pretended to be asleep when he carried her. He wouldn't carry her if she was awake. She'd peek up at his red beard as it moved, like a dry brush, with the motion of his walking.

"You pretend to be asleep just so Daddy will carry you up," teased Polly from her bedroom.

"I do not. I never pretend."

"Yes you do. I can tell. I can always tell."

"It's none of your business."

"Oh Janie. You're Daddy's pet. You wrap him around your little finger. Everybody knows it."

She sort of understood. She watched a miniature Daddy circle her thumb. Like that, she thought.

Johnny Porteous had wanted a boy. He never said it, but that's how it was. Two girls were enough, and although he never admitted it to himself, he fancied his Little Janie an in-between sort of girl-boy; one to throw the ball around with in the backyard, or go for a skate. He bought her first pair on her eighth birthday and walked her to Rowen's Pond. Gave her a push. In a few weeks she picked it up, spinning around, making fun of Johnny's slow pace. He'd retire pond-side, take out his pipe and watch her.

Rowen's Pond, or the Corner, as they called it, wasn't a pond at all. It was a flat section of Peterborough Park, shaded by copper beach trees and edged by the post-and-rail fence that ran along Fountain. Wilma persuaded the city to let her flood it in winter. It froze over smooth as glass.

Today it was snowing and the air was clear as needles, and Wilma had gotten their man, all-around workhorse Ben Ruggers, to slosh Rowen's the night before. She had been right to do it because it froze over "tight as a grin," ready for hockey by Sunday. Janie waited outdoors. She sat on the stone wall, her feet heavy in unlaced skates. She looked over her shoulder, waiting for the nod. For Wilma to come to the window, pull at her shawl, and drop her head – the Signal. Not until then would Janie lace up her skates and stilt-walk on pointy toes to the Corner. She ached with impatience. She wanted to get there early. If she was late the boys would choose up sides for hockey and Janie, good as she was, would be overlooked. She needed the half-hour of extra time to practice her backwards glide.

She waited and waited. She would not budge without clearance. She was put off by her mother's sternness. She had not, in girlhood, spent much time with her. Daddy loomed too large to leave room for a difficult, criticizing Mother. But she knew Wilma was a good woman. The Corner was proof.

Wilma paid Ben Ruggers to edge the rink with bricks, lug the hose across and water it silver-smooth. Then she'd light a fire and thaw him out. Had she not been insistent, the Corner would never have come to pass. Old Ben would have kept to his room. He hated the cold and turned away from her, the tiny Portland society lady, wife of the beloved Dr. Johnny, wrapped in furs and walking alongside as he went to work each season. She sat on a low wall and cheered him on with peeps of enthusiasm, which frosted the air in front of her lips and made it appear that she was smoking – an impression she made no effort to conceal, and a habit she would add to her repertoire years later, a false Bohemian self-portrait.

Each winter, as far back as even Polly could remember, on cold mornings, the Corner appeared like magic. It filled up with neighborhood kids, and it was particularly exciting on Sundays, because it was then that the Porteous girls were allowed to play hockey.

Wilma was strict with her children. She encouraged them to believe that this sport, designed for boys and men, was a reluctant reward for good behavior and homework well done. Janie, being a good athlete, spent Saturday night polishing her skates, setting her long red underwear and mittens out to warm on the mantel and falling asleep dreaming of miraculous, winning slapshots that winged through the legs of a baffled Jamie Sullivan or Bobby Mayfield, making her team captain. She'd come home to cookies and hot chocolate with floating marshmallows, prepared by Arma-Jean, the Haitian cook.

"You gonna get fat, little girl. Fat like me."

"You're not fat, Arma."

"I'm big as a boat."

"You just look like Arma to me."

"Armageddon, maybe."

They'd laugh. Repeating the joke.

"Armageddon's the name of Uncle Spaulding's dog!"

They would howl in unison at an imaginary moon.

So here she sat, awaiting the Signal. She knew it would come. She knew it would be drawn out. She knew that Wilma despaired of her over-the-top enthusiasms. Polly and Franny were already on the ice, breaking in their sticks. This was taking forever. But then she appeared, a half-smile at the window. Wilma held her daughter's eyes for an uncomfortable moment and then, like a reluctant general to impatient troops, nodded.

Janie saluted, yanked the laces tight and tied them off. Walking on skate toes was natural for her. She'd done it a thousand times. She looked like a crane on a mission, torso jutting forward, eyes luminous, heart pounding. She clicked along *en pointe* until she reached, in minutes, center ice, where she was chosen by Jamie Sullivan with a shrug. It was as if he was saying yeah, you're a girl, but you're the best there is out here, and although I won't admit it out loud, I know it and you know that I know it. We'll win this game like we won the last one, like we'll win the next.

Janie wasn't conscious about this wordless communiqué, but the import was clear. She saw the puck in slow motion, zinging across the ice toward Bobby. She blocked him. The puck hugged her stick and the goal – two top hats lent by her dad – in the crosshairs. Then something happened. A twig or bit of cloth caught her skate and she tripped up, backwards. Her feet lifted into the air, and the sky opened above like a sheet. It seemed to last forever, that fall, but in seconds her head hit the ice with a crack. She tried to get up. She pushed with her hands. Jamie and Bobby leaned over. Then Polly and Franny. They saw blood, an expanding stain soaking the snow and ice shavings under her head. Polly screamed. Franny pulled off a mitten; she was going to put it under her head to stop the bleeding.

"Don't move her!" shouted Bobby. "Go get your dad!"

Franny ran home, tears streaking her face.

When Janie woke up, Dr. Johnny stood over her, Wilma grimly beside him. Janie's head hurt. Mother and Father looked like dolls.

Weeks later, she explained that she had to wear a horrible hat (she hated hats) because her hair was growing in funny, and it wasn't blonde anymore. It was brown! She was mortified. She missed being the only blonde in the family. And then there was that hole, the hole in her head.

"Here," she said, "feel it."

She took Polly's hand and brought her fingertips to the spot.

"There?"

Polly snatched her hand away. There was an indentation, and she felt something soft and squishy beneath it.

"I can feel your brains!" she cried. "I can feel your brains!"

The bad news was that that was the end of it as far as hockey was concerned. She could not be coaxed back to the Corner to watch. She didn't want to hear about it. She stayed home doing odd chores for

Wilma – sewing, rearrangements of glass horses on the mantel, folding laundry for Arma-Jean. Wilma paid her a dollar a job. She saved the money and counted it every afternoon in her room. She kept it in an old sock she stuffed under her mattress. Polly caught her counting.

"What are you saving for?"

"Secret."

Little One (the letter began)

As I sit here in my red leather chair, the bowl of my pipe warm in my hand, I realize how much I miss you. As you well know, I love all my daughters with the deepest unmitigated affection. But it was you, Janie, who sat in my lap those early winter evenings and whom I carried to bed each night. And thus it is quite impossible to sit here with only myself and my pipe and not be reminded of you. Your hair was blonde then, cut into a bob like Mother's, short bangs like a waterfall stopped in a photograph. Your eyes, your big sea-glass green eyes, would look up at me with such wonder. Believing Sammy was real and in deathly trouble. That his story existed without my telling it, and that sooner or later you'd find him winking at you from the waves at Prouts. Did I ever mention how worried your mother and I were the afternoon of your accident? At Rowen's? We wept that long night, before you woke up. It was indeed a miracle that you survived and have become a young girl, away from home and away at school. No doubt you will perform well at Emma Willard, much like your sisters before you. Mummy is planning a wonderful Thanksgiving, and Grandpa has promised to carve. You know how shy Horatio is about being asked. But yesterday he volunteered. He left a scribbled note informing that, as it was in fact Thanksgiving, he felt it his duty. I often wonder if Grandpa's stilted formality is something his son, your father, will inherit with age. Polly writes that you have written something about me. I don't know if you'd consider it appropriate for me to read, but as you can imagine, I'm dying to. Polly said it was lovely. I am planning a short trip to Harvard next week. Mother insists that I buy a new suit for the speech I am expected to give. She's even suggested I trim my beard! I promised her I'd consult you on that one. Alas, my hand cramps from writing. This is a relatively long letter from your silent old Daddy. I do miss you very much and hope to see you in a few short weeks.

Father

Janie looked up from the letter and wept.

"Anything wrong?"

"Just a letter from home."

Dr. Porteous packed a slim suitcase. He borrowed a suit from Frank Mitchell. He trimmed his beard to a point.

"You look like that dreadful Freud."

Wilma saw him off from a drizzly Boston & Maine platform. The coastline zipped by at a musical clip. Johnny put his forehead against the glass and thought backwards. His life seemed to be moving as quickly as the train. Horatio would soon be gone, the girls married.

They changed conductors in Andover. A new man was to take it in to North Station. He was drunk. As they chugged into Manchester, he misread the signals and barreled into the caboose of another train. It burst into fragments and fire. Johnny's car derailed. He was thrown out of his seat, across the aisle and through the window, splitting his head open. He was killed instantly.

The coffin was closed at the funeral, but Janie leaned up and kissed the top of it. The rosewood surface was cold. She was startled. She made a face. Franny pinched her leg. Dr. Johnny was buried up behind Portland General and the girls returned to school. Janie felt estranged, lost. She remembered how brave Wilma was, that she had cried only once, briefly, at the service. If Mummy could be strong, then she would too. She finished the first semester third in her class.

Party Shoes

Same as work shoes. I wish I could own some real party shoes. A pair of kick-ass boots. A pair of hip-hop Day-Glo sneakers. Smart, slim boy leatherettes that ride cool under a nifty cuff. But duck feet and busted toes make that impossible. What I wear to work I wear onstage, at weddings, funerals, bars. The heels erode and unbalance my posture so that in a year or two I need to head back to Marathon Sports and pick up a new set – DK black. Yanked off after work, slathered with pizza juice, ranch dressing, ginger ale and beer, the laces are *hors d'oeuvres* for the kitties. They gnaw, pull, chew and lick, even before they're free of my throbbing feet.

At Reagan International, when T.J. and I flew to D.C. to film the Tomb of the Unknown and the Vietnam Veterans Memorial for the video of the song "Unknown Soldier," I got me a first-ever sneaker shine from a cute Latino. My "dogs" (as Dad called shoes) got the full burrito. Three layers of sauce, each sneaker slap-polished and buffed. Skillful hands on feet. I think the dude knew my deal. Felt the customer attraction and rolled with it. Part of the gig: humor the homo. I would have stooped to conquer behind a monument wall and had a moment with him if it had been remotely possible.

"My beautiful wife," he said, showing me her picture.

"Totally," I answered.

(One never forgets these encounters.)

I doubt many people actually notice the shoes we wear. Girls in stilettos? Different story. Those beauties sashay sexy legs down the runway of dreams. You don't need to be gay to notice that shit. But dudewear, not so much. I mean, yeah, I notice. The crisp shine of dark maroon leather under a pant leg. The latest low-boy sneaker. The chef clogs (which seem miserably uncomfortable). The so-gay penny loafer.

"That one's high in his loafers."

Of them all? The flip flop is my nemesis. I won't wear them. I can't wear them. They slide off my feet. I cringe at the soft up-slap against heel: *plip, plip, plip.*

There was one time, however, that I got over myself. I met this kid who told me his name was John (which, now that I think about it, was the perfect pseudonym), and he wore those bastards. Black 'n' white horizontal stripes over the instep strap. Worn down. No socks. Big feet. Pretty toes. He was taller than me. Short black stallion hair, brown eyes, smooth skin. Sicilian. I met him at Doyle's. He showed up out of the blue with a co-worker from a nearby restaurant. He seemed to like me, so I slipped him my phone number while his friend was taking a piss. He called me the next night.

Thus began my return to ganja. I hadn't smoked in years. The annoying paranoia onset turned me off.[84] But John had weed and wanted to smoke. Was I gonna say no? He lit up a bowl and the earth shifted. Nothing happened, although we hugged goodbye, and the smell of his hair, the softness of it against my face, was hot as hell.

Thus began a series of encounters. A late-night booty call. A pick-up. Smoke. Talk. Head. I loved his angular body. His cock. Ass. Armpit hair. The gasp he made when I fingered him. We did it in my car, hand up his shorts, unable to wait.

"Dude. You make me so fucking horny."

---

84   See "In the Weeds" *(The Paragraphs)*

He never slept over. Drove him home after orgasms. Then it stopped. He disappeared. The flip-flops no longer pit-pat in the Factory parking lot.

A classic "John."

Peter Barrett & Moosup, The Musical

Backstory

1968. You could get a draft deferment if you were a teacher. No boot camp. You wouldn't have to train to kill or be killed. Done with Yale, I found a job teaching what they called "Special Class" and art to middle-schoolers in a tiny, one-street town in Connecticut called Moosup. Less than an hour's drive from New Haven.

I brought a Smith Corona portable, an acoustic guitar (which I could not play and never would), a book of *The Collected Frederick Nietzsche* (seriously?) and a camera. I moved into a boarding house on Main Street, Mrs. Grenier's. A narrow bedroom with a walk down the hall to the john.

I settled in. Began teaching five mentally challenged students in Special Class; beleaguered Down syndrome kids, wonderful to be around. They did take flak from the un-special. I had to rescue Tony, who'd been lined up against a gym wall as seniors fired basketballs at his head. He was laughing. Drool fell from his mouth. Cynthia wore high heels. They pocked on the linoleum. She wore a ballerina's tutu to class every day. She had a Jack-o'-lantern smile. We took a class trip to Mystic Seaport. I loved how wildly different we were from the "normal." If I remember accurately, flattering myself, I got them out of school and into paying jobs where they would be OK. Then I quit. (I'll get to that later.)

I also taught art class to 4th graders. Kids that age have an already-art gift. What they paint or sketch has an un-self-conscious freedom and beauty. I mailed one of their brightly colored landscapes to Ethel after Bobby was assassinated. I doubt she got it.

The heart center of my time there was not at school. It was across the street at the Aubert house – a grey, two-story shingled shack at a nervous tilt above the river. Camille, the mom, had left her husband in Pennsylvania, fleeing abuse. I'm not sure how it went down, but I wound up with Cam and her kids nearly every single night. She'd cook dinner and tell stories. Scary stories. One about a killer back in PA who'd sandwiched a murdered child under a bloody mattress. She knew about the body and turned the guy in, terrified he'd find out and come after her. As she was telling the tale, one of her boys snuck outside, pressed his face against the living room window, tapped on the glass and screamed. We hit the floor in mock terror.

Since early adolescence (with one unremarkable gay bar visit), there'd been little going on in the sex department of my repressive life. My Zanzibar roommate (Yale) took me to a Manhattan whorehouse where, duh, I couldn't get it up, even from an overly solicitous *"just relax, baby"* prostitute. But that was it. I avoided any pretense of acting on or even hugging a boy I was interested in.

I knew, like a fever in my gut, that I was attracted to Cam's eldest son, Leo. I think she knew this in some back-in-Pennsylvania coal-mining-town way. That bisexuality was not considered unusual or frowned upon. It wasn't gossiped about or shamed. Boys with boys. Men with men. Boys with men.

She had me tattoo a butterfly on her upper thigh, the thread wound around a hot needle (as instructed), Cam squirming and giggling underneath. She had several boyfriend visitors. I imagined one or two of them shared Leo's bed. I assumed that because of what happened later. He seemed to know his way around that block.

One night she chased him all over the house, wrestled him to the ground and announced that she was going to "de-pants" him. She hung him upside down by the ankles and pulled off his red corduroys. He was laughing, that sort of sex laughter that has a smell to it. I couldn't look away. I swear it seemed as if they were both looking at me as if to say, green light, Rick. It's OK.

"If you want, you can sleep over. There's room in Leo's bed."

So up I went. Slanted ceiling. Posters of Brando, Elvis and Dean. A sway-backed mattress. Clothes all over the floor.

This happened just about every night. Dinner. Bed. Desire requited. Up at sunrise, climb out his bedroom window, clomp across the porch roof, drop onto the grass, hurry across the street to Mrs. Grenier's, shower, dress and get picked up in a truck by another teacher and driven to school.

We were inseparable. We ran all over the fields and woods, out of breath, laughing, eye-to-eye. We'd meet up after school on the big yellow school bus and ride in back, bouncing off the seat into midair. We huffed glue. I floated up to the ceiling, stuck up there looking down at this kid; black and blue hair, black eyes, no front teeth (he wore a denture clip that he clicked in and out of his mouth). I bought a Kawasaki 650. With Leo on the back, we drove all over the place. To a nearby lake incredibly early one morning, riding through the frost, his arms around my waist. To Providence, Boston, Northampton. Spending *Lolita* nights in motels.

Eventually, I decided that I had to leave Moosup for good. I couldn't handle it with Leo and Cam and his family any longer. It was ripping me apart. I was becoming possessive, more demanding of his time. Jealous of his other friends. He even began a campaign against me, calling me a fag. The unmentionable. I refused to call it that. To call myself that. To think that the gentle, circuitous love-making that took place in his room, in the moonlight when the rest of the house was asleep, on his bedspring-noisy bed, was anything to be ashamed of. That he loved me there was no doubt, but I began to worry. Even though this was not an episodic aberration, and that I was not the only man he slept with (there had been the sailor he told me about who stayed over in his room), I was terrified of the mob, of pitchforks and torches, of community exposure. Maybe I could have survived, but how was Leo processing what we did together in his head? In his heart? Best for him with me out of the picture. So I fled. I ran away. I quit the job and climbed onto the Kawasaki and rode home to Philadelphia. The bike I sold to buy the blue truck that carried me across the country to Steamboat Springs, Colorado, and my next (and last) abortive teaching job.

I dropped off the 650 in Newtown Square and drove back to Moosup in the fucking Oldsmobile. I packed it up with my stuff and crossed the street to say goodbye to Cam. She made coffee. Leo was at school. We talked about him. She didn't mind. She must have known about us, this Tennessee Williams *Rose Tattoo* of a woman. Very little got past her.

"I know, Rick," she said. "I know. For you, the sun rises and sets behind my boy."

I asked her to wash my hair in the kitchen sink. She used to do that a lot, the country music station blaring in the next room. I asked her to do it as a final ritual, and she did. It was grand. Then his sisters came home and hugged me. They had helium balloons from school. They put them in my car. I kissed them all goodbye and drove away crying. I could barely see the road. Somehow I made it home, ending the longest, the most enduring emotional and physical current between myself and another human being I had known. I drove straight to Newtown Square. When I opened the car door, one of the kid's balloons floated out onto the driveway. I didn't see it and stepped on it.

Bang!

I looked down at my foot and saw the shriveled yellow scrap of rubber dead on the asphalt. It was like the gunshot that George used to kill Lenny. I went upstairs to my room and closed the door and burst into tears. Ugly, choking sobs. I went inside myself and closed off to everyone. To my parents. To my sisters. To my friends. I started wearing black, all black. Black turtleneck, black pants, black socks and black shoes – the *Hamlet* ensemble. I didn't speak to anyone for days. I drove downtown to the dangerous part of South Philly, got out of the car and walked around in the wee hours, hoping to provoke an attack on myself, a chicken suicide. But nothing happened.

And now look at me: a card-carrying queer. Disco bars, New York baths and blather. Emotionally, I was far afield from Moosup. Leo and I slept together every night for months. I'd wake up and look at his sleeping face in the moonlight and in the morning sun. I'd get dressed and climb out his window and jump down into the grass, scramble across the street and get ready for school. Avoiding scandal. Avoiding everything. But we were, for that brief, shining Camelot moment, fully a part of each other's lives.

I've written pages and pages about you, Leo. I mailed long, wordy letters of love and assurance, hoping to keep us together from far away. But what counts, and always will, is the timeless quality of how we were together. I see it now as if through a prism, a sliver of glass that looks in on those days and nights, at the two of us laughing and falling into the arms of love and cool sheets when nothing about it was ill-conceived. I imagine your thoughts of me every day, as you, I wonder, imagine mine. Do you still have my letters in a box, and the Bowie knife? Do you remember me and know that I still love you? Who can say? I try to picture you as you must be today, but I can only see you as a kid.

Walking home last night, under the stars, I realized that only once in my life, and for only ten minutes, was I embraced by someone, for real, both of us naked, an embrace of heart and passion in your bed. An upstairs room on Main Street, Moosup. I can still feel your arms around me, your hair against my neck, your breath at my throat, my surprise at this sudden burst of undisguised emotion. Your knees against the side of my legs. Your body pressing against mine.

When Lilian and I visited you at your father's place in PA, we took a long walk up the hill that rose behind the house. It was dusk, and we sat on a rock and gazed out into the valley. Your brothers were racing around and shouting in the distance. You turned and looked at me. Your eyes were super dark, the blackest black. Deep pinpoint light shone out, flashing.

"Do you remember that night?" you asked. It had been a year and a half ago.

"How could I not?"

We sat there awhile and then ran down the hill. There was no way we could arrange to sleep together. Lilian and I had been given the upstairs bedrooms. His Dad and his brothers were stretched out on the couch and on the living room floor.

"Leo has all your letters and the pictures you took and the Bowie knife you sent him in a box up in his room," his brother confided.

He looked more handsome than ever. His body was longer, leaner, country strong. I fantasized that he slept with that older kid who lived on the neighboring farm. The one who played accordion. It was the last time I saw him. When Lilian and I drove back from California, we looked them up at their supposed change of address. A shanty-town, a coal town up in the hills, with one decrepit, abandoned ware-house. But there was no sign of them. Wind blew newspapers about like leaves. One lost-looking kid was leaning against a streetlight.

"You know the Auberts?"

"Nope."

I have a photo of Leo and his friend, laughing in a tree. I shot it. Developed it. Framed it. He'll always be a part of who I am, even as I have, until now, hidden the details out of respect for that time, for him, for us. But as much as it was so intense a physical attraction, what it was, honestly, was love. Body, heart, soul – that rare trifecta. More than once I have passed someone on the sidewalk, at the airport, on the trolley, who looked like Leo grown up. How odd it would be if we looked right through each other, unable to recognize the person we loved, whose bodies we held so tight.

Several years later I was able to find his phone number. He was living down South. Married with kids. His son picked up the phone.

"Is Leo there?"

"Who *is* this?"

"Tell your Dad it's Rick."

"Rick!? From Moosup!?"

"Yup."

Leo called me back later. He said he was no longer "that way" and that I wouldn't like him anyhow. He'd gotten fat, had a potbelly, and was going bald. I said if he ever got up to Boston we should hang out, grab a beer. We never did.

So now what? Write a musical about it? Are you fucking kidding me?

It starts with **Peter Barrett**...

...about great men: they are often a little odd, they inspire in us a feeling not so much of respect as of intimacy. We detect in those who possess grandeur something of our own spiritual essence, what is best and most pleasing in us, and we laugh at them in just the same way we laugh at ourselves."
– Marcel Proust

I met Pete in New Haven. He lived upstairs with his boyfriend, Hank, at our big three-story house on Howard Avenue. None of us had money. Howard Ave. was in the sketchy part of the 'hood so it was rent-cheap. Pete shopped artfully at thrift stores. Hank, a seamstress, would upscale crappy throwaways and make them Milan fabulous. They were a perfect ethnic black-and-white couple, the first actual gay relationship I'd encountered. Hank was the guy who made Peter look at himself in the mirror and realize that he was handsome in spite of an upper-back scoliosis curvature. Hank turned Pete's self-deprecating sense of how he looked upside down, and his encouragement in front of "the dusty mirror" wound up in "Doris Dreams," Orchestra Luna's signature composition. Being totally out and living just upstairs, these two nudged me so far out of the closet I never went back.

"I'm going back in the closet. I've had it with all the 'we're here, we're queer.' I'd rather *not* get used to it." Peter, 1980s.

Of course he didn't mean it. He was just making his familiar wry, un-PC Barrett remarks.

He met and knew many of the fifteen-minutes-of-fame personae in the big city. Fran Lebowitz, Rene Ricard, his pal Buddy, Gerard Malanga. Peter was a New Yorker living in New Haven. One night he took me to the Continental Baths, the Manhattan equivalent of the Roman. The lighting was designed to flatter the body, to make one look one's best, one's sexiest. Even old men look as if they had smooth skin and attractive shapes. There was a swimming pool with a lion's-head water spout and designer tiles, two steam rooms, a pool table, massage rooms, grope rooms so dark you had to "feel" your way through, an orgy room, a dance floor (where Bette Midler famously got her start), two white baby grand pianos, non-stop pounding disco, porn flicks, a health food and juice bar, and your choice of book locker, full locker or a room, which cost $12.50 for the night. You could stay as long as you wanted, or as long as you could stay awake. It was impossible to get any sleep even in the quietest of rooms, because sex was whimpering and hissing and groaning and screaming at you from all corners.

Everyone wore a plain white terrycloth towel or went completely naked, wandering up and down stairs, in and out of steam rooms, checking out the possibilities and hoping to score a perfect one-time fantasy. You never had to talk. It was pure, anonymous, zipless fucking and sucking. The place was hygienically immaculate and nobody bothered anybody. It was safe as could be (before AIDS).

I talked it up with Joey, who worked there changing beds, hauling piles of dirty towels, jacking up the exercise bars, tucking in the waterbeds and refilling the mouthwash dispersers. He polished and wiped down the luxury-liner disco mirrors, the jukebox glass and the bathroom porcelain. He'd worked here for months, making people smile, a cute, on-the-floor and at-your-service Puerto Rican. He was the youngest in a family of five boys, and they all slept with him secretly. He'd never known sex as anything other than gay. He was a popular soldier boy in Vietnam, and just as popular here at the Continental. Gay life in this building, shut off from the outside world, was as frictionless as K-Y jelly.

Upstairs were prison rows of single rooms, the size of a sleeper suite on an overnight train, except that they were made of grey metal walls and had chicken-wire ceilings with a single orange lightbulb in the center, often shaded by a pair of underwear or a T-shirt. Everywhere the sound of men sucking, farting, kissing and choking on cock pervaded. Some of the doors were left open, and you could watch guys jerk off or pose in clichéd pornographic positions, or make it as threesomes for passersby to witness and get off on. All ages, all types. Boys as young as fifteen (although accounted for by some well-heeled sugar daddy).

I arrived with Pete around two in the morning: show-time at the baths. We'd driven down from New Haven. It was not until the early hours of the a.m. that I met someone I liked, a blond-haired *Freewheelin' Bob Dylan* lookalike who turned me down flat. He preferred a thirty-five year old, balding department store salesman who still had his shoes on. I saw him French kiss a grotesque-looking fat man in the steam room. To each his own. I wound up with a plumber from Cape Kennedy. He'd driven all the way here for a four-day weekend. He looked terrific. Eighteen, had a build like a wrestler and ice-blue eyes. We fooled around for about ten minutes, until he had to leave for the long drive home. He had a stash of Black Beauties to keep him awake. He left me his room to sleep in, but that was impossible. The guy in the stall next to mine was being given a loud and graphic lesson in the art of the proper blowjob. His first fellatio, apparently.

The lighting never changed. You couldn't keep track of the time. It's always dark, fireside-psychedelic, warm and protective. It never seemed debauched or sick or wrong or bad. It made you think that life should be more like this – instant sexual gratification, without games, in a totally sensual environment. Shower up, do it again, no clothes, no explanations, no autobiographies. I felt my gay identity clearing up like the air after a rain. I felt calm, without love, but oddly loving.

One Saturday night I was approached by an Armenian businessman, around thirty-eight, with a Richard Burton pockmarked complexion.

"Would you like an Indian massage?"

East or Native? He had a hairy body and was short and wiry. He reminded me of a dwarf Rasputin. He wore black-rimmed glasses. I was nervous and thought a rub-down would relax me. Stupid Rick. It hadn't occurred to me that he wanted sex. I said no.

"Do you want money? I'll pay."

"No thanks. I wouldn't feel right about it."

But he persisted, and a hippie from Allentown said I should accept the dough, but only on my terms, and for not less than ten bucks. So I searched around and found the Armenian in the grope room, and he wanted to do it right then and there. I insisted that we have privacy. He went upstairs and rented a room. I was completely passive. I shut my eyes and fantasized about the plumber as he rubbed my back and happily finished me off with fifteen minutes of sloppy head. I wouldn't let him kiss me and I wouldn't go near his dick. He told me I was beautiful and, in a way, we both satisfied each other. My one and only hustle, and I made two bucks! Two fucking bucks! I was too embarrassed to make a scene. He must have seen right through me.

"Don't tell anybody about this," he said.

(My tombstone: a two-dollar blowjob at the Continental.)

I met a boy who'd been a Salvatore Dali model. Dali had him strip naked and wander around a Paris party cradling a red silk pillow with a centered pearl. Dude wore fluffy feathery coats and wanted to visit me at Howard Ave. Kid was sweet, but fifteen minutes of Surrealism was enough.

Back to Barrett.

He'd stop downstairs, stand silently, and take in whatever it was I was working on. I'd be painting my wall on an acid trip and his eyebrows would rise above his glasses. He'd turn and leave the room; a mute *harrumph*. I always, always wanted his approval. He presided at the local porn store with a dry expression and a circumspect disdain for the customers. I'd visit, check out the mags and clientele, one eye on Pete, my guide to all that mattered in art, porn and gay.

I heard him read his poetry at a tiny local storefront gallery. He rotated a spindly aluminum chair backwards, sat down and read, legs outstretched. It was astonishing to watch and to listen. I'd never seen anything or anyone like it. He wore his trademark hobnail red-and-black boots, which he'd painted and stud-decorated. My eyes went from boots to face, his words pounding in my head.

Once the band began to coalesce, I asked him to move to Boston and join up.[85] A wildcard spoken-word singer-performer who capped off

---

85   See "In the Dunes"

an already bizarre concept. He arrived, named the band and settled in, more or less. He seemed restless. Wondering if he should move on, if Boston was the right town for him.

We tried several absurd money-making projects. "Two Typists" – farming ourselves out as rewrite stenographers; a bust. "Boys' Underwear for Girls" – our graphics on tighty-whiteys. Another bust, but good for a laugh. We considered ourselves brilliant imaginers.

Moosup, the Musical

If you've read the backstory, you know what an absurd idea this was. But the songs and the principle characters were terrific, as was Barrett's book. I wrote the songs that made Moosup go 'round. Pete, the story. A love story between a young man and a boy. Good going, Kinscherf, an obvious hit, right? The *Springtime for Hitler* investors will flock.

We worked it up, songs OL2 actually performed: "Special Class," "Moosup Is Dead City", "Dear Kate," "Long Distance." Peter's script is dead in a drawer somewhere. I doubt anyone would put something as incendiary as that on stage, but we were crazy free back then. I would still love to see it mounted. I really would. Won't happen in a million years, unless as a drag show at Machine on an off-night. (Ryan Landry?)

At the dead end of OL (Pete had been in both versions), he took off for San Francisco, the homo heartbeat of the U.S.A., and formed No Sisters with his two brothers and a fourth. It was truly the end of an era, the end of the most liberated art epidemic I've known. A profusion of unrestrained ideas and liberties taken. Peter was the shining caboose on the end of that train. None of it would have been half as interesting or groundbreaking without him. I can still picture him in an empty Orpheum writing up the OL setlist in his trademark handwriting, as we took for granted how easy it was to be opening up for Roxy Music, the Boomtown Rats, the Mahavishnu Orchestra, the Pointer Sisters, Split Enz – riding high without the constraints of real-world Icarus vertigo.

Pete contracted AIDS. My roommate Charlie and I went to visit. He was the same. Had a boyfriend – when did he not? Was clear-eyed about his decline. He had become, for a skeptic, out-there spiritual. Trying all remedies, just in case.

God, I miss him. I miss his fraught belief in me, my writing, my sputtering, helter-skelter artistic landmines.

"Will you stop having so many ideas!" he'd yell at me outside rehearsal.

There has never been anyone remotely like him in my life. My biggest regret is that my friends of today, those I've made post-Barrett, never got to know him.

A NIGHT OUT WITH HUSTLERS

Peter, Charlie and I would hit the Other Side (a Mafia-owned gay bar and Frenchie restaurant across the street from Jacques – Nan Goldin did a full book on the place). It was there that I met Holly Woodlawn and stood face to-face with David Bowie after a Ziggy show at the Orpheum. More to the point, it was where I met Timmy, Mario, Frankie and Billy, who became the Orchestra Luna II song "Greyhound."

The three of us decided to go to the Howard Johnson's on Boylston St., where the hustlers and the Other Side lowlifes hung out after the bars closed. The view of the city from our cab looked like Wonderland as reflected in the Charles. I pressed my forehead against the taxi window and looked up at the stars. The restaurant was jammed with drag queens and hustlers with acne and waitresses jacked up on too much coffee. I nodded out at our table, head in arms. We had to wait a half-hour to be served. We gave up. Raked a few cups of jelly and marmalade into our pockets and left. On the way out the door a young queen, seventeen, the one in a Cleopatra wig, threw us a big glossy smile.

"*He-ey*," she crooned.

"Seen Timmy?" I asked.

"Yeah. I'm livin' with him."

"Where?"

"436 Marlboro. Way up."

Next day I stopped by. A tough-looking teenager with a poodle shag met me at the door; short, brown-bruise rouge, tight leather jacket.

"Timmy live here? Or Frankie?"

"Yeah."

"Can I see him?"

"Wait."

She looked at me suspiciously, chewing gum and tapping one foot before going inside. She left the door ajar. I could see a mattress on the floor in front of an empty fireplace. A blond kid was asleep, twisted around pillows. A single light was on but didn't do much good. The apartment was bleak and dark.

"He's in they-ah." Pointing.

It was a small, square room just off the living room with a double bed that took up half the floor. I imagined a lot of sweaty Quaalude fucking. Three, four at a time. Cigarettes afterwards, casual affection. Timmy was passed out on the bed. His hair was in his eyes. A Springer Spaniel was on the bed with him. The dog looked like a junkie, yellow scum on his eyelids. So did Timmy, but what did I know? I'd never met any for-real junkies. Maybe he was exhausted. Up all night, night after night. I pulled his big toe.

"Hey, Timmy."

He lifted up his head.

"Yeah? Uh... Rick?" He smiled.

"How was New York?"

"Crowded."

"Did you like it?"

"I hated it."

"Wanna go out?"

"You kidding? I can hardly stand up."

"Tired?"

"Yeah. This is my dog."

The girl came in.

"Where's Frankie? He out workin'?"

His face got real hard, a lot of lines. He almost screamed. She left.

"This picture is great," I said, pointing at a small framed photo hanging above his bureau. Five kids. Looked like kindergarten or first grade. All leaning against each other and laughing. It had an offhand feeling about it, the opposite of this place, this life of drugs and sex and anger and paranoia and desperation. Maybe I arrived at the wrong time.

"Gotta go. Late for rehearsal. I'll be back."

The blonde on the bed in the living room was the same one who was at Howard Johnson's last night in the Cleopatra wig. He got up and stumbled into Timmy's room, flopping down on his bed, pressing his sex into the mattress.

I left. I imagine they did it afterwards. Maybe not. I felt like the little old lady I saw in the Arboretum. She'd accidentally bumped into a couple making out in a small grassy enclosure. It was a sunny afternoon. The girl was giving her boyfriend passionate head, bobbing slowly, rhythmically up and down, up and down. His eyes were closed. It probably got them off, doing it out in the open like that. The little old lady had to catch her balance on her cane. She stared silently and then shuffled along. A walk in Nature on a lazy blowjob afternoon.

On my way back to the subway I heard a shout. Sounded like *"Rick!"* I turned around and all I saw was a couple, arm-in-arm in *Saturday Night Fever tawps* and *bawttoms,* staring romantically at the sidewalk in front of them. A far cry from the boys of Boylston.

"Timmy and Mario. Frankie and Billy. They come to the city, leaving their families so far behind..."

KITCHEN

Pete got up from his chair at the table to get a napkin. He left a glass of water behind. I didn't know this. I emptied the glass of water and filled it up with apricot juice. I sat down with my plate of rice. Peter stood next to me with his napkin.

"Get up," he said.

"Get up?" I asked.

"You're sitting in my seat."

"Sorry."

I moved and started in on dinner. Mindless eating.

"Where's my water?" he asked.

"What water?"

"I had a glass of water right here. It was in a glass just like yours. You probably dumped it out and then filled it with apricot nectar, and you probably didn't even realize it."

"Sorry."

"I'll just drink the apricot nectar."

"OK."

POST SCRIPTUM

The sound in the back of his throat when he let go. – a lyric from a song I wrote about Leo, quoted by Chet as something he had to accept when we played shows.

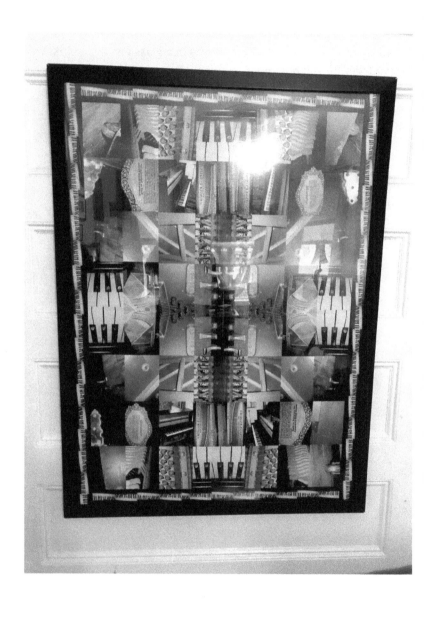

Piano

Musicians Who Make Visual Art: a theme for an exhibit at the Paradise Rock Club. Let's see. Hmm… I'll do two. Photoshop collages. One based on the Green Street neo-hippie house, the other of the upright at my Piano Factory loft. Art pal Jeila Farzaneh,[86] a phenomenal originalist painter, saw both and assured me, "They'll fly off the walls, Ricky."

They did not. Cost close to a G-note apiece to frame. Nobody wanted either, but I got to keep 'em.

Here's the thing. As a kid, I learned to play on a baby grand. A Steinway. A gift from Mom 'n' Dad. With no room for it in any of my railroad apartments, it was sold, the money divvied up between the three of us. From then on it was church-discard uprights, hoisted and edged into third-story windows by drunken piano movers. Those tallboys were old, hard to tune, but gorgeous furniture. What made 'em cool were the tacks I pressed into the hammers; a harpsichord ping to each note, more whorehouse honky-tonk than Horowitz, but the brassy burst inspired me. Best of all? With the tallboy you get the sound smack in your face. Open up the levered panel and it's brass-band loud.

The fella above was the last of the breed. Each sector of the collage is a clip of one section of the instrument. Gorgeous in the melancholy absence of the full monster.

An acoustic piano is almost human. The keys smile. Step on its toes and it sustains. If you lower your forehead to the ivories, it's like head bumping a cat. It's musically versatile. You can play rhythm, chords,

---

86   See "The Mouth That Roared"

bass and melody all at once. You don't need to be some hot-shot whiz-kid prodigy to make it happen. I'm self-taught. The fingers land where they land, and sometimes a song rises to the occasion. When I shut my eyes and play, on a good day, worlds collide and lead to an unexpected planet.

Mine's electric these days. A bright red Swede Nord.[87] Durable for all my banging, but not cheap. A heavy carry. I envy the guitar player who can sling his arrow-quiver axe over his shoulder and write on a hillside. Piano is not that. I have to actually fire it up, sit down and hope. I miss the ol' acoustic. Miss it like a phantom limb.

---

87   See "The Big Red"

Picture Bats A Thousand

I met Eddy deSyon at the Paradise (a bleak gay bar on Mass Ave., now defunct). My roommate Charlie and I were out and about as usual, hoping for anything or anyone. There he sat at a small café table in the dark, a slender pencil of a boy, super smart in the eyes, as if nothing could get past him, blond, chain-smoking unfiltered *butts* with a mellifluous French accent. He was sitting with a friend who wondered why Eddy would be talking to "those old guys." So the fuck what. We hit it off (friendship karma). One of those we-will-never-sleep-together-but-will-always-love-each-other things. Eddy remains, as Charlie put it, my Friend-for-Life. He calls on my birthday (I seem to forget his). I can hear him light up. Big inhale. Big exhale.

My sketch of him as a small child listening in his father's inner sanctum (his dad was a famous Swiss shrink) hangs above his desk in his office at Sal de Bain (his house in Geneva), as does the above in my bedroom (his art). When we visited him *en Europa* (at his expense), he and I took turns on his massive concert Steinway: my song, your song, a musical show-and-tell. I flashed back to his tiny room above Kenmore Square where I hammered away on his rented spinet, gagging on fumes from the India Quality restaurant downstairs, inspired by his detached expression, as implacable as Gertrude Stein's, his omnipresent *Gauloises* and espresso cup.

It was there that he witnessed an unspeakable horror: a homeless man walking up from the basement engulfed in flames. His overcoat soaked with whiskey, a lazy cigarette dropped on the alcohol wet and ignited. He was stumbling up the stairs just as Eddy was leaving his apartment. Smoke was everywhere. He called 911 and then he called me. The alarm in his voice I'll never forget. The man expired in the hallway, blackened, a burnt match of a human being. I wrote "Man in Flames" about it. The one time I performed the song, a woman spoke to me afterwards.

"Please. Never play that song again. It's excruciatingly terrifying and sad."

It was a near-empty Paradise that first night, dropping names, bragging about my songwriting (trying everything). After countless beers and countless cab fares, we sort of fell in almost love. We wrote poetic, non sequitur letters back and forth, sometimes every day, but never kissed. He'd play Schumann's "Scenes from Childhood" (especially the delicate, near-whispered movement, which I've asked him to perform at my funeral) as I sat on the floor of his kitchen. We never made out. Our hips never touched when we hugged goodbye, but when I'd leave the building, I'd turn to look up from the sidewalk and he'd be standing there in the window looking back. Always.

He is, or was, obsessed with the music business. His ambition, immaculate. Everything came into play: his repertoire and gift as a classical pianist, his historical cognizance of contemporary music and biography (Serge Gainsbourg, his idol), his tongue-in-cheek pose as pretty-boy-of-the-week for industry pederasts, the spending of the family fortune on studio time and session musicians and even throwing champagne parties for, I shit you not, the King of Cheese (a Swiss zillionaire).

He learned all about *Whatever Happened to Baby Jane?* from Charlie, mastering and recalling all the favorite quotes. *Yes, fine. I'm pleased that you have a friend. That's what you need.* He loved Charlie even as he was, like many, confounded by him (another story).

Our friendship is proof of my belief that once one is truly soul-connected, it is, regardless of maintenance, a forever thing. Catching up is elucidating, but unnecessary.

Eddy loved the Orchestra Luna record. He was the instigator for our reunion at Ryles Upstairs. He programmed his synthesizer to include the full orchestration for "Doris Dreams," achieving what seemed an impossible feat.

So, yeah, this guy matters. He's been through a few battles of his own and survived. He "comes from money" but is one of the least lazy people I know, and he has a mountain of work to show for it. His first band, Les Joyeux Hippies, was wonderful, young, innocent and kid-sexy.

The drawing? An endearing composite of details personal to our time together while he was at school at BU in a double major, Proust/Piano. The inevitable taxi, the cock 'n' balls matchstick, the many homo conversations, the curious eyebrows (his and mine), the snow mountains of Switzerland, the burnt edge, the guitar as well as the meth-scratchy rush (he was a fan) of the pencil.

I wonder. Will someone, long after we're both gone, find this drawing and make sense of it? Probably not, but he or she will make their own interpretation, and that's exactly as it should be.

Pull Hard

After Doyle's shut down, they held an auction to sell off the one-of-a-kind memorabilia that made the place what it was physically. I refused to go. I didn't want to see the clothes ripped off her body, the rape of beauty and memories. Everything went. They even sawed off the four barstools attached to the floor at the front door. Sawed 'em off at the ankles, an amputation. A Mafia hit. Having that place go down hurt badly enough as it was. Many of us still have Doyle's PTSD.

My friend, bartender and server Jill Petruzzielo, snagged this puppy for me. A JP Music Festival beer pull. A local company gave Doyle's a full keg for free, which, when sold, would plunk a donation into the festival bucket. Not sure how many bought the beer. It might have been shit, who knows? But here sits the pull, cockeyed on my bureau. A reminder of two major parts of my life and countless friends. I love how whacked it is. I love that Jill thought to get it and save it for me.

Here's what she wrote about Doyle's. (She gave me permission.) It says, better than anything I've written or read, what it was like to work in that place.

GOODBYE DOYLE'S

I have calluses on my hands from years of carrying ice buckets, scars on my right-hand index finger from opening thousands of bottled beers, and my arms have random burns from carrying trays of hot food. My knees are in bad shape and will most likely need to be replaced before I'm 50, my hips hurt every time it rains, and I have bruises all over my body from years of Sam bumping into me with his bony elbows. I only have two sets of clothes in my wardrobe: Doyle's clothes and office clothes for my other 40-hour-a-week job. I have used and abused at least twenty pairs of running sneakers, and I am convinced that the only reason my dog cuddles me is because I constantly smell like cooking grease. The last time I didn't work six days a week was before I graduated college in 2013, and I have missed countless cookouts, gatherings with friends and birthday parties because of it. My body is used to not sleeping and running on autopilot, to the point that I've considered getting "Now We Literally Lay Jill Down to Rest" on my tombstone. If I had a dollar for every time someone told me that I worked too much or asked "why do you do this?" I would have enough money to buy the Celtics. So, why do I do it? Why do I sacrifice my personal time and my body three nights a week even though I have another full-time job? Because love isn't a strong enough word to describe how much I enjoy doing it. Do I get sick of the food? Yes. Am I ever just not in the mood? Yes. Am I too tired to work sometimes? More often than I care to admit. So, what gets me through it? What drives me to come to work not just on those days, but every day? The people. What makes Doyle's closing so hard? Leaving these people.

THESE PEOPLE. I have never met a more selfless group of people in my entire life, and I will never work with a better group ever again. I started at Doyle's when I was 16 years old, and these people have truly molded me into the person that I am today. I will never forget everything you guys have done for me. You guys tracked down my North Face jacket that a customer took by accident three days after Christmas when I was 17 and brought it to my house. You got me a goodbye cake when I moved away to college for my freshman year. You called me on my 21st birthday when I was away at school and made the front room sing "Happy Birthday" to me. You helped me write my college essay. Even two weeks ago in the middle of the craziness that was Doyle's closing, some of you took the time to drive to Foxborough to go to my grandmother's wake. You taught me about loyalty, teamwork and how to take care of others. and I'll never forget it. Don't get me wrong, I learned a few things from my parents, too, but you are the second family that I never asked for and now can't live without. I love all of you, except you Erik. From the bottom of my heart I'm so grateful for all of you, especially you, Gerry, for bringing us all together. I wish we could have done more for you.

That is just a list of the stuff that you did for me, never mind the other people in the community. It is so admirable the way all of us, including the ghosts of Doyle's past, drop everything when one of us is in need. We have been dealt our shitty situations over the years and rallied through them together. From putting on a fundraiser at Florian Hall for Joe when he had his stroke, the golf tournament for Billy Shaw, muckball for Gary, the party in the backroom for Billy when he got cancer, covering Rick's shifts when he had his surgery, to passing an envelope around to cover Sarah's rent when she suddenly lost her mother at age 21, we truly look out for each other. We need each other now more than ever. This doesn't just go for the staff, this goes for everyone that comes into Doyle's or feels connected to us. Losing Doyle's is terrible, but losing the customers who made it so special doesn't have to be included in that. Please stay in touch. It has truly been the experience of a lifetime getting to know all of you and watching some of your families grow up. I have enjoyed it more than I can ever begin to tell you.

I always knew that there would be a day that I would leave Doyle's, but I never thought that it would leave me. I so looked forward to someday having my rehearsal dinner, my kid's birthday parties, and future "I don't feel like cooking" pizza nights there. I'm still light-years away from having children, so there is plenty of time for me to plan what other bar I inappropriately take them to, but it saddens me to think that I won't be able to share a huge part of my past with my kids the way that my family shared theirs with me on our many trips to Triple D's (my grandfather's bar). Finally, I want to thank everyone who reached out to me when they found out about the closing. I haven't changed my profile picture in four years, but I took the time out of my day to share this five-paragraph essay with you, so clearly Doyle's means a lot to me. I appreciate your support and encouragement during this time because I really needed it. I know that we'll all land on our feet and we'll all get other jobs, but I dread that process, because I know it won't be the same.

There will be a day when I won't have calluses on my hands, the scars and bruises will all be gone, I'll have the best knees that modern technology can give me, but I guess only time will tell if this heart ever heals.

Scrapbooks

One

Two

Three

I keep them hidden under the bed, collecting dust mice and cat fur.
They're huge, heavy and in disarray – seams torn, plastic split, photos deteriorating. I was obsessed with them a couple of decades ago,
Scotch-taping photos from boxes of memorabilia into full-page collages. Bits ripped from porn mags, discarded flyers, rock-club dressing
rooms, letters lost. My early and midlife categorized and imprisoned
between black cardboard covers. Little Ricky at a picnic. My sisters with
frozen expressions, hating to be photographed. The face of a boy I once
knew whose name I've forgotten. The skateboard hero with a boner
hidden under a flower stick-on. Two friends, one who looks exactly
like Kafka and the other like DiCaprio during his *Gilbert Grape* period.
My nephew, Sam, as a baby, naked in a tub. I hide 'em because of the
ubiquitous state of undress. HBO up-front caveat: Adult language.
Nudity. Weird. After I'm dead I won't give a fuck. Maybe those left
behind will unearth the big books and alarm those who never knew
or only suspected that side of Berlin.

I considered an art gallery exhibit. Each scrapbook page mounted on
pristine alabaster walls. My songs playing softly in the background.
Plastic cups of shitty Chardonnay. Moldy cheese and crackers. Rotting
grapes. The curious confronting the disturbing. These scrapbooks
were just one more art project. A frantic activity of torn tape, scissors,
jigsaw placement and eye candy. They are not my heart or dick, even
as they encroach upon them. My heart belongs to, well, if you've read

any of these, you already know – youth. Eroticized emotion, re – or unrequited, taser to the solar plexus.

NARROWING DOWN A DILEMMA

The Freemen were supreme in that quality the ancients called "Spannungsgenen" – which is the self-imposed delay between desire for a thing and the act of reaching out to grasp that thing.
— **Frank Herbert,** *Dune*

The younger one **always** *has the power.*
— **Dr. Hooker**[88]

If it had been given me in that period to create my God, I would have fashioned him with the body of an adolescent – like an ancient Kouros, with thick fuzz on his cheeks, solid knees, slender waist and holding the world on his shoulders as though it were a calf.
— **Nikos Kazantzakis,** *Report to Greco*

I'm not a pedophile, but if I were to put into a time capsule a photograph of what I thought most beautiful, it would be that of a fourteen-year-old boy.
— **David Sedaris (loosely translated)**

I was essentially not interested in making it with the young, because if I was interested in sex only, then heart truth (which I idealized) would wind up in the garbage. Once the idea of sex surfaced it would be mishandled, communication dissolving into charade and nothing left except instinct: the chance to see and touch that place underneath clothes, to feel his erection, to taste him, to embrace his naked body or to imagine his now-safely-controlled, on-the-edge-of-control self, his too-cool persona, break into abandon. All and none of the above.

---

88   Who got into trouble during the '60s when he wrote medical deferment slips for draft dodgers

Put another way, I was more interested in the give than the get (who isn't?). Even though fantasy loomed large, the aching thundercloud of desire had me worried he would miss the point. That he would interpret flat-out sex as an absence of love, or worse, that there had never been anything like Real Love in the first place; that he had been "had." That he was just another pretty boy that I wanted. A sex object that I didn't really give a shit about and that the whole buildup of getting to know each other was a sham, that it came to this, his nakedness. And so there was a weight, a heaviness about my loving, the heightened intensity of the withheld. There would always be an elaborate, unspoken hands-off policy. If sex was ever to occur, when you came right down to it, *they* had to seduce *me*.

Jake comes barreling in the front door and sits down, legs out front, heels on the shag rug. He looks amazing. Black hair, long to his shoulders, thick dark eyebrows that connect at the bridge of his nose, full eyelashes that make feathery shadows. His eyes are enormous, dark and deep. They look right inside you. He has a mustache. It isn't bristly and it isn't fuzz; more like a watercolor brush stroke. Sharp cheekbones. His face blooming with life. Long fingers, a tall, thin body. Eighteen years old. Accomplished sophisticated B 'n' E's with middle-aged Mafia dudes. Stealing Persian rugs from Harvard professors' houses in Cambridge. A lot of heavy drinking and drugs. I imagine him semi-naked, outdoors, a river, twilight, an unwavering regard, frankly sexual. I remember that Brick told me that he saw some guy blow Jake once in the basement and that when it got hard his penis curved inwards, towards his belly. Jake asks if there was anyone I was in love with these days. I said I was solo, heart in mouth.

A few months later, in warmer weather, I stopped to watch a Krishna chant on that cement island in the middle of Brattle Street.

"Hey, Rick! How ya doin'?"

It was Jake on a bike.

"Where ya livin'? Still over in Allston? Wait! I'll get some paper. Pencil. Hold my bike. I'll be right back."

He disappeared into the crowd. My heart was beating like Thumper. Minutes later he was back. He wanted me to dictate to him so he could write it down. I rolled the bike his way so he could use the seat to write on. He said no.

"Put your leg up."

He wrote down the address on the paper. On my thigh. Got hard right away. He said goodbye and vanished. Next I heard, he was in jail.

THE EVIDENCE QUEEN

You, Dirtbike, recalled a few nights ago that this second attempt at a book is the result of the Joni Mitchell Syndrome: the need to be in love to make art. Much as I archive, much as I want to litigate proof of us, it could never be as vital as hearing your voice at the end of your video clip of a field in Santa Barbara as you zoom in on the roofs of buildings:

"This is the airport."

That scrapbook could never be built. It lives elsewhere, undiluted by the inaccurate. It cannot be frozen on a scrapbook page under my bed.

Stars & Stripes & A Gilded Eagle

Dad brought home the bird. Nailed it above our walk-in fireplace. You could almost hear it squawk, "Ready the rifles, gentlemen! Fire!"

It annoys me that patriotism and weapons are in bed together. "The Eagle has landed" (on the moon) is a happier reference.

I was naïve. I thought Mom 'n' Dad, lifelong Republicans, knew whose side to be on. I had a signed letter from Dwight D. on my teenage wall. In retrospect I admire that rare Republican, Mr. Call-it-like-it-is-a-military-industrial-complex, outing the lethal money grab that is on perpetual war footing. If anyone could get away with it, it was Ike.

I Like Ike.

If my parents were alive today, how might they have voted after 9/11? After "Mission Accomplished"? In 2008, for a black president? For Trump's fake tan, fat ass and con-man persona?

Patriot?

After running all over Mexico, nearly imprisoned in Guadalajara, Montezuma's Revenge in Mexico City and a regrettable sexcapade in Acapulco, I breathed a sigh of relief when my bus drove past the checkpoint into Texas. Home to the familiar. I remember seeing a kid throwing rocks at a stop sign.

"Yes," I thought. "My country 'tis of thee."

After two weeks in Europe and the plane landed at Logan, I wasn't about to kiss the tarmac, but I was happy to be back. What I realized is that I *am* American. It's what I know. It's where I live. Patriotism based on the home fires. On friends. On family. On those who pierce my heart. I'm not French. Or Canadian. Or Czech. I'm Ugly American. I do, however, loathe the strident salute, the self-righteous hand-on-heart hard-on for the National Anthem, when we've become increasingly income-lopsided, fearful and cruel. If it made a difference and I had the right forum, I'd take the knee with Kaepernick. *That* sings Anthem to me. *That* feels American.

Still, I like the crisp, carved golden feathers. Hoisting it high in my room reminds me of Dad, as it inadvertently focuses a foggy brain on what's really at stake. That we are One Planet full of at-odds nation-states. An alien invasion, please. Bring us to our senses, all for one and one for all.

Yup, naïve.

Steve Brown Frames The Band

I love this photo of us taken at Porchfest one summer when we set up outside the McLean garage. I pinned it up in the small kitchen at Doyle's as a poster advertising a gig. It was taken down, the removal of the out-of-date. I forgot about it until, weeks later, I got a present from Steve. He'd framed the photo. I was floored.

Steve bartended at Doyle's for as long as I can remember. We pissed each other off. I was impatient to grab drinks while he was jawboning regulars. Oil and water. Went on like that for years. What pulled the rabbit out of the hat and calmed the antipathy was my friendship with his kids: Sam and Molly.

Molly is the girl who at seven wrote a short story called *WHY??!!,* which, at that age, is the Number One Question. I can hear her seven-year-old voice screaming it out loud and clear in a pretty-in-pink little girl's bedroom. I cast her in the Nickel & Dime video "Daddy's Got A Girlfriend." She played my father's college girlfriend (whose name was also Molly), pretending to write him a love letter and trying to cry.

Her brother, Sam, is as shirt-off-his-back a guy as you could ever hope to meet, and crazy clumsy. Breaking glasses into the ice chest, over-pouring beer, squirting whipped cream like a subway tag all over the walk-in door, spilling creamy Italian dressing on the floor. As a dropper of everything, I can relate.

At long last, Brownie and I buried the hatchet. We respect each other. Keep texting tabs, share the pre-melanoma skin condition and dermatologist. His is worse than mine. His day job is outdoors, sun blistering a bald head. Doc had him burn off epidermis and hide in the shade. When IBEW (the International Brotherhood of Electric Workers) Local 2323 went on strike, he gave me a T-shirt.

> *A scab is a traitor to God, his country, his family and his class.*
> **— Jack London**

I wore it proudly. (They won the fight.)

Funny, how the once inimical can sail into a safe harbor and respect each other. Steve taught me that.

THE BAND

How incredible it is to be a band for ten-plus years running. How rare, given the musical chairs of drummers and bass players. The songs hang together like the junk in Ricky's garage. Each musician, like each garage artifact, seems to appropriately fit, to belong both as person and player. The records are proof. In the jagged little pill that is the deteriorating music industry, we found no home but live well on the street, lucky to have scored countless shows and fans. We've been fortunate to know each other in the rush job that is the high-speed honeymoon all bands face when they "marry." Somehow, with the amicable divorces of former players, we continue to bloom. The quick photo (Jane Mangini Photoshopped into the upper right corner, barely visible), shot by a friend that afternoon, happy in front of the garage, more than any hi-res glossy tells our story, Dimes and nickels scattered haphazardly on a sidewalk next to chalk art drawn by a little girl.

Stop Action

… is an iPhone app. Painstaking, one-at-a-time single shots collected and stored in my phone that make it into a music video edit. I keep the kitties locked out. One false jiggle is fatal – the whole shebang falls apart. The careful placement of a toy car or dog miniature could be nosed off the grid by a curious critter. I'd have to start over from scratch. For always-in-a-hurry Berlin, such a catastrophe is unthinkable. Just look at Carlotta in this picture. She's down to hit that shit.

A tripod is essential gear in stop action. The aluminum stork was the best I could buy for the money. Spindly, skittish, but sufficient. The cam must not move. I need to keep my phone plugged in and powered up while taking one clip after another, a process that can take an hour and a half.

One day I'll have Carlotta see how far she can get with a project of her own.

"You try. You try to make a stuffed toy mouse twitch-move in Stop Action so you can stare at it and chase the beastie in *your* kitty movie."

Stud Shades

A present from gal-pal Kelly Ransom. I sat on and cracked an earlier pair. She replaced them, a solid back-atcha. I wear these fuckers proudly, knowing how bitch-queen they look as I get compliment after compliment from total strangers.

"Dude! Those shades rock cock!"

I should have been Rita Hayworth wearing these in a red convertible, a flaming scarf Isadora Duncan-ing out behind in the Hollywood breeze. Or a dark dude in a dark bar, with shades promising a more dangerous person than I could ever be. Or Herbert the Pervert on the beach, surreptitiously ogling the nearly-naked from behind rose-colored lenses.

I lose the best ones. Leave 'em on a table, under a chair, crush 'em in a rush to grab a seat on the subway. But these? Hang on, Berlin. They define you. I'm not sure if they block the ultraviolets, but I don't care.

Lady Ransom is a special breed of woman. A whirlwind. A shaker and a mover. Fearless in the face of obstacles. Works for under-the-radar folks in need. A City Hall maven. I've never seen her in a bad mood. This girl shows up. Keeps her promises. Dresses loud. Makeup out to here. A torch song of hot. A friend at a glance, not requiring coffee talk, dinner dates or extended conversation. She reads the lay of the land like a tweet on her omnipresent phone. Hate the overused expression, but here it applies.

Kelly Ransom is a force of nature.

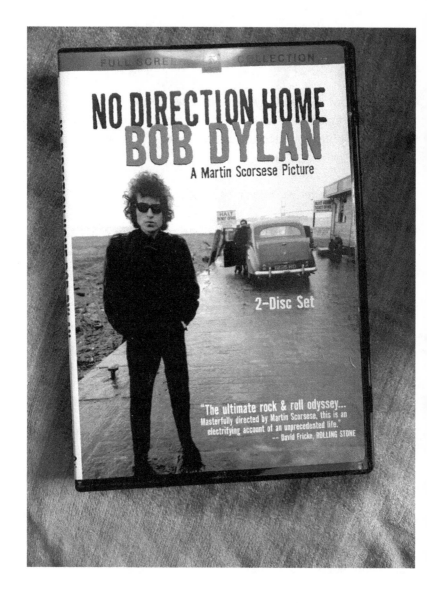

The Blue Ox

... is our JP Big Man, Shamus Moynihan.

Where to begin?

One thing's for sure, he won't like it that I'm writing about him. Keep-Your-Personal-Cards-Close Moynihan is an Empire State Building of intimate secrets. He'll hide his and keep yours. He's not a blabber-mouth, even as he likes to gossip.

No Direction Home, the DVD which he gave or loaned me a few months back, is monumental Scorsese. Shamus is the hardcore fan of what I'd call "true" music – unproduced, or under-produced. Not that he looks down on the weird, electronica or over-the-top. Case in point: as we parse through the 100-plus applications from bands to play the JP Music Festival, we take turns shifting course in the selection process. Shamus will pick a glam band. I'll tip my hat to Americana. A cynical job, axing out music that bands have labored over for years. Berlin/Moynihan, a pair of fake A&R reps. Thank god our conversations aren't recorded.

"We balance each other out," he says about our co-sponsorship.

Not so sure about that.

Shamus handles the permits, the odious, frustrating trips to 1010 Mass. Ave., the long table meeting with department heads of everything to do with the city. He books the food trucks, hires PA and stage, cuts the checks that pay the bills, wanders the field on the day-of to collect and squirrel away the gate donations, hires a crew to move the leftover crap into Bethany McIver's basement, orders T-shirts and hoodies, rents and returns the errand truck, nudges Mayor Marty onstage, locates the bus stop ads and the solar panel speed limit sign at the corner of Perkins and the J-Way. It's an endless list of horrors I couldn't and wouldn't ever want to be responsible for. At meetings with the important, my fucked-up ears misunderstand everything said. I sit there mute, pretending to listen, as Shamus bats away every question and concern. The massive JPMF tent would never go up without this "very powerful person"'s (a Nick Blakey quote) hands on the steering wheel.

What do I do?

I manage and chase down bands and MCs (before, during and after), sort and hire the backline, run John Casey's Bar Wars, Della Street the notes from the infrequent committee meetings, create the two-stage set-up and set lengths, dream up crazy shit like the stuffed squirrels in the basket – that hilarious flop[89] – compose the Dear John letters to the not-chosen, flyer the town with ads and scare up volunteers for Mike Condon's barker-teams-for-cash-donations (the sole reason we are able to pay bands), and hit the Behan when it's all said and done for ten minutes before I collapse at home.

Together we wander the hood with a tin cup, soliciting local businesses for sponsorship dough. Together we hang the glossy Burke Distro banners, choking them off with zip ties in all the optimal locations, and take check-it-out selfies. Together we back 'n' forth wacko-vs.-workable ideas.

How's that for balance? Shamus's weighted end of that seesaw hits the ground. I'm up in the air with a paper stick of spun candy. OK. I came up with the idea. Well, not really. It originated with Ben Crouch after a joint gig at the Lizard Lounge.

---

89   See "These Guys"

"Why isn't there a JP music festival?" he asked.

I took that ball, ran into Shamus at the Laundromat, and the rest is history. Honestly, I don't think we ever gave Crouch the credit he deserves. But fuck it, we started the motor, and the damn thing took off like a rocket, nine years running.

> *I don't care whose idea it is as long as I get the credit.*
> **– Barry Keating**

Met the big man at the Behan when he was doing a lot of walking back 'n' forth, back when he was drinking. A lot. More than I ever realized – Berlin, the Oblivious. At the fest, before he gave it up, he'd fill a bottle with vodka and drink throughout the day. I thought it was water. The sauce caught up with him, and after a couple of relapses, he's been on the wagon for at least six years. Like many drunks, he's the same person to me, fucked up or sober, the difference being a healthy liver. When he was drinking, he'd be right up front when a band was onstage, singing his lungs out, eyes closed, one hand on his heart. I have a photo of him that way at a CD release for Nickel & Dime. We were playing his favorite: "All in This Together."

We rarely just hang out. He has his world of work and friends; me, mine. We spend time when the festival heats up. He bought his own car. We used to do a lot more driving around before that, but the Berlin Taxi is now obsolete. Thing is, we don't need to spend undue hours together. Neither of us requires unnecessary personal attention.

He works for the city, a glorified meter maid. Got bumped upstairs (typical for the indispensable hire he soon becomes), and is now the dude *in charge of* meter maids. Great money, a pension (which is to me an unheard-of miracle), a fabulous schedule and a lot of war stories. He's a fantastic storyteller. Comes with the Irish. I've heard him speed-talk the same anecdote more than twice, repeating it word for word, without sounding bored with himself or the re-tell. In a roomful he can hold serious conversational space. I retreat.

He has an encyclopedic memory. Names, tales, rules and regulations, assholes to write off, laws to follow, new start-ups, meat bodegas buried in Eastie. He could write the book on common sense (of which I am consciously ignorant). He'll make – he already is – a superstar politician, the beneficiary of years of skeleton-closet wisdom. He's a great self-taught cook. Grows vegetables and ganja like a Green Giant. He can build a tip into a tipping point. If there's a new pot shop in Somerville with a Weed New Deal, he's on it, and he tells the 'hood. He's the go-to guy when you land in trouble. He loves all kids and animals. He works his iPhone in a Millennial frenzy. That thing is attached to him like a third arm. He has an ever-expanding circle of friends, and he looks after them like a non-invasive parental hovercraft. He initiated, count 'em, four GoFundMe's for friends in need, myself included.[90] Mountains of relief money raised. Shamus just gets it done. You don't have to ask twice.

There was one time when I pissed him off, asking, "Are you OK?"

He was passed out, or nearly, on a couch in the stinky "green room" basement at the Midway that first year, when we tried to keep things going after the music ended at Pinebank. We booked bands who hadn't made the cut for an afterparty – a freaking disaster. Nobody showed up. He looked dead to the world. I asked again, "You OK, Shame?"

He went ballistic.

"Don't you ever, *ever*, ask me that question again!"

I have not.

I'm lucky to have this guy in my life. I am honored that he's my friend. We all are.

---

90   See "My Benefactor(s)"

WALL OF GLASS

It's hard to sort this out, the closeness and the distance I feel in groups. I'm an inveterate one-on-one dude. The intimacy foxhole. I have never been a raconteur. I don't tell tales well. I'm impatient. I omit detail. I can write it, but I need to edit, revise, think through and clarify the story beyond a cloudy recollection. I never had the gift of the live retell. I admire those who do, but I am not among them. So it's weird at times to find myself on the shy periphery of a group of friends where I contribute nothing to the cacophony. I don't get drawn in, nor do I draw in. It's as if there's a fuzzy invisible shield between myself and my friends. They are, for real, nine times out of ten, true compadres. I've had memorable one-on-one conversations of depth, humor and reveal. But in a group, there I sit, lost in my head, looking elsewhere for a solitary barfly, or a spot for myself alone as I mentally sketch a Lautrec art-watch. This doesn't make me sad or lonely. I like it like that. It's always been this way. If I thought that nobody I cared for gave a shit, I'd be upset, I suppose. What is it Adam Wells said the other night?

"Rick, you are a fly on the wall, and I am a flyswatter."

Sums it up.

The Coffin

... is what Dad called it. It has that look, but without the corpse. A small child could fit in there snugly playing hide 'n' seek. Other than the Grandfather clock, this is my fave after-they-died artifact from Mom 'n' Dad. Initially I used it to prop up the flat screen, the $150 piece of shit I bought from Nepal. Nepal?! (It took three deliveries for one of them to make it to my apartment in one piece.)

It's been promoted to my bedroom. It looks handsome there, the pine lid chipped and scratched from wear and tear, but still gorgeous. I keep towels and linen in the wooden vault. In the smaller side section: old photos, a passport and memorabilia. Wasabi plays Mozart harpsichord on the curved edges.

Maybe I'll write it into my will that I should lie there, jammed in, forced into a human origami on my way to the crematorium. They'll burn up me and the coffin in one fiery furnace. I do have a Plan B for my final moment. A flimsy Viking canoe filled with hay, my body stiff under a sheet as I am nudged out onto Jamaica Pond at midnight. Miller Lites for all and a sourly performed, *a capella* "Walkin' in the Hood." A good-looking archer would light an arrow and fire it into the hay, igniting boat and body. Adam Wells promises to set off fireworks, and Michael D says he knows an archer in Florida. Someone will have to buy off the cops. Shamus?

The Fierce Urgency
Of New Love

Not sure how long ago this was done, this pencil sketch by my friend Lilian Voorhees, drawn on her flagstone porch across the street from our house on Atlee Road in a diet-pill rush. It resembles work by Kahlil Gibran, though with a more frenetic ferocity. I loved Lilian. I told her everything. I shouldn't have. She was hurt, her feelings for me larger than mine. I was, for too long, pathetically unaware.[91]

She drew it after I told her about my friend Derek, who was in the Duke's Men of Yale singing group with me. I was out of my mind over him and barely admitting it even to myself. How fierce the urgency of new love. How on fire the sheet music.

"You can't hurry love."
– The Supremes

At this I fail. I *am* a hurrier. Ask Dirtbike.

Looking back, it seemed sophomoric, our time together, more soap than Shakespeare. Letters written back and forth, mailed on a daily basis. Dinners in dark dining halls, leaning forward to compel, to persuade a resistant heart. Were we out of balance? Can love be Geiger-countered in the first place?

A letter from Derek (below) illustrates the dilemma. All I know is how oceanic it felt, our conversations, locked eyes, poet vs. philos-

---

91   See "My Girlfriends" *(The Paragraphs)*

opher. We'd argue constantly about the difference. He, the realist; I, the emotionalist. Somewhere in between, we met. Laughter, argument, a bipolar romance.

I have no idea how I explained him to Lilian, but she caught it in one straight-up sketch. How we were with each other. How I've been with others who captivate in spite of caution, in spite of self-destructive impulse and fear of loss. What might be the original cause of romantic repetition.

I want to forever Lilian's drawing as a tattoo. It represents, for good or ill, how I love. How it comes at me like a cyclone. These beautiful boys who karma-claw their way into my life. I cannot find them. They find me. Bit by bit I learn how to love. How to not keep score. How to create the Other on new canvas. On the other hand, I fuck up. I have a mean mind about myself in the contagion that is romantic love. Jealousy, terror, obsession – a snakepit of horrors.

We are both human *and* being. The being side of the coin practices selfless love, an even keel in a towering emotional wave. The human: a chaos of contradictions, miscues, misinterpretations and possessiveness. Just the way it is in my pulsing heart corner here on planet earth.

"And in the end, the love you take is equal to the love you make," right? Miles to go on that one.

Derek's letter (located in a scrapbook):

Rick,

Last night I read over the letters which you wrote during the last two years. I read them carefully, several times, and for the first time I understood them. You were dealing with an illusion, loving a creation, someone who resembled me, but who in the most essential respects was far from the boy who sat across the table from you in the Silliman dining hall and talked about a Bach cantata. The astounding thing about those letters is the way in which you continued to speak to me, knowing all the while that I was not the real one for whom the words were meant. And that is exactly what I am doing now, writing though I know that there is no longer any way for you to feel what it is that I am trying to say. You once loved an illusion, and I now love a memory. The power of that memory is actually what causes me to write now, for as I read over those letters I suddenly understood who you were, and those parts of the letters which I had been unable to understand suddenly became the expression of feelings which are very much a part of me now. And overwhelmed with love for him who wrote those things, I now write you much as a man feels compelled to talk with the close friends of a man he has loved very much soon after that man dies.

It astounds me that I should now become so exactly the person that you were then; I could well write every word of what you wrote me. Seeing in every word of those letters the expression of my own feelings, that is proof to me that we have indeed missed each other. No greater tragedy is conceivable to me, for we are both so rare that so near a miss is unthinkable.

I don't think you can destroy the past any more than you can preserve the future. God knows we tried hard enough to preserve the future in those days, and we have failed completely. But the same futility lies in your efforts to say that what happened was an ugly mistake. Your letters are all that remain, but they are enough to prove to me that your love was real. Written to an illusion then, they are now the only real base on which I am building my own illusion. And though you cannot accept my love now, I know you would have accepted it then. I am just beginning to return a part of what you gave me, and though it is too late, I will not let this stop me.

Derek

I went back to New Haven for a reunion. My 25th. For the most part I didn't hang with anyone. The howdy and hellos to classmates were friendly enough, but lacked depth. The town, buildings, streets, restaurants, quadrangles enthralled with unexpected nostalgia. I walked around campus alone and wept, realizing that it was not the waste of a formal education, it was not the singing, the bouts of booze, the baby steps with weed and acid that came back. It was the river of emotion that surged as I realized that it was here, at fucking *Yay-ul*, that I first felt the ravages, the beauty, the power and the heart invention that is True Love. I "fell" here, in this crown of a university. I fell in love for the first time. It changed me once and for all.

Isabel Hickey says that you can never lose synapse with any soul you truly love. That seed, once planted (if planted honestly), comes inevitably and patiently to fruition. That when two people spend time together, they create a spiritual "birth." A spiritual child. Much of the relationship is based on nurturing that child. If they separate, the child still exists, and love won't die until that child dies. Or, in reverse, the child will die as soon as love ceases. If you want to be rid of an attachment, you can do so only if you consciously "kill" the child you created together.

"Why would anyone ever want to do that?" she asked.

THE QUINTESSENTIAL ARIA

Come back! Come back! Dearest friend! My only friend come back! I swear to you I shall henceforth be kind! If I was nasty to you it was all a joke, a joke in which I persisted. I am more sorry than I can ever say! Come back and everything will be forgotten! How unfortunate that you should have taken that joke seriously! For two whole days I have been doing nothing but weep! Be brave! Nothing is lost! You have only to cross over again and we shall live together bravely and patiently. I implore you! It's in your interest as well! Come back and you will find all your things here! I hope you realize that there was nothing really in our quarrel! That awful moment![92] But you, when I asked you to leave the boat, why didn't you come? Have we lived together for two years to come to

---

92   They were at a hotel in Brussels when a distraught Verlaine reportedly yelled, «Here›s how I will teach you how to leave!» at the 18-year-old and fired twice with the six-shot Lefaucheux revolver. Verlaine bought the 7mm six-shooter in Brussels on the morning of 10 July 1873, determined to put an end to a torrid two-year affair with

such a pass? What will you do now? If you don't want to come back here, would you like me to join you wherever you are? Yes! I know it was I who was in the wrong! Oh! Say you won't ever forget me! No! You can't forget me! For my part you are always in me! Do answer at once. Are we no longer to live happily together? Be brave and answer quickly! I can't remain here much longer. Only follow the feelings of your heart. Quick! Tell me if I am to go to you. Yours for all life.

P.S. If I can't see you again I shall enlist in the army or the navy. Oh! Come back! At all hours of the day I weep! Tell me to come to you and I'll come! Tell me! Wire to me immediately."

— Rimbaud, to Verlaine

The letter shows traces in the handwriting of having been composed under intense nervous excitement and in a state of mental instability. There are also visible traces on the paper of what must have been tears.

---

his teenage lover. The 29-year-old poet had abandoned his young wife and child to be with Rimbaud, who would later become a symbol of rebellious youth.

The Guru Is You

As a hardcore acidhead hippie living in an Igloo tent in the Law School Quadrangle at Yale while I was attending the Drama School, I ran into a couple of guys who, high as kites, would take me on as a fellow traveler – someone who was asking incessant but puerile Big Questions and who had a give-it-a-shot spiritual take on the Unanswered. Two brothers. We smoked a lot of pot, talked simultaneously and tripped our brains out.

Two favorite wanderings:

1. A glade in the woods where the trees were rooted in loose dirt, so close to the surface that they could be pushed over with no effort and come crashing to the forest floor. When they showed me how to do this my brain went numb
2. East Rock, a big red forehead pushing above flat New Haven, where you could climb, hide and hurl stones at whatever or whomever was scurrying in the underbrush

They introduced me to a new New Haven, a populace outside the university, beyond the walls of college dorms; a Beat collection of wacko artists, poets and musicians. It was a formative upending of whatever I thought was my life trajectory. This rare collective of friends sparked the fuse of what became my abnormal, asymmetrical approach to life, art and music.

Around the same time my sister, Janie, tapped into Transcendental Meditation[93] and encouraged me to be initiated. Back then, in the

---

93 "It is the teaching of Maharishi Mahesh Yogi that the Individual is cosmic. Indi-

'60s, learning to meditate was inexpensive. A buck to be taught your personal mantra. Stop smoking weed for two weeks, bring a white handkerchief, a piece of fruit and a flower, and off you go. I dropped acid for the ceremony. I learned my mantra backwards and a year later had to be reinitiated at a retreat in Maine. Been meditating ever since. Twenty minutes, twice a day. It's not discipline. I do it because I love it. It begins my day, sorts out what's eating at me, and calms the static in my head. I have no illusions about nirvana. It just feels right and good.

I gave other transformational practices an audit. The Horrible EST. Tina Turner chanting. Gurumayi (encouraged by my friend, Peter Walsh, whom I dearly loved, his hope being that with her blessing I would never contract HIV). When I met her as a potential devotee I grabbed her ostrich feather as she was "anointing" me, as if on each shoulder she would lay the queenly feather. I have no idea why I grabbed it. I laughed out loud. She scowled, but I've been HIV-free ever since. It was an act of pure love on the part of my friend. He bought me a scarf that had been consecrated by Gurumayi. I keep it under my pillow. I think of him every morning when I make the bed.

The thing is, as my sister points out, it's "difficult to take two boats to the island." So I've stuck with TM, as have my immediate family. Dad called him "the Haharishi" or "the Hiroshima." We were not dissuaded.

Favorite Maharishi quote: "Funnily enough, all love is directed to the Self."

Something enthralls those of us who've read *The Autobiography of a Yogi, Siddartha,* Timothy Leary, Hermann Hesse, *The Doors of Perception,* Baba Ram Dass, Castaneda. Through them we entertain the possibility of

---

vidual potential of life is cosmic potential. It is divine. Transcendental experience awakens that divinity in man. It's a human right to live divinity. Gurudeva (above) developed a modified practice of meditation, suitable to the householder engaged in the affairs of everyday life. This method was spread globally by Maharishi Mahesh Yogi." (Wikipedia)

other dimensions, other consciousness, beyond emotion, reason or proof. Planet Earth as a way station. One's intuition whispers and some of us, some of the time – or all of us in an unexpected, inexplicable moment – glimpse that rare view of the Bigger Picture.

HORSESHIT THEORY?

This lifetime, each lifetime, if you buy the concept of reincarnation, is a visit to this Schoolhouse Planet of ours. Like Arthur (*The Prince and the Pauper* – Twain), who exchanges his crown for rags and is able to learn, in real time, the true lives of his subjects, we similarly enter life in search of essential lessons. Our "high self" chooses a particular handful. How to love in wisdom. How to ride the horse of ambition. How to rise above jealousy. How to forgive. We instantaneously forget the lesson list as we enter this time around. We arrive innocently; our self-chosen, pre-lifetime slings and arrows find their mark in hopes that we can lift the stuck needle above the vinyl of repetitive karmic mistake. When we gradually wise up, gather bits of truth, treat our friends properly and evolve, we "graduate" – we're outta here 'til our next time at bat. New lessons, new axes to grind.

The guru we've been seeking, whom we think will make our journey a snap with an easy ET touch to the forehead, is, in fact, within, already a part of our being, ready to awaken. An undiscovered, done-deal Dharma path.

The House That Margie Built

Margie Nicoll. How long have I know this woman? Lost track. I met her at the Behan through her friend Richie, an all-dressed-in-black kid, a diabetic, a card sharp, handsome, brooding. He predicted the precise date of his death. He died on that exact day. She always looked after him. She looks after all of us, even at the expense of her own well-being. Of late I think she's grown out of that a bit. Climbing the precarious ladder of the Solo Self.

She was the creator/editor of Compost, an art and poetry 'zine. A true voice singer who can cut loose, especially on a Patti Smith cover. A supreme chef and caterer. A photographer with an unconventional eye. A cat person. A dancer. A solitary who still holds out for love, for a life partner. If she has one fault, it is job loyalty. No matter how demanding a situation, her boss, the debilitating hours, she hangs tough. Works her body to the bone beyond what her friends consider fair or healthy. She just won't quit.

The house above is a collage. You're not sure until you look closely. What at first seem to be watercolors are actually bits of paper, glued down. A combo, an artful, askew sense of proportion, surprise and placement. The house is real. It exists. She'll snap a photo or remember it or both, but once completed, it's hers. Her house. The one she built on paper from scratch, as she did so perfectly for the cover of this book.

When she shows, work sells. She has a knack for what's commercial without purposely aiming for it. Personally, I think it's her humanity that shines through. Just about anyone can feel it and want to own it for themselves.

Most affecting is her smile; generous, a flash of sunlight. Friends of mine, meeting her for the first time, immediately feel at home. She takes you in that way. Clairvoyance and trust in those big eyes. Which is why she is so ideal a choice to represent JP in this video: "Walkin' in the Hood."

She's a believer in the supernatural, the mysterious cosmos, the pull of the planets and moon. She keeps those theories close to the vest if she thinks you think it's hogwash. But if you are so inclined, she'll open up: everything out on the Gypsy table.

As your friend, she's an encourager. She can see, or guess, what it is you're aiming for as an artist or whether you're tuning up a dream of any sort. In a sentence or two, she lets you know that she gets it, gets what you're chasing. Hears the heart of your song. Pulls essence from the words you write.

She reads people with a forgiving skepticism, as she can cut though the bullshit. She can thumbnail-bio a friend in common, but with a more severe suspicion than the gullible might expect. Margie tells it like it is, but is quick to see when she's off and 'fess up.

In New York she finds a city I've never known, as often as I've been there. As if a New Yorker herself who lives in Boston, synthesizing both cities in one embrace. She has that downtown art-scene sensibility. Hip, but not haughty.

One wants the best for this woman, her desires realized. Some of us lucky ones find an end-rainbow pot of gold early on. Some late. Some never. I think Margie has a shot. After all, she owns property in Prince Edward Island with a lighthouse, right?

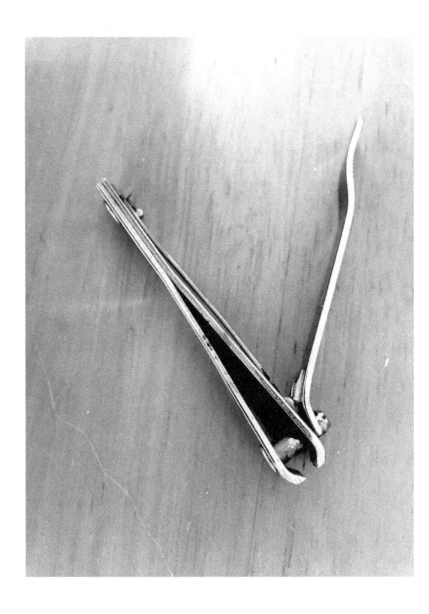

They Don't Bite

... properly, but I wish they did. At least a closer approximation to a nail salon, where those laughing ladies know what the fuck they're doing with my toes.[94]

Finding the right position, the bend-over, is impossible. How can I macro-contort myself into the pretzel shape required to a) reach my foot and b) properly cut? I've tried edge-of-bathtub; the light is good in there, but it's too low a seat. The toilet: too much sliding around. The couch: too squishy. They all suck in one way or another, as do my amateur pedicure gouges.

No way, during the pandemic, can I hit up PS Nail & Spa for an expert pedi. I went last month and was the lone client. I think, given that the provider ladies are Asian, it was an avoidance zone. I was lucky. I got my fave practitioner. She takes her time and is surgically precise. She edges those nasties as short as possible, back where I want them. I don't need length of toenails made pretty-for-paint. I don't want to return more frequently than once a month. She gave me so close a shear that it should last two.

Sooner or later I'm going to have to do this on my own. I dread it. My toenails are tough as petrified wood. It hurts my hand to squeeze and snap. The fungus, which at Nail & Spa gets dug out, will remain. Lifting the alpha-keratin like a roof and nicking out the muffin dough with a lobster-claw tool ain't gonna get the job done. My toenail will rise like a rattlesnake ready to strike. The cuticle moons will also stay put, as will the tiny skin tags that margin the nails like miniature v-shaped

---

94 See "Fantasy Nails" *(The Paragraphs)*

insect wings. Mine will always be an imperfect, frustrating attempt. I can't wait for C-19 to come to an end and return to the salon in gleeful celebration.

Three As One

I cannot imagine what it must be like to be an identical twin, let alone an identical triplet, *and* make collaborative art, but that's who the Casilio Sisters (a.k.a. TRIIIBE), Sara, Kelly and Alicia, are and do. I was lucky to meet and interview them for an ultimately unrealized video documentary about Jamaica Plain.[95] They lived in an apartment on the corner of Boylston and Dresden. They painted, as three, the ceiling of their living room as an optical illusion, a dome, painstakingly transforming a squared-off ceiling into a tiled, arching blue, black and white Muslim Mecca, incredibly cool. You could see it from the street. It took your breath away.

These three are honest, funny, and fiercely close (a sometimes annoying challenge to whichever boyfriend-of-the-moment).

"If I break up with my boyfriend, will he look at my sister? Does he realize that he has not only to deal with me and my schedule, but also with my sister's?"

Their work makes artistic and multi-layered statements that can be political, cultural, personal or all three at once. In reaction to the Iraq War (above) they stood on the steps of the capital dressed as businesswoman, soldier and Muslim. Each square inch of the red cloth represented the death of one of those disparate souls. "Blood" flowed down the steps of the capitol. They also stood (same way) at Ground Zero until arrested. A photo appeared in *Time* magazine.

---

95   See "Good Idea/Never Happened"

They have been wonderful to me. Arriving at Doyle's late for work one afternoon, Alicia rounded the corner.

"We have something for you," she said, handing me an envelope. Inside was a check for $1,000. "We had some extra money, so we decided to give it to you."

I was floored.

I don't see much of them anymore. Now you're with 'em, now you're not. But in some alternate universe we are timelessly joined.

They have exhibits in major galleries around the world and work tirelessly. They are beautiful inside and out, and they challenge each other and the world with their brilliant, compelling and inspired art. Would that my songs have a tenth of their impact.

Watchman

Not a fan of weddings. Never have been. Sure, I love to be there as friend or family in support of the betrothed. Honestly, I do. In the back of my mind, however, like the ex-wife of Logan Roy (*Succession*), I wonder: "How long do I give them?'" Can't help the snark. On the other hand, when it seems "made in heaven" and they are the two best people for each other in the whole wide world, I am exuberantly happy.

Still, I'm a drive-by attendee, jumping out of my skin. Can't wait to get the fuck outta there. The sciatica hits hard during the ceremony, no matter how brief or originally composed. I float at the pre-dinner snack table and shove finger food into my mouth like a sow. I rarely drink much before midnight these days, so at weddings, especially Irish weddings, I'm not a fucked-up-'til-dawn participant. I get it. Two families about to be enmeshed with each other for decades and who hardly know each other have to sort out the get-along. Booze will lubricate, although it could also exacerbate any future friction.

Then there's the set-up: The bride and groom stuffed at a tiny table center stage and apart from where friends and family sit, located after weeks of chair roulette trying to make happy campers of everyone without insulting anybody. So there we park, catered to by the disin-terested, forced-smile help. Notably, there's one or two who keep my eyes wandering, but a quick encounter behind a delivery truck is out of the question.

The speeches by the best man and best woman I look forward to. They provide the least dishonest part of the proceedings. A skewering of bride and groom followed by a tearful memory.

The dancing. The first dance to the first song carefully chosen by the happy couple as I avert my cunty, judgmental eyes. There was one time, however, when the First Dance made me cry. My former roommate, Travis, and his fab girlfriend Danielle had me officiate (I brought up their love of the Fart. The Kerns laughed out loud. The Hollingsworths squirmed in their folding chairs). And they faked me out. They chose a song of mine, "My Friend" (*Paper Airplane*), for their first dance, and I cried my eyes out in spite of myself as they laughed and kissed and danced.

But once the DJ button is pressed (or, if they have the dough, a Real Band) and the crowd, pumped up on booze after the open bar, clump to the floor and bump and grind to all their favorites, that's when I start to check my watch and plan my escape.

The watch. I was one of my friend Jeff Chasse's four best men. We got these fabulous pocket watches as keepsakes. Mine hangs like a single silver testicle on my wall. It opens and shuts with a musical click. It has Roman numerals and elaborate engravings. I love it, but I never wear it. Watches on my body break, on wrist or in pocket. But I like seeing it on the wall. It mitigates my aversion to the betrothal behemoth, the Wedding Industrial Complex: insane money spent for one night only. How about a down payment on a house, for Christ's sake?! The bridesmaid's dresses that have to be bought, fitted and never again used? The rented morning suits and tuxes? The presents? The money spent is out of control.

> *If I buy you a wedding present, can you buy me one when you*
> *get divorced?*
> **– Laurie Sargent**

A terrific idea.

The Overseer. The clipboard lady with the grim smile who chases caterers, hurries family and wedding party to be where they need to be when they need to be there. Who shoves the photographer into everyone's business and encourages overenthusiastic smiles. I want to punch her in the mouth.

My most curmudgeonly self surfaces at these affairs. Would I, given a gay green light, want a version of this for myself? Two dudes in pink tuxes? A rainbow balloon arch? Can't say. I doubt a wedding is in the stars, though Forever Yours unrealistically occurs of late with a certain Person of Interest. There is something to be said about friends showing up in belief and support. Like the teaching creatures in *The Once and Future King* (T. H. White), gathering in the clearing as the Wort (young Arthur) pulls sword from stone like *buttah*. The anointing by your nearest and dearest of this profound one-of-a-kind moment.

But for real? I think a ritual formalization can only jinx two souls in love. You can't get divorced unless you're married, right? I get it, the financial benefits, the made-legal visit to the deathbed, the middle finger to rejecting parents. But should that really be an incentive? Elope. Fucking elope. Give each other a pipe clamp ring. Drink wildly expensive booze, take drugs, go somewhere awesome, and adventure yourselves into a meaningful, original bonding. You deserve it. But beware Berlin on your wedding sidelines. He has malevolent thoughts.

Wayfaring Stranger

I bought it online from Wayfare. Dave Goodchild, Nickel & Dime Band's bassist, was working there and promised a discount. Turns out he left the company before he could get it done, but I went for it. I needed a new one. My cats scratched the other one to bits. It looked like your back after a sunburn, with the skin peeled off.

I miss the former. I had it for decades. Liz Gallagher – Lunette in both Orchestra Lunas – found it on the sidewalk outside the OL house on Ridgemont.[96] When she moved, she gave it to me. It had curved, feminine edges, a coin tray in the top drawer, a sock slot and two doors at the bottom that the cats would pry open. I was afraid they'd crawl in there and shit; shutting them tight was an insufficient deterrent, so I sealed them forever with packing tape. The clawing continued unabated, but the doors remained shut.

It eventually failed the pretty test. Much as I was enamored, it was time to put it back out on the sidewalk. Thankfully, it found a home with my friend Jay Cuneyt. Jay has a cat, however, so its condition has likely worsened.

So I bought the Wayfare chiffarobe. Problem was, it came in a box. A narrow box with instructions. The shape of the box looked like a plank, nothing like a bureau. It had to be assembled from scratch, instructions followed to the letter. If there's anything I hate, anything I refuse to follow, it's instructions. The print is too small even with reading glasses. I have to photograph and magnify in order to decipher. Even then they make no sense, seem to be an hysterical Chinese-to-English

---

96   See "Ridgemont Street"

translation, and I screw up the construction. An able roommate can do the job if it's not too complicated or time-consuming, but I'd rather not ask. I paid the extra bucks to have an installer, a professional, equipped with the tools, the time and the know-how to get it done. He would follow the instructions brilliantly and put it together shipshape.

Dude showed up in a bad mood. This was his part-time gig. Maybe he had to deal with a prior OCD customer who ragged on his every move. I asked if he wanted a glass of water.

"No."

I let him go at it, pretending that he didn't notice the YES WE CAN[97] framed ink poster of the black slave working Thomas Jefferson's dick, just to the left of where the new bureau would park. It took him over an hour, but he built it perfectly. I didn't tip him. I figured that would come out of the put-together fee. Dave corroborated, but maybe I should have. I'm a fucking waiter, for Christ's sake. I always tip. But this time I didn't. Chalked it up to his sour mood.

I wonder if it will last longer than Liz's. I worry that it might develop Ikea Murder Syndrome. You buy it, build it, and it's solid until you try to move it. Then it falls apart. I'd read that an Ikea collapsed on a child and killed her. Ikea sucks balls. Robby had to throw his out. It fell apart when he tried to move it a paltry six inches.

Hey, Wayfaring stranger, I got you, but don't kill my cat or injure a visiting child.

---

97   See "Master/Slave? Slave/Master?"

Wear It Like Ya Mean It

I thought I'd die with my apron on and a microphone in my fist. Go down, server Moses. Then Doyle's came to its bitter end, The Squealing Pig had to close (C-19), and all music venues, the same. They might rise to the surface when this nightmare is over, but god knows when, and if so, will there be a job and stage waiting for a near-octogenarian to mount in a walker?

The apron. You can't be a proper server without it. In those pockets: pens, a paper to write down orders and cash to make change. Behind my back, strung on twisty apron strings like a donkey tail, the towel. It swings like Tarzan behind your ass as you skate around the premises. Tying it in back, unable to see what you're doing, is like the first time you tie your shoelaces: it's not an acquired skill, it does it by itself. As natural as strapping on a server's six-shooter and heading out to the floor to take on an impatient Neanderthal customer.

For now, all my aprons are stuffed in a drawer, clean as a whistle, smoothed out, unused. When working, however, a mere one hour into my shift, it's a wreck, caked and crusty with kitchen sauce and beer. Since I can't use a tray, since I *won't* use a tray, glasses and plates in my hands teeter and spill. Beer is jerked out of pints onto my sleeves and accumulated in abstract patterns on the apron. Salad-dressing spots and pizza-dough flour freckle the cloth. You hope the customers won't notice and reflect their revulsion in your tip.

A filmmaker, Bill Anderson, was shooting a documentary about me. Slated and financed by WGBH. Loaded with mortifying moments. I think his ultimate goal was to study the effect of "the Muse" on an artist. On me. About me and Dave Berndt (the Shelley Winters Project), whom I was obsessed with. The interviews got heavy. Anderson was scouring for prurient details. Much of what was said could be read as diatribes from a couple of complainers, caught off guard. Dave ultimately shut the project down. He didn't want to hurt me or broadcast himself as an inflammatory manipulator (which my roommate, Charlie, thought he was). A part of me would have liked to have seen it finished, seen what Bill had done with it, as humiliating as it might have been. But it never got off the ground, and the funding had to be returned.

I bring this up because at one point Bill stopped by Doyle's to film me at work and to interview the staff. He followed me all over the joint and I got to see, on camera, how silly I look. The Berlin Waddle, head bent uncomfortably forward, the sloppy carry. I can see it now. I think of it when strapping on the apron and lacing the back-assward towel as I prep for my shift. Or used to.

I miss the damned gig. The running around – my exercise for the day. Clocked five miles one night on a walk-o-meter. I miss the crazy team. The laughter. The gossip. The girls. The Colombians. The "get-over-here" regulars. The personal threads that led to inspired friendships all over town. The exquisite handsomeness that was Doyle's. What a shame it's gone. What a fucking shame.

Zerbe's Box Of Three

Dad's friend at the bank, Zerbe (no "Mister," no first name) had a hobby – self-carpentered objects that he tailored to look antique. A Geppetto in a basement. I wound up with this one. I store tiny things in there for safekeeping. A fob, a thumb drive, a stamp, a Buddha blood bead necklace, pennies. The drawers pull smoothly and purr. The brass knobs have lost their luster like a legit antique, the nicked wood looks even older than the 100 years required, and all seem wise improvements.

I'm pretty sure Zerbe and Dad had a falling out. Could have been the booze. Dad could be nasty and insulting after one too many vodka tonics. This baby survived them both. No idea what possessed him to make it or give it to my father. I doubt it came from a book of instructions. More likely he made it up, already had the knobs and wood lying around the shop. Maybe there's a secret compartment, a hidden document that solves a perfect crime or has a dirty phone number. I won't look for it. Not until *I'm* an antique.

Epilogue

It's love's illusions I recall...

A summer night. Big sky, fragrance of weeds, lilacs, pine trees and, in the dark, heat lightning.[98] Flashes of illumination. That is how Mike infiltrates, how he is awake in the margins and in between the lines of this book. So why is it that I haven't written about him in detail? The guy who inspired me to write the damn thing in the first place? (No "Dirt." No book.)[99]

I love my friends. My family. My roommates and band mates. They, me. Without them I'd be meaningless. What I've written about past relationships, however incomplete, was an easier undertaking. I've known those guys for years. In some cases, decades. I can write about them, about them with myself, words based on a shared history. Mike and me are too new, too brand new. We were making it up second by second. We thrived in that invented, preposterous beginning, the preface to a book not yet written; a chrysalis not to be codified by anyone, least of all ourselves.

> *I wrote this song before I knew who it was for.*
> — *Babylon Berlin*

Now that I think about it, this whole thing, this *Balloon*, is a chance for me to investigate the unanswerable all over again. Love. What the fuck is it? Sexual attraction? A platonic construct? A psychic/emotional

---

98 A flash or flashes of light seen near the horizon, especially on warm evenings, believed to be the reflection of distant lightning on high clouds.

99 See "Double Dedication(s)"

collaboration? Like/un-like-mindedness? Open windows in a parallel universe? The tension of the incomplete? Dopamine? A self-inflicted fantasy? All or none of the above? And how do we know when it's there? When the heart has Hindenberg'd us off the ground and caught fire? But we do, don't we? We really do, because what I re-remember is that love is a simple, a very simple thing. It is about being "known." Known by another in a way that is as unmistakable as it is ineffable; that knocks the stuffing out of your preset sense of who you thought you were. It's not a perfect sentence or a paragraph. It's not biography or anecdote. It is a startling, can't-fool-you cognition. An ego that has become an out-to-lunch sign on the door of one's "personality."

It happened that very first night we met at the Behan. Thinking back, it was at-first-sight instantaneous. The following weeks just played out; boozing at the Behan, walking each other home, yakking on the big couch, downloading new movies, visiting the Harvard lab, breakfast at the Dipper, Jacques, Brookline Ramen, the Gehry building, endless texts, razor-blade cutting prosciutto-thin slices of gummies as a THC experiment. All that for shit-sure. But in the end, or in the beginning, it was in that first split second that we got it. That we "knew" each other. Found each other. How the fuck!? It's crazy, right?

Michael Dirtbike:
"It was frantic, but easygoing at the same time."

What I saw in your "can I call you, Ricky?" face that night was the whole deal. The Everything. The reason any of us are alive on this vertiginous planet. Both of us, at the same time, "knew" each other, right then and there. I live for this shit, but I can't look for it. It happens or it doesn't. It finds me or it does not. You know this as well, Michael. You've been lucky, like me, to have it happen in spades, the big L. We are fortunate to have found it with each other. If God is love, dude? We got religion. I've kept us secret, you and me, wanting to avoid the contamination of misunderstanding. I think in some ways love is a private thing. No parades. No brags. Though I bet some of those barflies at the B were onto us.

Our time here in the 'hood, a mere eight weeks, felt like an acid trip you never want to end. No bad vibes. No nightmare hallucinations. Not one bad time spent together. Challenging, comical, brilliant, gorgeous, affirming. In one flashbulb burst.

Michael Dirtbike:
"...we bring out the best in each other."

The pandemic sent him home, where he should be. Olivia. Boogey. Surf. Bike. Friends. Work.

Therefore we hover, dragonflies in an afternoon sky. Who knows, it might be over. One or the other of us could have already chosen to end it for whatever reason. If it's you, Mike, I'm OK with it. I wouldn't fight to save us against your will, or against the exigencies of where life takes either of us. Against the "fate" you partly believe in. Who can say? Perhaps even I could become the exciser of out-of-sight-out-of-heart atrophy. Our time was our time. Who the fuck knows how/where we wind up. Does it matter? Will we evolve into forever and eradicate my romantic precondition of doubt?

"Rick. There's nothing to worry about."
— MD

rick berlin:
one question: your name in this thing. as it stands: using it as-is. Michael Dirtbike or in spots, shortened. you ok with it? i could change it to something weird, or just MD. honestly, i think yll be fine with it, but don't want to presume

Michael Dirtbike:
— 100% trust you

Berlin and Dirt. Carve that in a tree.

I picture *The Big Balloon* opened on your lap, a beer on a side table, under a table lamp in Santa Barbara (or the UK) as you re-investigate my weird life and our mirrored reflection, clear or dull, good or ill, real or imagined, true or false. Love, the great mystery.

There's a feeling

That creeps up on you

When you're sure

That you are not alone

Anymore.
– "Green Street"

No words can describe.
– MD

I really don't know love... at all.
– Joni

What?

You are so fucking beautiful.

You *are* beautiful.

"Красота спасет мир"[100]

---

100   "Beauty will save the world" – **Fyodor Dostoyevsky** *(The Idiot)*

FIN

About The Author

Rick Berlin is a Boston-based singer-songwriter, videographer, formerly the frontman of Orchestra Luna, Luna, the Suitcase Band, Berlin Airlift, Rick Berlin: The Movie, the Shelley Winters Project and the Nickel & Dime Band.

His discography includes:

Rick Berlin w/ THE NICKEL & DIME BAND
ALWAYS ON INSANE

WHEN WE WERE KIDS

BADVILLE

THE COURAGE OF THE LONELY

GREAT BIG HOUSE

7 SONGS

Rick Berlin/Jane Mangini
THE CHA CHA CLUB

Rick Berlin (solo)
HALF IN THE BAG

RICK BERLIN LIVE@JACQUES

ME & VAN GOGH

OLD STAG

PAPER AIRPLANE

The Shelley Winters Project
EP

I HATE EVERYTHING BUT YOU

FORCED2SWALLOW

CATHEDRAL

Berlin Airlift
BERLIN AIRLIFT

PROFESSIONALLY DAMAGED

Orchestra Luna
ORCHESTRA LUNA

Other works by Rick include *The Kingdom: A Musical, Go For It Girl: A Queer Travelogue, Armchair General: A Fictional Autobiography of Dick and Jane, The Paragraphs (A Memoire),* all published on his website: *www.berlinrick.com*